BEAUTY FOR ASHES

The Spiritual Transformation of a Modern Greek Community

Beauty
for Ashes

The Spiritual Transformation of
a Modern Greek Community

Stephen R. Lloyd-Moffett

ST VLADIMIR'S SEMINARY PRESS
CRESTWOOD, NEW YORK

Library of Congress Cataloging-in-Publication Data

Lloyd-Moffett, Stephen R. (Stephen Robinson)
    Beauty for ashes : the spiritual transformation of a modern Greek community /
Stephen R. Lloyd-Moffett.
      p. cm.
    ISBN 978-0-88141-341-0
    1. Orthodox Eastern Church—Preveza—Greece—History.   2. Preveza
(Greece)—Church history.   3. Nikopolis (Greece : Extinct city)—Church history.
4. Meletios, Metropolitan of Nikopolis, 1933–.   I. Title.

    BX310.L56 2009
    281.9'4953—dc22

2009038906

Copyright © 2009 by
Stephen Robinson Lloyd-Moffett

ST VLADIMIR'S SEMINARY PRESS
575 Scarsdale Rd, Crestwood, NY 10707
1-800-204-2665
www.svspress.com

ISBN 978-0-88141-341-0

PRINTED IN THE UNITED STATES OF AMERICA

To appoint unto them that mourn in Zion,

to give unto them beauty for ashes,

the oil of joy for mourning,

the garment of praise for the spirit of heaviness;

that they might be called trees of righteousness,

the planting of the Lord,

that He might be glorified.

Isaiah 61:3

Table of Contents

Introduction

On the twenty-eighth of March 1980, the new bishop arrived in town. All the government officials, the local army battalion, the town band, and all of its citizens awaited him in the central square. The bright sun beamed upon him as he exited the car. Unlike his predecessor, a portly and worldly man, the new bishop was thin from fasting and otherworldly in demeanor. People in the crowd had heard that he was a living saint. To them, he seemed weak and simple. His face reflected a curious glow and deep serenity. He was followed by five young, zealous monks—his spiritual children, his disciples. Even their presence was new and a bit strange; the local Church[1] had lacked functioning monasticism for at least a generation. For the monks, their plans for a life on Mt Athos had been unexpectedly interrupted by the election to the episcopate of their *geronda*, spiritual father. The peace and solitude of the Holy Mountain was only a dream now; reality placed them in the center of a bustling provincial town with the seemingly impossible task ahead of restoring the faith of a scarred and distrustful populace. As for the bishop, he looked upon the people with compassion and wonder—compassion because the people had been scandalized by the Church and its representatives in one of the most infamous church scandals of the modern period; wonder because he had heard they were suspicious of outsiders, guarded with their feelings, and "bishop-eaters." Bishop Meletios began to speak . . .

This book is a study of what transpired after this moment. Based on numerous personal visits over a decade and a year of formal ethno-

---

[1]Note on capitalization: "Church" will be capitalized when it refers to the body of all Christians and remain uncapitalized when it refers to a building. Metropolis will be capitalized when it refers to a specific metropolis and remain uncapitalized elsewhere.

graphic research, this book is about the spiritual transformation of a town and the role the bishop and monastery played in it. The transformation has been profound. In 1980, the Metropolis of Nikopolis and Preveza was the embarrassment of the Church of Greece. Riddled by scandal and spiritual neglect, the spiritual life of the people of Preveza was undoubtedly at its nadir. A quarter-century later, it is one of the most spiritually vibrant towns in all of Greece. The Metropolis has changed from one of the most dispirited in Greece to an archetype for others. This dramatic reversal did not happen overnight and offers no miraculous solutions. Moreover, the struggle continues today. However, what occurred and occurs here is both instructional and inspirational. My hope is that understanding it will bear fruit elsewhere.

This book began with a desire to understand this spiritual transformation so as to provide a practical model for other parts of the Orthodox world to follow. This book provides no such ready-made solutions and even comes to question the very value of developing such models. In the place of such a guide, it offers a story. I have deliberately sought to let the story stand on its own, without drawing direct parallels to problems in churches outside of Greece. I will allow the reader to draw his or her own conclusions. The themes of the story—the role of the bishop in the modern world, the relationship of monks to contemporary society, the transformation of a community—are universal for the Church. I believe they are also timeless. Our challenge is to apply them to our current situation and current age.

This study is largely contained in this three-way relationship between the bishop, the monks, and the people of Preveza. As a result, my analysis is always relational: it attempts to detail the history, surrounding context, and resultant outcomes of these relationships. The relational dynamics are neither always positive nor always reflected upon deeply by those involved. However, they are the concrete happenings that yield real change. Analyzing them has led to broader questions, especially about my own work as a scholar and member of the Church. Can the relationship between a bishop, his Church, and a monastery ever be captured in words or are relationships so inherently dynamic that writing about them is to inevitably alter them? And if the dynamics at work can be identified and analyzed in a meaningful way, would it really have any value for other contexts? In other words, which relationships are universal and which are unique?

THE STRUCTURE OF THE STORY

As this story came together, it took the form of the analysis of a play. Chapter one is dedicated to the setting, the city of Nikopolis/Preveza and her story from the time of Paul to the contemporary period. The second chapter is a character study of the main protagonist in the play, Metropolitan Meletios of Preveza and Nikopolis; the chapter follows him from a boy to his decision to become a priest and then eventually to the place where he would become a rather unlikely bishop. Chapter three sets the stage for the dramatic tension that drives the story: the scandal that emerged in the church of Preveza that led to the arrival of Bishop Meletios. Chapter four provides the story itself—an inspiring tale of transformation guided by an ancient faith tailored to the modern world. The next chapter might be seen as a character study of the primary supporting actors—the monks of the Monastery of Prophet Elias, a diverse and sometimes quirky group of men driven by their faith and their common attachment to their spiritual father, the bishop. The final chapter examines the monks' unique role in the transformation of Preveza.

In the end, this study is a story about a bishop, his young disciples, and the town they arrived in on March 28, 1980. In telling the story, the goal has been neither hagiography nor exposé but rather to provide detailed presentations of the concrete mechanisms behind social and religious change. For this reason, throughout the book I have sought to interweave the histories of the main characters with my analysis of the motivating principles that underlay their behavior. I have also tried to be liberal with the details; while some details may appear superfluous at first glance, they are intended to flesh out the character of those who are acting and to reveal both their virtues and their shortcomings. In the end, this study offers no "exportable" paradigm for ecclesiastical success but rather numerous examples and vignettes of a living organism in the midst of change. It is an incredible tale about a bishop, a monastery, and the town that was forever changed by their presence.

CHAPTER ONE

The Setting: The Apostolic City of Preveza and Nikopolis

I t is the evening of Great Friday and the streets of Preveza are filled with people holding lanterns, processing behind wooden sepulchers adorned with flowers of various hues and type. Each sepulcher contains an image of the Crucified Christ, which have just been taken down from the Cross. The passion of Christ has been relived once more, as it has every year for nearly seventy generations in these parts. The tradition has remained largely the same throughout these years, though the composition of the people has changed remarkably—now there are Lefkadians, Vlachs, Kephalonians, and at least this past year one foreign scholar alongside the "indigenous" population. The crowds seem to get bigger each year, one local tells me. The procession winds through the narrow streets, illuminating ancient buildings placed amidst modern concrete and glass edifices. The city seems stuck midway between its ancient past and modern future. The lines of light converge at the central square, where a warm glow reaches out to the cloudless sky. Each sepulcher—and the sweating men who hold them upon their shoulders—is blessed by the bishop who awaits them. His face glows brighter as each new procession arrives. A monk-deacon stands to either side of him, their faces cast down. One deacon holds the tri-part candle representing the Trinity while the other a two-part candle representing the two natures of Christ. Few in the crowd seem to know what they signify, but at least one old man needs to share his knowledge with me. By 11 p.m., nearly the whole town of 15,000 people has gathered around the bishop, literally encircling him. Eight sepulchers—one from each local parish—remain hoisted above the heads of the crowd. The bishop speaks like a father to his extended family. He offers words of encouragement, education, chastisement, and above all, inspiration. The pinnacle of Lent will occur in two nights with the celebration of Pascha (Easter), but the communion of the people of Preveza will not be stronger. The community is formed anew each Great Friday.

This chapter is dedicated to the history and character of religious community in the region of Nikopolis and Preveza, from the inception with the Apostle Paul in 63 CE to the arrival of Bishop Meletios in 1980. The importance of this community in the wider region, nation, and empire has risen and fallen numerous times over the years. Neither the composition of its people nor the quality of its leaders has been consistent. Much of the most important information, like the annual Great Friday meeting of the sepulchers described above, was never recorded. From what is available, however, a "biography" of the Church in Preveza can be constructed, which will be useful to set the stage for the arrival of Bishop Meletios in 1980.

The Ancient Church of Nikopolis[1]

Octavian Caesar, better known as Augustus, founded the city of Nikopolis in the spring of 29 BCE to commemorate his final victory in the civil war over Marcus Antonius at nearby Actium. This city of victory (Nike = victory, polis = city) was built to be a major regional center. Never known for his patience, Augustus ensured that it would become an important city quickly by forceably resettling the inhabitants of the surrounding territories into the new city. The city stood for hundreds of years as a testament to the beginning of the the great Roman peace, *Pax Romana*, in the area. The city must have been glorious: it had three ports, a mint for copper coinage, a stadium, a gymnasium, a theater, an odeum, an aqueduct, and several temples that

---

[1]I am greatly indebted to Stephen Balestra, a graduate student at the University of Ioannina, for use of his painstaking research and access to his useful chronologies and bibliographies. This section, while the first attempt in English to sketch the history of the metropolis, can offer only a brief synopsis of the events. A fuller account will appear when Mr. Balestra's work comes into print.

are still visible today, though in ruins. It was home to quadrennial "Aktian" games, which rose in stature to be equal to the Olympic games. During the games, the population swelled substantially but, even outside these years the city maintained its status as a major regional center.[2] In 66 CE, the Emperor Nero, the famous persecutor of the Christians of Rome, came to participate in the games.[3]

In Nikopolis, Nero must have been personally disappointed to find Christians already present. A few years earlier, the greatest and archetype of all missionaries, the Apostle Paul himself, had arrived in Nikopolis and had spent a winter with the people.[4] In his Epistle to Titus 3.12, he writes (possibly from Philippi in Macedonia), "When I send Artemas to you, or Tychicus, do your best to come to me at Nikopolis, for I have decided to spend the winter there." The people of modern Nikopolis, the city of Preveza, believe that Paul references their town and their belief is not unwarranted. There were, without question, a number of cities named Nikopolis in the ancient world: Alexander the Great founded a Nikopolis in Syria after the battle of Issos;[5] Pompey founded a Nikopolis in Lesser Armenia after his victory at Dasteira in 60 BCE; Octavian founded a Nikopolis in Egypt east of Alexandria to celebrate his final victory over Egyptian forces around 30/29 BCE. With the tremendous academic work given to reconstructing Paul's itineraries, the Greek Nikopolis is the most likely candidate for Paul's visit.

Most scholars believe that in Paul's final years he traveled from the lands of the eastern part of the Roman empire to Rome, where he was eventually martyred. The Greek Nikopolis would have been a natural place to sojourn on such a journey, as people would travel along the

---

[2]Although the commonly quoted temporary population of 300,000 cannot be accurate.

[3]P. Chrysostomou and F. Kefallonitou, *Nikopolis* (Athens: Ministry of Culture, Archaeological Receipts Fund, 2001), 13.

[4]Some scholars, particularly in the West, doubt that Paul is the author of the so-called Pastoral Epistles, in which his letter to Titus is grouped. The authenticity of this letter is beyond the scope of this chapter and can never be determined absolutely. Nevertheless, the weight of the tradition will be accepted here and we will assume that Paul is the author of the Letter to Titus.

[5]Strabo XIV, 4, 19.

coast from port to port in a system known as *cabotage*.[6] Titus, who was in Crete, would have also naturally passed Nikopolis on his journey west. By contrast, there is no recognized itinerary that would place Paul in Armenia, Syria, or Egypt during this period. The Greek Nikopolis thus fits best with what is known about Paul's travels.

Furthermore, Paul usually stayed in towns with Jewish populations as he traveled. Several indications suggest such a Jewish population in the Greek Nikopolis. The famous Jewish historian Flavius Josephus states that King Herod of Judea helped finance the construction of Augustus' Nikopolis. In all likelihood, this support would be given due to the presence of a Jewish population there. In addition, according to Eusebius, the Church theologian Origen made a comment in the third century that there was an original copy of the Old Testament in Hebrew in Nikopolis. Both these points support the hypothesis that there was a Jewish population in Nikopolis, which would had been consistent with Paul's mode of travel.

Beyond doubt, however, is the strong belief among the people of modern Nikopolis, the city of Preveza, that their faith is tied to Paul directly. No one less than Paul himself is the founder of their church. They even locate the precise spot where Paul taught near the Church of the Lithari, in the eastern part of the province. As a result of this direct connection to the ancient faith, the Metropolitan of Nikopolis bears the title "*Apostolic* Metropolitan of Nikopolis" even to this day. The first representative of the Church, then, should be considered St Paul himself, probably in 63–64 CE.

Despite the rich memory of Paul's visit, no Christian archeological remains have been discovered that can be verifiably dated to the first three centuries of Christianity in Nikopolis. This dearth of evidence is not rare in the early Christian world, because few permanent and lasting buildings were built anywhere for Christians during the

---

[6]Navigation on the coastal routes, known as *cabotage*, was the most common and safest type of sea travel at that time, in particular for merchant ships, and generally speaking St Paul traveled along the established commercial routes. The more dangerous open-sea routes were usually taken only in times of emergency, such as war, or as an unintentional result of unexpected adverse weather conditions (see Acts 27).

era of persecution. Despite its apostolic foundation, it is likely that the number of Christians around Nikopolis was few during these early centuries. In the early 300s, the Latin writer Arnobius described the region of Nikopolis, known as Epirus, as an area in which Christianity had already put down roots, though later he qualifies this statement by noting that Christianity was not yet widespread.[7] Nevertheless, the era has been remembered for the numerous stalwart examples of faith in the face of persecution.[8] Church traditions note that a mother named Evanthia and her son Eleftherios were martyred in 120 CE; Saints Donatos and Therinos were tortured to death in nearby Bouthrotos around the middle of the third century; in 283, Saints Isauros, Basileos, Innocenzo, Felix, Ermeias, and Peregrinus, having refused to sacrifice to Emperor Numerianus, were tortured to death at nearby Apollonia. In the minds of the people of modern Nikopolis, the faith of the people is rooted in ancient examples of those who gave their lives for their religion.

If the rise of Christianity in Nikopolis is murky, the founding and organization of the Metropolis itself is still more obscure. Eusebius in his work *The Life of Constantine* mentions bishops from the province of Epirus attending the First Ecumenical Council at Nicea, though he does not mention any bishops by name.[9] It can be presumed then that some degree of ecclesial administration was in effect at Nikopolis, and it is known that a Bishop Apollodoros of Kerkyra, which is nearby, attended the Council. However, the names of the early bishops of Nikopolis and the early functions of the Metropolis of Nikopolis are unknown.

The first reference to the Metropolis itself occurs in 347 CE when Bishop Eliodoros of Nikopolis took part in the Synod of Sardiki, along with a bishop from nearby Nafpaktos, Martyrios.[10] Nothing

---

[7]William Bowden, *Epirus Vetus: The Archaeology of a Late Antique Province* (London: Duckworth, 2003), 109.

[8]See Φώτιος Οικόνομου, *Η εν Νικόπολει και Πρέβεζη Εκκλησία* (Αθήνα, 1973) 35–37.

[9]*Life of Constantine* III,7,10.

[10]See Βιτάλης Φιλάρετου, *Μητρόπολις και Μητροπόλιται της Νικοπόλεως Ηπείρου* (Αθήνα, 1972), 12–13; and Οικόνομου (1973), 31.

about this Bishop Eliodoros is known beyond his name, though he is the first known bishop of the area. At the Second Ecumenical Council of Constantinople in 381, Bishop Donatos of Euroia, which is near Nikopolis, attended and would later be canonized a saint.[11] There is no mention of the presence of the bishop of Nikopolis specifically, but there is some indication in the Acts of the Council of Nikopolis' importance in the Church hierarchy. The Acts of the Council place Thessaloniki, capital of the Metropolis of Macedonia, in sixth place of the administrative hierarchy of the Church, behind the five Patriarchs of Rome, Jerusalem, Antioch, Alexandria, and Constantinople. Within this Metropolis, Nikopolis held the third place, behind the renowned cities of Thessaloniki itself and Corinth.[12] Thus Nikopolis was placed in prominent company in the ancient world.

At the end of the fourth century, Nikopolis figures prominently in a controversy that would become familiar over the coming centuries as the bishop of Rome came to claim the doctrine of Papal Supremacy. Around 390, Pope Siricius (384–399) of Rome set a precedent by pressing the claim that the bishop of Thessaloniki had the power to consecrate all metropolitan bishops in the metropolises of Macedonia, including Nikopolis.[13] The bishop of Thessaloniki saw himself acting on behalf of the Pope as his *vicarius* or representative. It is apparent, however, that not all the bishops of the region recognized this chain of authority, and the Pope of Rome during the next half century repeatedly distributed encyclicals reminding the bishops of eastern Illyricum of their allegiance to the bishop of Thessaloniki and through him to Rome itself.[14] This incident will not be the last time that Nikopolis will find itself stuck between Rome and Constantinople.

Perhaps the most famous of the ancient bishops was Donatus of Nikopolis (*c.* 425–432), who appears to have gained some prominence

[11]Οικόνομου (1973), 27, 37; and Φιλάρετου, 12–13.

[12]Μητροπολίτου Νικοπόλεως Μελετίου, "Ο Νικοπόλεως Ευγένιος και η Σύνοδος της Χαλκηδόνος," εν *Πρακτικά του πρώτου Διεθνούς Συμποσίου για τη Νικόπολη, 23–29 Σεπτεμβρίου 1984* (Πρέβεζα, 1987), 269.

[13]This claim included Macedonia's northern neighbor Dakia (shortly thereafter comprising the eastern prefecture of Illyricum).

[14]Γ. Θεοχαρίδου, *Ιστορία της Μακεδονίας* (Θεσσαλονίκη, 1980), 115–17.

as a delegate to the Third Ecumenical Council at Ephesus in 431 and a correspondent to the great church father Cyril of Alexandria regarding the threat of the heresy of Nestorianism.[15] However, one of the most intriguing stories of the diocese involves the character of Bishop Attikos of Nikopolis (446–451), who in the mid 440s was ensnarled in a controversy with a Bishop Anastasios of Thessaloniki regarding the right of Metropolitans to choose local bishops without the consent of other local bishops.[16] The controversy began when Bishop Anastasios consecrated the bishop of Thespies, within the Metropolis of Corinth, without the support of the local Church. Bishop Attikos of Nikopolis and several others in the region refused to attend a synod called by the bishop of Thessaloniki to ratify his authority in consecrating bishops at the local level. For their insubordination, the bishop of Thessaloniki had Bishop Attikos and the others arrested and transported to Thessaloniki. Some within the group perished along the way. Bishop Attikos was forced to winter in Thessaloniki where he was coerced to sign the declaration. Eventually, he was restored to his position through the intercessions of Pope Leo I (440–461), who describes the episode in a letter from 449.[17] Pope Leo I defended the bishop of Thessaloniki's right to interfere in local affairs but deplored his treatment of the local Bishop Attikos in particular. In the end, he sided with Bishop Attikos that the election of the Metropolitan should be a local affair but added that the candidate must have the consent of the Pope's representative in Thessaloniki, which should be given without delay as long as the election was made according to Church guidelines.[18]

---

[15]Ε. Μπιτζιλέκη, *Νικόπολις: Ιστορία – Μνημεία* (Πρέβεζα, 1966), 12; and Οικόνομου (1973), 27–31. Also, Μ.Β.Σακκελλαρίου, ed., *Ήπειρος 4000 Χρόνια Ελληνικής Ιστορίας και Πολιτισμού* (Αθήνα, 1997), 160.

[16]The right to choose Metropolitan bishops was recognized, but here the question extended this right to local bishops.

[17]Σακκελλαρίου, 160.

[18]C. Pietri, "La Geographie de l'Illyricum Ecclesiastique et Ses Relations avec l'Eglise de Rome," in *Villes et Peuplement dans l'Illyricum Protobyzantine: Actes du colloque organise par l'Ecole francaise de Rome, 12–14 May 1982* (Rome: Ecole Francoise de Rome, 1984), 27–28.

Despite his rift with the bishop of Thessaloniki, Bishop Attikos appears to have been a thorough team player. He attended the so-called Robber's Council of 449 in Ephesus that supported the position of the leader of the non-Chalcedonians, the Patriarch of Alexandria, Dioscoros, whom the Orthodox considered a heretic for his doctrine that Jesus had only one nature. He signed the decrees of this council in the 34th position.[19] However, when the theological winds shifted a few years later, Bishop Attikos switched positions and supported the Fourth Ecumenical Council in 451, held at Chalcedon, which among other things invalidated the council of 449. In this council, Bishop Attikos of Nikopolis signed in the 47th position, effectively denouncing his own participation in the council two years prior.

Midway between Rome and Constantinople—literally and figuratively—the metropolis tended to side more often with Rome. In 457–458, a provincial synod was held in Epirus to ratify the decisions of the Fourth Ecumenical Council of Chalcedon. Bishop Eugenius of Nikopolis wrote a letter sometime after to Pope Leo I of Rome regarding the status of this local synod and in response to a query by Emperor Leo I (457–471). The Emperor, also named Leo, was trying to gauge support for the Council of Chalcedon and for the legitimacy of Bishop Timotheos of Alexandria, who usurped the previous Bishop Proterios with the consent of the Governor Augustalius in a caper of typical intrigue for the Byzantine Empire.[20] In his letter, Bishop Eugenius of Nikopolis offered his unqualified support for the Council of Chalcedon and his opposition to the usurper Timotheos, interestingly invoking the authority of the bishop of Rome in his argument, a position not lost upon those debating the doctrine of universal Papal authority over all Christians.

The ancient Christianity of Nikopolis may also have developed its own unique liturgical practices. The earliest of the six main basilicas

---

[19]Ibid., 29–30.

[20]The letter has been preserved in Latin in a collection called the *Codex Encyclius* and has been translated to demotic Greek by the current bishop of Nikopolis, Meletios: Μητροπολίτης Νικοπόλεως Μελέτιος, "Ο Νικοπόλεως Ευγένιος και η Σύνοδος της Χαλκηδόνος," in *Πρακτικά του πρώτου Διεθνούς Συμποσίου για τη Νικόπολη 23–29 Σεπτεμβρίου 1984* (Πρέβεζα, 1987), 269–77.

of ancient Nikopolis, constructed sometime between 450 and 470, is unique in design for the ancient world with five aisles, a three-part transept, a three-part narthex, and two symmetrical annexes to either side.[21] The location of the annexes suggests that the officiant would bring the ceremonial items, such as the Holy Gospel and the gifts from the narthex area, through the main nave to the altar rather than have the liturgical items near the altar as was customary elsewhere.[22] Over time, the church was remodeled to conform to the standard practices of Constantinople.[23]

In the fifth century, the Church came to play a more prominent role in the administration of the society, and Nikopolis came to reflect this shift.[24] The most loved and important bishop from this era was undoubtedly St Alkyson, whose reign (491–516) coincided with the reign of Emperor Anastasios I (491–518). The emperor continually worked to undue the decisions of the Fourth Ecumenical Council at Chalcedon. In 511, he disposed the patriarch of Constantinople, Macedonius II (495–511), for refusing to sign a document which formally condemned the Council of Chalcedon. Locally, Bishop Alkyson responded in 512 by convening a synod attended by forty bishops from throughout the region that condemned the document

---

[21]This basilica is called 'B' in the contemporary complex. The basilica labeling system was determined by the order in which archeologists discovered the basilicas, not the order they were constructed. So, awkwardly, Basilica 'B' precedes Basilica 'A.' Moreover, although Basilica 'B' is usually called "Of the Bishop Alkyson," this ascription was determined by an inscription found on a later addition to the basilica and thus it was most certainly not built by Bishop Alkyson, who was bishop from 491 to 516. For dating, see Bowden, 2003, 123; D. Pallas, "Monuments et textes. Remarques sur la liturgie dans quelques basiliques paleochretiennes de l'Illyricum oriental," *Επετηρίς Εταιρείας Βυζαντινών Σπουδών* 44 (1979–1980), 37–116.

[22]See Δ. Παλλάς, "Οι Χαρακτήρες και η ακτινοβολία της εκκλησιαστικής αρχιτεκτονικής της Νικόπολης," *Πρακτικά τού πρώτου Διεθνούς Συμποσίου για τη Νικόπολη, 23–29 Σεπτεμβρίου 1984* (Πρέβεζα, 1988), 226–229.

[23]This hypothesis is supported by renovations done by Bishop Dometios circa 525. Archeologists believe that he converted the transept into its current three-aisled form to allow for the liturgical practice as it was performed in Constantinople, which had increasing influence during this later period.

[24]See the arguments of W. Bowden, who argues that the bishops came to supplant the *potentiores*, who had been the primary power brokers within the government structure during most of the fourth century and the first half of the fifth.

and the all the activities of the emperor, despite the public threat of persecution. From 512 to 516, persecution of the Orthodox bishops became more severe as Emperor Anastasios used his political influence to dispose bishops that disagreed with him and replace them with loyal ones. In 515, this purging led Bishop Alkyson and most of the local bishops to align themselves with the Pope of Rome, Hormisdas (514–523), and broke communion with the Patriarch of Constantinople and the Archbishop of Thessaloniki.[25]

In 516, Emperor Anastasios called a new Ecumenical Council to formally condemn the Orthodox position of the Council of Chalcedon, inviting some 200 bishops who he hoped would support his cause. The emperor had the bishops who opposed him, including Bishop Alkyson, arrested and sent to the prisons of Constantinople. After surviving the gulags for five months, Bishop Alkyson was martyred for his defense of the Orthodox faith in September of 516.[26] The Council never occurred and Chalcedon remains foundational to the Orthodox faith today. Through the efforts of the contemporary bishop of Nikopolis, Meletios, Bishop Alkyson has been recognized as a saint by the Orthodox Church.

The replacement of the martyred Bishop Alkyson, who was already being seen as a saint for his confession of the faith in the face of persecution, led to yet another episode with Nikopolis being stuck between the powers of East and West. In 516, a local synaxis of bishops chose a certain Ioannis to replace Alkyson. Archbishop

---

[25]Later that year, the bishops were briefly re-united with Constantinople due to the diplomacy of Bishop Alkyson. See Pietri, 45, based on Euagrius Scholasticus, *Church History*, 3, 31.

[26]His body may have been recently discovered among the ruins of ancient Nikopolis. In the altar area of Basilica 'Δ,' which by material and design is known to have been produced in Constantinople, was discovered the relics of somebody who had been beheaded. This person was undoubtedly seen as holy because fifteen other people were buried immediately adjacent, and it was common practice to want to be buried next to saints. Archeologists have speculated that this body is that of St Alkyson, who died as a martyr in Constantinople and was undoubtedly returned to Nikopolis. If he indeed built Basilica 'Δ,' then it would have been a likely candidate for his burial. While such identification cannot be proven beyond doubt, the discovery of the burial of a holy man within Nikopolis from around this era is at least intriguing.

Dorotheos of Thessaloniki attempted to interfere and appoint someone more friendly to his cause, but the Pope intervened and proclaimed the end to his privileges as *vicarius*—an important role
legitimating Thessaloniki's power.[27] Afterwards, the newly ordained
Bishop Ioannis of Nikopolis sent a deacon, Rufinus, to the Pope of
Rome Hormisdas reaffirming their steadfastness in the faith and his
allegiance to Rome.[28] Interestingly, there is no report of any message
being sent to Constantinople.

For the remainder of the sixth and seventh centuries, references
to the Metropolis decrease, though archeological evidence suggests
that the Church continued to grow in Nikopolis, including the first
monasteries being built.[29] Nevertheless, there are indications the

[27]Pietri, 45–46.

[28]Οικόνομου (1973), 33.

[29]According to the Synekdimos of Ierokleos of 535—a sort of political, historical, and geographical encyclopedia—the Archbishop of Nikopolis had within his See
eight bishops: Adrianopolis (modern day Dyrinoupoleos), Dodoni, Euroia, Angchi-
asmos, Phoiniki, Photiki, Bouthrotos, and Kerkyra (Corfu). This division of the
ecclesial responsibilities was maintained until the Fragkokratia. In 596, Pope Gregory
wrote to the bishops of the region validating the election of Bishop of Nikopolis
Andreas. In 625, Pope Honorius I (625–638) wrote to Bishop of Nikopolis Hypatios
regarding the difficult travel conditions that prevented the latter's visit to Rome. In
the mid-sixth century, there were two successive bishops with the name Doumetios.
The first built the grand basilica 'A,' with extensive series of floor mosaics. The dating of this basilica is subject to some debate. Nikopolis, p. 21 dates to 525–575, Gkɪ–41,
dates to 525–550, Kitz–92 dates to 530–550, Mous. p. 35 dates to 540–550, Foss-204
dates to after 551. Furthermore, around this time some reconstruction work was carried out on the older grand basilica 'B' known as 'Alkyson,' and a three-aisled basilica 'E' was built near the ancient harbor of Magarona. Bishop Dometios II apparently
finished basilica 'A' and built basilica 'T' nearby. These basilicas were richly adorned
with floor mosaics and some degree of imported marble. While their building mate-
rials were not as precious as basilicas in major metropolitan centers, their construction suggests a thriving Church in the local area with a bishop in a central position
for harnessing the local resources. See Bowden, 135–51. The bishops seem to fade in
importance in the following centuries. Nothing is known about them beyond their
names: Bishop Anastasios of Nikopolis signed the Seventh Ecumenical Council
(787), and seals bearing the names of Ioannis II, Leon, Vasileos, and Antonios have
been found. The eighth century also saw the establishment of the first monasteries
in the Metropolis, the most famous of which is at Zalongo, which is still occupied.
According to Seraphim Byzantios, a bishop of nearby Arta who wrote a history of
the region in 1884, the monastery at Zalongo was founded in the eighth century,

perennial role of being stuck between Rome and Constantinople continued to shape local affairs. In 732/733, Emperor Leon III transferred
the region that contained Nikopolis from the ecclesial jurisdiction of
the Pope of Rome to that of the Ecumenical Patriarch of Constantinople. From that time on, the bishop of Nikopolis is given the title,
"Metropolitan" and continues to be responsible for most of the other
bishops of the region.[30] Telling, the last reference to a bishop of
Nikopolis comes in the context of the perennial divide between East
and West. The last known bishop of the Metropolis of Nikopolis was
Metropolitan Daniel, who is reported to offer support in 887 to St
Fotios in his fight against false union with the West. From 929
onwards, there is no mention of a bishop residing in Nikopolis itself.
The first golden period of the diocese had passed.

The "Dark Ages" for the Metropolis of Nikopolis

Due to its location adjacent to the sea on a plain, the city of Nikopolis lacked any natural defenses. As a result, a series of foreign powers
plundered it beginning in 474 CE, when the Vandals sacked the city,
and continuing sporadically throughout the next four centuries. The
city began its final decline in the tenth century when the Bulgarians
sacked Nikopolis in a series of raids. With the town nearly abandoned, the Metropolis of Nikopolis was merged with the nearby

---

though little is known about it until the nineteenth century. See Βιτάλης Φιλάρε-
του, αρχιμ., Ἡ ἱερὰ μονὴ Ζαλόγγου, (Αθήνα, 1959), 10. Likewise, the monastery near
Lamaris dedicated to the repose of the Theotokos is said to be established in 774 CE.
In the eighth or ninth century, the monastery of Lekatsa, dedicated to the birth of
the Theotokos and the Holy Trinity and located between the villages of Myrsini and
Riniasa, was founded. At the end of eleventh century, a monastery dedicated to St
Paraskevi Podogora was established within the Metropolis. See Φώτιος Γ.
Οικόνομου, Η ΕΚΚΛΗΣΙΑ ΤΗΣ ΗΠΕΙΡΟΥ (Αθήναι, 1982), 152.

[30]Σ. Τσαγκαρόπουλος, "Ο ΑΠΟΣΤΟΛΟΣ ΠΑΥΛΟΣ ΚΑΙ Η ΕΚΚΛΗ-
ΣΙΑ ΤΗΣ ΝΙΚΟΠΟΛΕΩΣ," εν ΠΡΕΒΕΖΑΝΙΚΑ ΧΡΟΝΙΚΑ 27–28 (1993),
56. Nikopolis is referenced in the Parisian Code (731–746) as the metropolitan of the
province of Epirus Vetus with the following suffrages: Adrianoupolis, Euroia,
Agiasmos, Fotiki, Bithypotos, and Dodoni. See Οικόνομου (1973), 24.

Metropolis of Nafpaktos to form the "Metropolis of Nafpaktos of Nikopolis." This Metropolis had jurisdictional control over all of ancient Epirus, but Nikopolis itself no longer existed. Over time, any reference to Nikopolis ceased and the memory of the golden era of the church of Nikopolis began to fade.[31] The bishop of Nikopolis had been eliminated, even in name.

THE RISE OF PREVEZA AND THE RETURN OF THE METROPOLIS OF NIKOPOLIS[32]

In the thirteenth century, local residents near the ancient ruined city of Nikopolis built a church dedicated to St Nicholas at the mouth of the great bay upon which Nikopolis had been built. A town emerged around it, and it faced the same plight as its predecessor, caught between Western and Eastern powers. In 1292, in the long wake of the plundering of Constantinople by Italians during the Fourth Crusade, Genoese warships plundered Preveza as it attacked their eastern enemy.[33] By the sixteenth century, the population of Preveza

---

[31]During the reign of the Andronikos Palaiologos (1259–1282), Nafpaktos was captured by the Italians and the headquarters of the Metropolis was shifted to Ioannina in 1285. Shortly afterwards, the city of Arta began to arise as the dominant city in the region, with the Metropolis of Nafpaktos Arta being formed in 1367 when the Metropolitan of Nafpaktos Matthew came to transfer the Metropolis to Arta and act as its first bishop. The identification with Nikopolis did not die altogether—despite being in Arta, in 1470 the Metropolitan of Arta called himself the Metropolitan of "Nafpaktos-Nikopolis." However, by 1507, the title was renamed "Nafpaktos-Arta" and references to Nikopolis ceased. See Οικόνομου (1982), 81.

[32]I am greatly indebted to Nikos Karambelas and the Aktia-Nikopolis Foundation, which he heads, for their support in this section. Mr Karambelas has proved to be not only an invaluable resource for local history but also a helpful discussion partner and good friend.

[33]In the Greek version of the *Morea Chronicle*. The French version reports the same event as the sacking of "Port de Saint Nicolas de Tort" (Port of St Nicholas of the Tower). While an absolute identification between these two references cannot be assured, it appears likely that St Nicholas of the Tower and Preveza are one and the same. A map produced nearly 400 years later by Coronelli in Italy about a journey that took place in 1684 places "Ressiduo della Chiesa di San Nicolo" near the present location of a church dedicated to St Nicholas. See Μηνιαίο Ιουνίου, εκδ., Δημ.

remained small but was growing. In the Ottoman registry of 1564, 30 households and 13 bachelors were noted (~163 persons); by 1579, the total had increased to 50 households and 20 bachelors (~270 persons).[34] While the report suggests that the population was exclusively Christian, the presence of a mosque in the large fort named Bouka suggests at least some Muslim population as well. Its geographic position would continue to shape its destiny, however. In 1684, the Venetians conquered Preveza for the first of what would be two periods of rule. Occupying the city, the Venetians promptly converted the mosque into a church dedicated to the Archangels. As part of a treaty between the Venetians and the Ottomans, this church—the second of Preveza—was destroyed in 1701. Preveza then remained a small fishing village, perhaps with as few as 1800 inhabitants.[35] However, the region continued to be caught between mightier powers to the East and the West. The Turks retook Preveza in 1701 only to lose it again to the Venetians in 1717. The Venetians then ruled it until 1798, building a Latin Church in a new castle dedicated to St Andrew.[36]

In the face of either Latin or Ottoman control, the Orthodox people of Preveza built private family chapels that later would be donated to the Metropolis. The names of the original families are still connected with the churches, though the stories of their origin have

---

Θεοδοσίου 1761, σελ. 3 in Ιερέα Ιωάννη Αλ. Κόλλια, "ΕΝΟΡΙΕΣ ΖΩΣΕΣ ΚΑΙ ΑΓΩΝΕΣ ΚΛΗΡΟΥ ΤΗΣ ΠΟΛΗΣ ΠΡΕΒΕΖΑΣ ΕΠΙ ΤΟΥΡΚΟΚΡΑ-ΤΙΑΣ," *ΠΡΕΒΕΖΑΝΙΚΑ ΧΡΟΝΙΚΑ*, 27–28 (1993), 81. Furthermore, a note inscribed on a liturgical book says that a "new" church was built upon the "old" church of St Nicholas in 1530, suggesting an earlier church of St Nicholas prior to the sixteenth century. Unfortunately for historians, because there is still a church dedicated to St Nicholas on the site that has been repeatedly renovated, archeological evidence has not been available to confirm the hypothesis.

[34]Delilbasi Melek, "The History of Preveza in the XVIth Century according to the Ottoman Taxation Registers," *Η Ιστορία της Πρέβεζας* (Πρέβεζα: Δήμος Πρέβεζας, 1993), 57–65. It is important to note that not all people were necessarily "registered." Further, it is difficult to tell where the boundaries of the city were. Did it just include the Castro or more of the surrounding area?

[35]According to Κ. Καρατζόγλου as reported in Γιώργος Μουστάκης, *Τα Πρεβεζάνικα* (Πρέβεζα: Δήμου Πρέβεζας, 2002), 11.

[36]This church was converted into a munitions dump and the importance of this third known church in the history of Preveza was lost. It still exists as a building, but no one has studied it for its historical importance.

largely been lost.[37] Monastic communities, largely isolated from imperial control, also thrived. By the beginning of the nineteenth century, no less than 14 monasteries were functioning in the area. In 1779, the great saint of the poor, Father Kosmas, came to Preveza and preached to the people in front of Sts Constantine and Helen church, where until recently a mosaic marked the spot. Later he wrote a letter to the people of Preveza, expressing shock that they did not have a school. The letter is as follows:[38]

To the Inhabitants of Preveza

My most noble beloved brethren, inhabitants of the village of Preveza, I greet you and beseech the Holy God for your spiritual and physical health.

I, my brethren, as an unworthy servant of God, travel about and teach the Christians according to my ability. I also came here and seeing that you don't have a school, I urged (the Christians) and they gave according to their ability and will for your school.

You also should always help your school from your own resources or from those of the village or from those of the religious endowments, so that you might receive wages from God and honor from men.

I too am a debtor and I beseech the Lord, who blesses all things, to bless your village, your school, your children, and to find you worthy to live well and pleasing to God here (on earth) and to put you into paradise to rejoice and be glad, glorifying the Holy Trinity.

---

[37]In 1742, the church of Saints Constantine and Helen was built by the Christodoulos family who immigrated from Corfu and then granted it to parishioners. In 1750, the church of St Athanasius was built by the family of Father John Gorgousi and then deeded to the parishioners. Recent restoration work on the church has confirmed this approximate date, as the wall paintings in the church were done in 1780. In 1780, the church of St Paraskevi was built by the Sergianni family and later funded by the Gabanozi family before being turned over to parishioners. The first church built after Venetian control was re-established in 1717 was probably the church of St Haralambos, which would later become the seat of the Metropolis. Although construction may have begun as early as 1715, it was built in a style consistent with Venetian overlords. The family connected with this church is unknown.

[38]Translation provided by http://stmaryofegypt.org/kosmas/letters.html, 8/1/03.

Amen. . . .

Hieromonk Kosmas
who prays for you
April 1779

As a result, it appears that a school was founded in 1779, which went on to educate many of the important members of the community. St Kosmas is also remembered by a chapel dedicated to him below the modern church of St Constantine, and his feast day (24 August) is a large festival in Preveza.[39]

As Preveza grew in the nineteenth century as a regional economic center, its religious life reflected its classical geographic position.[40] By 1884, there were eleven Orthodox churches in Preveza, all, with the exception of St Nicholas and St Haralambos, still in private hands, as well as one Roman Catholic church and two mosques. The nineteenth century also produced the most popular local legend, the saving of the city by St Haralambos.[41]

On March 10, 1816, a ship arrived in the harbor with a sailor who had the plague originating from some undisclosed location. The plague spread very quickly throughout the city, with many of the residents fleeing to the monasteries in the nearby hills. As many people perished due to the plague, the bishop of Arta, who at the time still governed Preveza, sent his assistant, a prominent man named Joseph, who would later become a great martyr during the Greek revolution five years later. Father Joseph worked day and night tending to the

---

[39]See Οικόνομου (1982), 243.

[40]In 1895, Ottoman sources report there were 5,168 Christian males and 4,840 females, as well as 3,512 Muslim males and 3,097 Muslim females. See Ali Cevad, *Memalik-I Osmaniyenin Cografya Lugati (Geographic Manual of the Ottoman Lands)* (Constantinople, 1892), 238–40, in Ilber Ortayli, "Preveza during the Tanzimat Era (1864–1895)," in *Η Ιστορία της Πρέβεζας* (Πρέβεζα: Δήμος Πρέβεζας, 1993), 241–48. A perhaps more-reliable report by British Consul Barker in 1871 reports 4,318 Christians and 1,724 Turks. *Parliamentary papers and accounts report of Vice-consul Barker (Preveza 1872–28 January)* p. 1355, in Ortayli, 242.

[41]The story regarding this event was discovered inscribed in the front cover of a liturgical book, the February copy of a Menian published in 1799, written by a priest named Evangelos.

sick and looking after the families of those who had perished. When the deaths mounted, he gathered all the people in the church of St Haralambos to entreat God to save his people through his saint. He took the holy relics of St Haralambos and made a procession throughout the town while the people chanted "Lord Have Mercy" and "St Haralambos help us." On the edge of town, the people began to see a very old hieromonk who was unknown to the people walking in front of the procession. Some people, especially small children, noticed that he did not appear to be walking but rather floating just above the ground. When the procession returned to the church, the old, unknown hieromonk seemed to disappear. First the priest and then all the people came to notice that the icon of St Haralambos had tears falling from his eyes. An all-night vigil commenced, and after this vigil, the death toll began to wane. The plague had ended with the help of St Haralambos. The people began to recognize him as the protector of the town. In 1835, St Haralambos was officially recognized as the patron saint of Preveza.

In 1881, the nearby town of Arta, from where the bishop governed Preveza, was liberated from Turkish rule when the Greek state annexed the area. However, the reach of the new Greek state did not extend to Preveza. The result was that the churches of the still-occupied Preveza were separated from their Metropolis home. Furthermore, Arta came under the authority of the Archbishop of Greece while the lands surrounding Preveza all the way to the river Arachthos, which was the border between Greece and Turkey, remained under Turkish control and thus stood ecclesiastically directly under the Ecumenical Patriarch. As a result, the Metropolis of Nikopolis was re-established after nearly a millennium and centered in the growing town of Preveza. The "new" Metropolis of Nikopolis *and Preveza* was thus created in August 1881 with 110 parishes and fifteen monasteries.[42] The first bishop built the house of the bishop with his own money.

---

[42]Patriarch Jacob III (1878–1884) wrote, "The Holy Metropolis of Arta was bisected due to political changes (the liberation of the regions beyond the river Arachthos, which until that time were under Turkish occupation) and became subject to the Greek State. For this reason, the Synod of the Ecumenical Patriarchate

Since its re-inception, fourteen bishops have been named head of the Metropolis of Preveza and Nikopolis. Most of these bishops were from outside the region, were well educated, and resigned their position long before their death. During the Turkish period up until 1912, the bishops not only were responsible for the spiritual needs of the people, they were quite literally the judge, headmaster, and spokesman for the Greek people. That is, the position of the bishop was an ethnic, political, and even economic position, as well as spiritual. For example, often times he was called upon to be the "go-between" for the Greek people and their Ottoman rulers in the system of bribes and payoffs by which the local economy operated. Likewise, the Church became responsible for setting up schools to teach Greek language, religion, and traditions, often under the dire threat of their overlords. Perhaps as a result of these multifaceted leadership requirements, Preveza became a stepping stone on the road of the Church hierarchy, especially during the tumultuous twenty-year period between 1890 and 1910 when no less than eight bishops held the throne. Among them were some interesting figures.[43] The third bishop, Joachim, was only twenty-seven years old when he took the throne, which he only held for twenty months. However, he eventually became bishop of the important city of Thessaloniki, a position he held for only two years before dying at age forty-nine. The prize for most meteoric rise, however, most go to Bishop Neofetos, who after less than three months as local bishop of Nikopolis was selected

decided that the sections belonging to the Holy Metropolis of Arta, which lie to the north of the river Arachthos and remained a part of the Ottoman Empire, (i.e., Preveza and the surrounding areas) form a separate Metropolis. Its spiritual jurisdiction will be under the Ecumenical Patriarchate. The new established Metropolis will bare the ancient name Metropolis of Nikopolis."

[43]Because Preveza was a port city, many of its bishops seemed to have international connections. Bishop Gabriel (1896–1899) studied law in France and theology in Constantinople before coming to Preveza. The nearby bishop of Paramithia passes on the intriguing description that while Bishop Neofetos was "good and thin, he was worldly in ways." One of the most dynamic bishops was Dorotheos (1901–1908), who retired to London. A full list of bishops can be found in Γεώργιος Κούρτη, Η ΙΕΡΑ ΜΗΤΡΟΠΟΛΗ ΝΙΚΟΠΟΛΕΩΣ ΚΑΙ ΠΡΕΒΕΖΗΣ ΚΑΙ ΟΙ ΑΡΧΙΕΡΕΙΣ ΤΗΣ (1881-2000 μ.Χ) (Πρέβεζα: ΙΕΡΑΣ ΜΗΤΡΟΠΟΛΕΩΣ ΝΙΚΟΠΟΛΕΩΣ, 2000).

to be the Ecumenical Patriarch of Constantinople. However, the bishop of the ancient city of Victory (Nikopolis) would once again emerge as an instrumental player in securing the freedom of the faithful during the Greek revolution.

In 1912, a rebellion was brewing in the hills around Preveza against nearly five centuries of oppression by the Ottoman Turks.[44] One of the important leaders of the rebellion was a priest from Preveza, Spiros Kurgios. His men, however, lacked adequate arms to fight, and the Turks controlled all the roads and ports. Small arms would be brought into the Preveza port on fishing boats and gathered by the priests—who were less likely to be searched—in the middle of the night. They would carry them under their robes to the house of the bishop, where they would be placed in boxes of candles that could be transported without suspicion to the monasteries that lined the remote hilltops of the region. Once at the monasteries, they would be distributed to the freedom fighters. By October of 1912, the freedom fighters were armed and prepared for a decisive battle. The location was fittingly the ruined city of Nikopolis, Augustus' city of victory. This time, however, it was not a Roman Emperor leading the soldiers but a local priest. The final words of Father Spiros before the fighting began would have been as appropriate for an altar as a bunker: "May you have courage and lean upon the Protector of the weak, the All-powerful God and our Savior Jesus Christ." Amidst the ruins of Roman stadiums and ancient churches, the descendents of Nikopolis defeated the Turks and liberated the people of Preveza. The next morning, the Apostolic Bishop of Nikopolis and Preveza, Bishop Joachim (1910–1931), signed a treaty on behalf of the people that united Preveza with the modern state of Greece for the first time. However, this victory was not just political but also spiritual. That night, the people of Preveza gathered at the central church of St Haralambos to give thanks for their freedom. All would be blessed by the bishop, who awaited them. His face grows brighter as the main sanctuary fills and then overflows. The bishop speaks like a father to his extended family. He offers words of encouragement, education, chas-

---

[44]The following account is taken from the history of the parishes by Κόλλια.

tisement, and above all, inspiration. They have come a long way from the Apostle Paul's first steps in Nikopolis, but curiously, little has changed.

CHAPTER TWO

The Protagonist:
The Story of Bishop Meletios

I greeted Bishop Meletios on a cold January morning in 1998 in the customary manner of kissing his hand. He held onto my head in an embrace and asked me a question in English: "When you look up "Greek" in the dictionary, what does it say?" I said nothing. "Rascal!" he said erupting in laughter. I wondered if this truism applied to him. Grabbing his staff, which was leaning against the door, he took my arm and walked down the quiet, empty streets. He was dressed as a common humble priest: pressed black vestments, pectoral cross, and black, rimmed hat; only his staff indicated he was the bishop, though I suspect everyone already knew. He inquired about my family and Orthodoxy in America, occasionally pausing to pass on some wisdom. We communicated in broken English, French, and Greek. His insights usually included a phrase I recognized from the Bible or a quote from the Church Fathers. We walked by a series of stores that I would later learn the bishop had constructed out of a ruined church in order to provide more revenue for the Metropolis. He made no mention of this shrewd act or anything else he had done for the town and the Church. Young university students spilled out of bars, completing their night of revelry early in the morning. Pointing to them, the bishop quipped, "Returning from their all-night vigil!" Older women came out of their homes in order to receive a blessing, which the bishop gave willingly yet with humility that could almost be mistaken for embarrassment.

We arrived at St Athanasius church around half past seven. The church, constructed in the mid-eighteenth century, was already half full. The church no longer had a parish, but by nine in the morning it and the courtyard surrounding the church was overflowing. As is the custom, all the faithful from the town came together as one Church to celebrate the feast of its patron. The bishop stood at the center of the church, looking thin and weak compared to the men and women kissing his hand and receiving a blessing. Among them were some of the communist civic leaders of Preveza, who had become Christians after their interactions with the bishop, and young children who were not yet in school. The Divine Liturgy began just after nine and the bishop served with his normal deep reverence. As was the case so many times previously, the people detected tear-filled eyes when the bishop came out of the altar to say, "Let us lift up our hearts unto the Lord." At the conclusion, he offered a simple homily, extolling the example of St Athanasius whose feast had just been celebrated. He spoke quietly, except for moments of accentuation when he was nearly shouting for emphasis. Afterwards, he passed out the blessed bread to each person. When the last of the bread was distributed, we walked back to the bishop's house. He bought some fruit along the way from a boy who called him simply *geronda*, old wise man.

This portrait of Bishop Meletios is indicative of his character. He is quick with the wit and a well-timed joke, but he is always serious about his faith and the tasks entrusted to him. He recognizes the gravity of his exalted position as shepherd of the faithful and heir to the apostles, but walks humbly among the people, affecting no pomp or circumstance. He is familiar with ten languages and has written high-level theological treatises, but he never flaunts his knowledge, always speaking simply. He is extremely ascetic and morally disciplined, but shows compassion and tolerance toward those he meets. He disdains politics and economic enterprises, but shrewdly manipulates them when necessary to benefit the spiritual life of the people. Bishop Meletios holds these various competing character traits together like few people can. This chapter aims to trace his development as a person and as a Church leader.

Biographical Sketch of Bishop Meletios

Alagonia (1933–1946)

Bishop Meletios was born in 1933, the third of eleven children. His father, Agisilaos, was a doctor and a particularly devout man, never beginning a day without prayers and in old age read only Scripture. His mother, Eleni, is remembered as one who "served in the holy ministry of being a housewife,"[1] as a woman of "amazing sacrifice . . . she was willing to serve the world and never said 'no' to anyone."[2] Although his parents were pious, he did not come from a tradition of dedicating oneself to the church—none of his immediate family or distant relatives had ever consecrated themselves to ministry. Furthermore, none of his numerous brothers and sisters would dedicate themselves to the church.[3] Nevertheless, throughout his clerical career he had the support of his family.

Meletios grew up in Alagonia, a small Peloponnesian village near the summit of the Taygetos mountain near Kalamata in the region of Messinia. When Meletios was a boy, the village had some 1500 people, though migration has diminished the town's population to 250 people today. The spirituality of his fellow villagers made a significant impact on the young Meletios. He writes:

> We did not have monks. However, we did have in my village many
> people who lived with a deep love for Christ and in purity; men for
> whom their life had boundless benevolence due to their love for

---

[1]In the introduction to Γιάννη Κείσογλου, "Ένας Σύγχρονος Άγιος: Ο δεσπότης που προηγείται της εποχής του και απολαμβάνει της καθολικής αποδοχής λαού και εκκλησίας," *ΕΠΙΛΟΓΟΣ* 5 (January 1996). Translation by author. Hereafter cited as "*ΕΠΙΛΟΓΟΣ*."

[2]Metropolitan Meletios, "Ο ΜΗΤΡΟΠΟΛΙΤΗΣ ΝΙΚΟΠΟΛΕΩΣ ΚΑΙ ΠΡΕΒΕΖΗΣ ΜΕΛΕΤΙΟΣ Μιλάει για τη ζωή του χριστιανού και το έργο της Εκκλησίας στον σημερινό κόσμο," *Orthodox Globe* (May 1996). Translation by author. Hereafter cited as "*Orthodox Globe*."

[3]One of his brothers became one of the leaders of the Communist party in Greece, a connection which at times has been a burden for Meletios, who consciously tries to shun overt political affiliations.

Christ; and who, while they were simple villagers, had the unceas-
ing memory of God.[4]

This "simple" devoutness appears again and again as Meletios' model
of Christian love and charity. He recalls a village family whose father
had been killed in the civil war, leaving the mother alone to raise their
seven children. Then, one day, the mother fell from an olive tree,
orphaning all seven young ones. The people of Meletios' village came
together to care for the orphans, taking turns to look after them all
day, every day, for nearly ten years. Quite literally, the village raised
the children. Eventually, the oldest moved to Athens and after set-
tling there, brought his remaining sisters and brothers to join him.
The family turned out well, and Meletios did not forget the village's
example of Christian charity and love.

Another early influence on the young Meletios was the particularly devout priest in his town, Father John Arfanakis. The bishop
recalled of him, "When he spoke about Christ and his Kingdom, he
wept from the emotions. And while performing the liturgy in church,
it was as if he was a genuine angel of God."[5] Meletios' parish priest
was the only example of a life consecrated to God available to the
young boy, as there were no monks in the local area and the next village was quite a distance. These circumstances may have contributed
to the paradigm of the consecrated life that Meletios would later
develop. Due to the remoteness of his posting, Alagonia's local priest
was insulated from the worldly affairs of the church; he could not
dwell in a *megaron* (bishop's palace) or work behind an administrative
desk. Furthermore, his entire life was open to the close scrutiny of his
fellow villagers. In other words, the circumstances demanded authenticity, total devotion, and simplicity from Father Arfanakis. Father
Meletios' earliest model of the sanctified life would establish the central characteristics by which he later would define his spiritual and
ecclesial purpose.

---

[4]Metropolitan Meletios, interview by author, unpublished written responses,
Spring 2003, Preveza, Greece. Translated by author. Hereafter cited as "Interview,
SLM."
   [5]*Orthodox Globe.*

Meletios did not grow up with an influential model of a bishop. Due to its remoteness, the village rarely saw the local bishop or any member of the Church hierarchy. He recalls:

> The bishop of that district, when I was in the village, paid us a visit only one time, in 1940–1941. He was very old and tired. There was not a road network. He came by mule. The entire village greeted him from a distance of a kilometer outside the village. When he drew near and raised his hand to give his blessing, all the people were found immediately on their knees! Afterwards, he remounted the mule and continued to the church. For all of this distance, the road was blanketed with brand new, unused sheets, blankets, dresses, etc. . . . all sorts of household finished fabrics, which were prepared for the houses of the girls who were waiting to be married the following year. They were spread out upon the dirt in order that the mule who was holding the bishop would tread on them and so they would receive a blessing! I don't ever remember seeing anywhere else such a reception! My fellow villagers welcomed their spiritual father like it was Christ himself.[6]

Perhaps Meletios learned from this single experience the sanctity of the place of the bishop. He also appreciated the spiritual love that could bind the bishop to his flock. Nevertheless, the young Meletios would have few early models for his future clerical career. But, then again, Alagonia in the 1940s was a very different world from Athens, where he would spend his intellectually formative years, and Preveza, where he would eventually become bishop.

Athens (1947–1954)

Meletios' family moved to Athens when he was thirteen. He finished middle school and high school in Athens, eventually studying theology and philosophy at the University of Athens. By his own account, Meletios showed little direct interest in the church during his adolescent years, when the "ideas of the Enlightenment and the mantra

---

[6]Interview, SLM.

about the death of God" influenced him.[7] Meletios has described this period as "living far from Christ" and "a deep adolescent crisis"[8] and a "worldly life,"[9] yet it was brief since his "conversion" to a life dedicated to God began at age sixteen. He recalls, "God out of his compassion did not abandon me to be lost. He drove me to awareness."[10] In this case, God used books to reach Meletios. He describes this process as follows:

> In the year 1950 (I was around sixteen years old), I had managed to gather up a small amount of allowance, which that season had supplied to me. So, I went to a cart to buy a cheap book (things in the bookstore were brand new and very expensive.) There I made the same choice as any boy of any age. First, I glanced at two books. The one was titled *The Galation, a Romance Novel*, by Polivios Demitrakopoulos. The second had the title: "The Apocryphal Acts of Paul and Thekla." I said to myself: "We caught the Apostle Paul in clandestine practices with a certain 'Thekla.' Before we make any decisions in our life, we better learn what this is and not just accept whatever the priest says." Afterwards, I also bought a copy of the Gospels and a book with the Lives of the Saints.
>
> When I read the romance novel (pornography for that era while morally benign for today's time), I detested it. I understood then I had not received anything at all from it.
>
> The other book, "The Apocryphal Acts of Paul and Thekla," was a book which referred to how St Thekla became a Christian by the preaching of the Apostle Paul and how she followed him with all her soul and in the end became a martyr. . . . It was a sublime book, which not merely fascinated me but also brought about the first spark of desire to become a monk.
>
> The third book with the lives of the saints strengthened this very desire of mine. The life of St Athanasius of Christianopolis particularly made an impression on me. And the New Testament became

---

[7]Interview, SLM.
[8]Interview, SLM.
[9]*Orthodox Globe.*
[10]Interview, SLM.

from then on my daily reading. By the time I went to university two years later, I knew it by heart.[11]

In other sources, Meletios consistently mentions the importance of the story of Thekla, as well as the lives of St Katharine of Egypt, St Antony the Great, and St Athanasius Christianopolis. The former three saints have inspired young people for generations to renounce the world and join the monastics, however, the life of St Athanasius Christianopolis is lesser known in the West and deserves further attention.[12]

St Athanasius of Christianopolis was born on the island of Corfu in 1665, though following the Venetian occupation, his family moved to a small village in the Peloponnese so that his father could be a governor. Athanasius' father greatly wanted him, the youngest child, to marry and have a family like all his older brothers and sisters. But from his youth Athanasius was attracted to the church, especially reading the Holy Gospels and works of the Holy Fathers. He wanted to pray more, to fast more, and to deepen his spirituality. He prayed continually, "Lord, teach me the way I should go, for to you I lift up my soul" (Psalm 143.8). At age 35, he still was not married and his parents arranged a marriage for him. Due to the respect he had for them, he agreed to get married to a wealthy young woman. He felt torn between respecting his parents and the Apostle Paul's observation that it is better to remain unmarried. He continually prayed about it, but respecting his parents he agreed to prepare himself for marriage by making his wedding garments. A few days before his marriage, he had a dream in which the Theotokos (Mother of God, Mary) appeared to him, saying, "You will become a chosen vessel and servant of my son. Send your servants with your wedding garments to your father because the girl will marry another man. You must go to Constantinople." Praising God and desiring only to follow his will, he fled from his marriage and family, arriving in Constantinople.

---

[11]*Orthodox Globe.*

[12]The following synopsis of the Life of St Athanasius of Christianopolis is taken from two unpublished homilies delivered by Bishop Meletios. The first occurred on May 19, 1986, and the second on May 17, 1999, in the Spiritual Center of Preveza.

There he became close to the courts of the Patriarch, who tonsured him a monk and ordained him a priest in 1702. In 1707, Patriarch Gabriel sent him to be bishop of Christianopolis, which is in the Peloponnese. His first activity was to tour his whole Metropolis and build numerous churches, recognizing that a person is sanctified by being in Church. Because the Peloponnese was still under Turkish occupation, he founded a school to teach the young Greeks how to read and write in Greek so that they could read the Bible and be fortified against the Catholic propaganda of the Venetians. Filled with the Holy Spirit, Athanasius began to do miracles, helping many people through his prayers. After his death, many more miracles have been recorded and his body remains undefiled at the Monastery of St John the Forerunner in Gortinia in the Peloponnese.

Bishop Meletios calls St Athanasius his "spiritual father" for he was instrumental in his decision to become a monk. Bishop Meletios says in one homily, "I love him and venerate him especially because it was due to him that I became a monk. No living person taught me to want to become a monk. I learned it from the life of St Athanasius, bishop of Christianopolis."[13] He later explains that after reading the life of St Athanasius, he realized for the first time that he had to make a choice whether to fully dedicate himself to God or live for earthly glory. "Seeing how one man chooses, with such circumstances, having made his wedding garments and then going to become a monk and dedicate himself to Christ, I made the sign of the cross and said: this is the road I must follow also. Glory to Christ and St Athanasius."[14]

Bishop Meletios also took other lessons from the life of St Athanasius. First, he would model his episcopal reign in part on St Athanasius, touring the metropolis and building churches for the people to gather. Second, he learned the value and power of words, noting in a recent homily the benefits of schools teaching classical Greek. Just as St Athanasius would educate himself as necessary and write for the good of his flock, so Bishop Meletios would do the same

---

[13]Bishop Meletios, unpublished homily, "Τὰ Σημεῖα τῆς Βασιλείας τοῦ Θεοῦ καὶ τοῦ Κόσμου," May 17, 1999, Preveza, Greece.
[14]Ibid.

in his career. Third, he observed the power of the Holy Spirit to work through individuals to create miracles. St Athanasius was not known as a commanding figure in his day, nor has his fame spread widely in the intervening years; however, in his simplicity as a monk, he was turned into a vessel of the Holy Spirit, performing great miracles. Fourth and finally, St Athanasius remained always humble. When parishioners noticed a warm light that shined like a bright star exuding from his mouth while celebrating the liturgy one time, he begged with them to tell no one and remain forever quiet. He did not want to be a saint; or rather, he wanted to remain one in anonymity and true humility. Bishop Meletios has consistently sought the same. I once asked Bishop Meletios what was the most important virtue. Recalling St Athanasius, he said, *afania*, holy obscurity.

It is important to note that the effect of reading the life of St Athanasius (and the other saints' lives that significantly affected him) was to lead Meletios to the Scriptures. In another interview, he describes this process:

> One fortuitous moment was when I read the life of St Athanasius, bishop of Christianopolis (May 17). It made me start to search within and seek without. So then, at the age of about seventeen, I read thoroughly the New Testament. I understood that Christ is the Savior of the World. And I made a decision to live near to him, to live for him.[15]

The lives of the saints led Meletios to Christ *via* the Scriptures, one might say. Furthermore, to this day, Meletios is quick to point out that the primary source of inspiration was and remains the Holy Scriptures themselves. In this sense, the saints point to Christ, as presented in the Gospels. Bishop Meletios recently commented that after immersing himself in the lives of the saints, "From then and since, I recognize only the splendor of Christ in the actions and mindsets of the saints."[16] Christ is fully revealed through the Scriptures themselves. Consequently, by the time Meletios went to university, he

---

[15]Interview, SLM
[16]Interview, SLM.

knew the Scriptures by heart. This thirst for the Scriptures must be considered the greatest fruit of that fortuitous visit to the book cart when he was sixteen.

The Monastery of Velanidia (1955–1957)

Meletios was tonsured a monk on December 28, 1954, at the age of twenty-one at the Monastery of Velanidia (Monastery of the Oak Tree) near Kalamata in the Southwest Peloponnese. He considers that day the highlight of his life, for on that day he formally began a life wholly consecrated to God that he had lauded in the saints' lives. Afterwards, he felt the same joy that he saw in many of the saints:

> I glorify God because from the time when I became a monk at the age of 20 years (now I am 60)—in other words, 40 years of a spiritual journey—I have not substantially felt what it means to lack peace and joy. I have felt bitterness and worry, but they were momentary and temporary for several reasons, but never were the gifts of Christ—joy and peace—lost to me. Through Him, I am happy, as I told you, and I consider the greatest moment and summit of my life the day that I was dedicated to Christ and became a monk.[17]

The fruit of his whole-hearted dedication to Christ has been the peace and joy he has felt since consecrating his life to God. The beginning of this peace and joy can be found in his brief experience living the cenobitic monastic life near Kalamata. Although he resided in the monastery for only two years, he yearns for that time even now. He reflected, "My soul still longs for the experiences of that period like St Symeon the New Theologian was longing to see a second vision of God."[18] Despite not living in a monastery for forty-five years, the experiences of that period are still very much present for the bishop.

The monks of the Monastery of Velanidia were not particularly educated and the monastery was not well known outside the local

---

[17] *Orthodox Globe.*
[18] Interview, SLM.

area. Nevertheless, Meletios found inspiration in his fellow monks. He discovered a simple but deep faith in Christ and reverence for his Church. He recalled:

> And the compassionate Lord closed for me other doors and drove me to a monastery where I joined the true angels. True angelic messengers of kindness, compassion, humaneness, charity, prayer, reverence, simplicity, and humility. All the monks were authentic. All their life was without pretense. Eternal be their memory. . . . In order to describe any one of them, it would be necessary to write vast amounts.[19]

The virtues of his fellow monks would serve as models for Meletios and provide the subjects for numerous homilies and spiritual counsel. He recalls how Father Ambrosios would cry every time he heard the Gospel.[20] One of them would sing the doxologia in all eight tones all night long.[21] Once, the elder who was responsible for the monastery when the abbot was away was so enrapt in prayer that he not only forgot to organize the preparation of the meals but did not notice when the meal was missed.[22] Undoubtedly, these experiences reinforced the image of the model Christian that Bishop Meletios found in his fellow villagers and in the lives of the saints: simple, pious, fervent, and humble.

The tasks and responsibilities given to the young monk Meletios were not reflective of an exalted university graduate but of somebody training in humility and obedience. He was responsible for minding the nursing sow in the sty so she would not roll over her piglets. He was also the assistant to the cook. In performing these obediences, he gained a reputation for being quiet and obedient. He privately told one of the monks about the relationship he had with the head cook,

---

[19]Interview, SLM.

[20]Monk A, interview by author, digital recording, Monastery of Prophet Elias, Flamboura, Greece. 3 December 2002 and 16 December 2002. Hereafter cited as "Monk A."

[21]Recalled by Nun E. Nun E, interview by author, digital recording, Monastery of St Dimitrios, Zalongo, Greece, 18 April 2003. Hereafter cited as "Nun E."

[22]Recalled by Nun E.

who always looked to fault Meletios for every trial of the kitchen. Yet when the abbot asked him if he needed help for something else, the cook said, "Yes, send Meletios to help me." The abbot reportedly said, "I think you love him very much." "Well," the cook replied, "he doesn't speak at all; he just says yes so I prefer him to come and help me because he doesn't object to whatever I tell him!"[23] Without a doubt, this period was a time of training in the monastic life for Meletios.

The hieromonks[24] in Kalamata during that era did not always have smooth relations with the Metropolitan. As so often occurs, the local bishop wanted the hieromonks to work in the towns, preaching and doing mission work, rather than secluding themselves in the monastery. Only those who were not ordained spent a great deal of time in the monastery. Over time, this procedure compromised the integrity of the monastic life of Velanidia and the monastery died out. The vivacity of the monastery was not a high priority for the bishop of Kalamata. Many years later as a bishop, Meletios would also have to employ the hieromonks "in the world" for the good of the local church. His experience with Velanidia undoubtedly sensitized him to the dangers of a bishop who over-utilizes the hieromonks at his disposal. As we will see, his need for hieromonks in Preveza was greater than the previous need in Kalamata, but he consistently worked to maintain the integrity of their monastic life first and foremost.

Kalamata (1957–1967)

In 1957, Father Meletios left the Monastery of Velanidia in order to serve the Metropolis of Messinia in nearby Kalamata. While in the monastery, he had become a deacon, a rank he would hold until August 20, 1959, when he was ordained a priest. However, his clerical career began in earnest in 1957 when he was commissioned by the bishop of Messinia to preach. He recalls:

> From 1957 to 1967, I was a preacher. I preached to the parishes of the Holy Metropolis of Messinia, to the people and to the youth. I was

---

[23]Recalled by Nun E.

[24]A hieromonk is a monk who is also an ordained priest.

not silent. I was speaking a lot. Very much. About the most substantial theme: the salvation of the world; about love and obedience to Christ. That period was a most fruitful period. Also for me personally. And for the pronouncement of the will of God. I was continually speaking. And I continually heard and saw the grace of the Lord and his mercy, which was pursuing me. I was feeling so satisfied from what I was experiencing in that blessed corner of Greece that I was wishing and praying to finish my life there in the same work.[25]

Meletios was known not only for the quality of his homilies, but also for their length—rarely finishing before forty-five minutes. Although he was extremely thin and his voice relatively weak, he spoke passionately, punctuating his homilies with brief moments of spirited accentuation, which some claimed bordered on shouting. Yet the content of his homilies were presentations of the Gospel of Christ told in simple language, as is still the case today.

His decade of service to the Metropolis of Messinia was also the most influential period for shaping his view of the ecclesial life. The experience was a positive one. He recalls:

The all-compassionate Lord had mercy upon me. He stretched out his hand. He placed me inside the beautiful world of his Church. He enlightened me to see her light and her beauty. And to place it deeply within me, that every one of His servants is a page, which speaks for "the great love with which Christ loves us." There were 250 priests in the Metropolis of Messinia and some hundred monks and nuns. And all of them, in their poverty and humility, had riches within! My ecclesiastical experience then taught me not only to not despise anyone, but rather to give thanks to God, who placed me in contact with them and I saw his grace, which stretched out so abundantly in young and old![26]

It was also here that he developed close relationships with two of his most important spiritual influences: the "colossal wisdom and holiness" of Archimandrite Joel Yiannakopoulos and the "tireless mis-

---

[25]Interview, SLM.
[26]Interview, SLM.

sionary of the poor of Jesus," Archimandrite Agathangelos Michaelidis.[27] Throughout Meletios' time in Kalamata, Arch. Agathangelos
was the protosingelos (primary assistant to the bishop) in Kalamata
while Arch. Joel was a fellow hieromonk and preacher. Because they
were so influential in shaping Bishop Meletios, their stories must also
be told in brief.[28]

Archimandrite Agathangelos Michaelidis was born in Asia
Minor in 1908 near Keysari, Cappadocia. Losing his parents at a
young age, he grew up in an orphanage. In 1922, he came to Greece
as a refugee, initially to Athens and then eventually to Thessaloniki.
He was tonsured a monk and ordained a deacon on Mt Athos at the
Monastery of Xenophontos. During the German occupation, he
came to Athens to study. While there, he assisted the poor greatly
during their struggles. In 1947, Bishop Chrysostomos of Messinia
asked him to serve in Kalamata as a hieromonk and then protosingelos. He gained a large following in Kalamata as a compassionate and
gentle spiritual father, more accommodating than many of the other
spiritual fathers and full of love for the people. He organized an
orphanage for the children, in which he did some of the cooking and
cleaning himself. He also began a Christian organization called
"Grace" that sought to educate the people about their faith. Although
he was protosingelos, he remained very simple, eschewing fancy vestments and cassocks for plain, worn cloaks. When he traveled by train,
he always asked to be placed in the lowest class of service. In 1967, he
returned to his monastic roots, leaving the metropolis to become
abbot of the Monastery of Pendeli near Athens. Finally, in 1983, he
retired, serving as elder to a monastery near Nafplio until he died in
1991.

Archimandrite Joel Yiannakopoulos grew up with a great love for
the Church. Even when he was in his teens, he would fast so severely
that he would have difficulty raising his legs to get on the bus. Eventually, he was tonsured a monk and made a deacon. Yet he did not

---

[27]Interview, SLM.
[28]Bishop Meletios has written a book about each one of them, so the following
is derived from these two volumes.

retire to a monastery but rather became a teacher of theology in the local high school. He had always been very ascetic and at one time his fasting became so severe that he had to be hospitalized. A year of recovery was required from that brush with death, during which time he began to learn foreign languages in order to study biblical scholarship from other Western European countries. He came to Kalamata in 1942 in the middle of the German occupation and served the people there. After the war, the political divisions of the civil war tore apart the city. Father Joel refused to take sides and this courageous act of non-partisanship even led to death threats. In the metropolis, he was known for the fervency of his homilies and his personal asceticism. He often walked in the cemetery in order to keep the memory of death fresh; he was known for the strictness with which he reproached people in confession; and he actively tried to isolate himself from all worldly aspects of life, especially in the politics of the Church. He wrote dozens of books, including a thirteen-volume commentary on the Old Testament for which he won a prestigious award from the University of Athens. He ended his career and life as an Archimandrite in Kalamata, dying on December 23, 1966. In his book on Father Joel, Bishop Meletios argues that he should be considered a modern saint.

In these two equally exceptional yet very different ecclesial figures—Father Agathangelos and Father Joel—one can identify many of the traits that define the ecclesial style and belief embodied by Bishop Meletios. Like Father Joel, Bishop Meletios is highly ascetic and strict with himself; both were known for being extremely thin and weak. Likewise, he has learned numerous languages and written scholarly and theological treatises like Father Joel. They also both share a strong distaste for the worldly aspects of political and Church life. However, like Father Agathangelos, Bishop Meletios stresses the importance of simplicity, humility, and compassion, especially in dealing with the sins of others. Moreover, Father Agathangelos never lost sight that he was first a monk and a simple priest, ultimately returning to his monastic roots for the last twenty-five years of his life. Bishop Meletios as well has never lost sight that he is first a monk and a simple priest. He, too, has been found riding with the common people on the bus to Athens and walking about Preveza in a simple cassock. The result of these two influences is a curious mixture that more than anything describes the ecclesial manner of Bishop Meletios: highly cultured and academic but at the same time simple and unpretentious; extremely strict and ascetic with himself but greatly accommodating and compassionate with others; a leader among the Church hierarchy but somehow insulated from Church and governmental politics; the first among the priests but still a self-effacing monk and self-sacrificing priest. This ecclesial persona—how Meletios sees himself within his ecclesial role—came into being during this time in Kalamata.

The Holy Synod (1968–1980)

In 1967, as the Junta came to control Greece, a new Archbishop of the Church of Greece arose, Ieronimos. He sought to purify the church from all complacency and corruption, reaffirming its commitment to traditionalism and holiness. Toward this end, he brought numerous archimandrites, many of them from the ZOE movement, into the leadership of the church. While not directly recruited by Archbishop Ieronimos, Bishop Meletios came to the Holy Synod during this period of revival and renewal.[29] He was appointed in 1968 as the Secretary for inter-Orthodox and inter-Church relations for the Holy Synod of the Church of Greece. He would hold this position for nearly twelve years until he was named bishop of Nikopolis and Preveza in 1980.

Although he had a parish in Athens (St Eleftherios near Alexandras street) and continued to preach often, his position as Secretary required the development of very different skills. He was called upon to represent the Church in various conferences and synods around the globe, including being a central figure in the ecumenical dialogues carried out by the Church of Greece.[30] This required the develop-

---

[29]In part due to this timing, Bishop Meletios would be charged after his arrival in Preveza by local journalists with being connected with the Junta. His response, which is of great interest, appeared in a local newspaper.

[30]This work continued once he was bishop of Preveza. He offers a very interesting solution to the dialogue with non-Chalcedonians.

ment of many different languages, particularly Russian and the Balkan languages. These tasks also required a thorough understanding and clear articulation of the doctrines of the Orthodox Church. He referred to this time when he said:

> I thank God and I am grateful to my parents who gave me the opportunity and the capability and the initial encouragement to gain some degree of education. And therefore I was formed into a "useful vessel," as the Holy Scriptures say, into a "deacon" of the Orthodox Church. From then, I was called into the Holy Synod, in the Office of Inter-Church relations. I went many times abroad to all the countries, in as many places with Orthodox Christians and to many other heterodox countries—European and even non-Church. And either in special missions or in theological conferences for communication and unity with the other churches, I tried to do the best that I could. I give glory to God for this. And I have the sense and satisfaction of my conscience that I did a lot based on the doctrines, the traditions, and the light of our holy Orthodox Church, which, in these opportunities, I learned to respect even more as the one and only true church: that which Christ handed down to the world.

Archimandrite Meletios was placed in a position to use his skills to represent the Greek Church abroad. The result was an ever-deepening love of the Church. However, one should not equate this growing love for the Church with a passion for his career as a cleric, a minion in the administrative hierarchy of the Church. Quite the contrary, as is evident from the two important lessons he claims to have gained from this period:

> One: Prayer is the great power of the church; mindful worship for the glory of God is: fasting, virginity, humility, anonymity. The other is: I once asked a pious cleric: what are you doing? And he replied: I am doing nothing. Unfortunately, nothing. However, fortunately, God is acting. Let him have the glory. It is enough for us not to lose what he has done with our sinful works.
>
> The beginning and end of every act of God is the salvation of the world. We must place the weight of our attention on this, not in the work of institutions.

These conclusions in many ways represent a peculiar dynamic at work: as Archimandrite Meletios moved increasingly into the center of the "institution" of the Church (the Holy Synod) and took on the most political of all Church tasks (ecumenical dialogues), he came to see the Church *less* institutionally and *less* politically. In many ways, the more he became involved in the administration of the Church, the less he came to see it administratively. Rather, he began to see the Church as much more than an institution. Faith should not be in the ecclesial institution but in the God behind the Church. This "otherworldly" recognition of the foundation of the Church reflects the position of his spiritual comrade from Kalamata Father Joel Yiannakopoulos and in many ways represents an extension of the "simple" faith of his childhood villagers and the brothers of his monastic experience. By the late 1970s, Archimandrite Meletios was ready to "retire" from the worldly life of the Church by going to the monastic center of Mt Athos.

While in Athens, a group of spiritual children developed around Bishop Meletios. Many of these spiritual children came out of a youth revival movement known as SOTIR (salvation) and naturally gravitated toward the charismatic Archimandrite who quickly gained a reputation for his holiness, asceticism, and erudition. As one of his spiritual children recalled:

> I first saw Father Meletios on September 15th of 1976 in Athens. This meeting for me was extremely influential. . . . [I saw] first of all, his spirituality, his humility, his goodness—all these things were for me attractive. . . . In Greece, we have a proverb that says the face of man reveals all things. . . . Some people have a genuine spirituality that comes with the Holy Spirit; God is incarnated in them. Do you remember Father Antonios [the Great of Egypt] when he went to Alexandria, many people could recognize his holiness. He did not become a priest, he did not preach; they just saw him and his face and his eyes . . . it is a different world, a heavenly world. With Bishop Meletios, when you look at his face you see a heavenly world.[31]

---

[31]Monk C, interview by author, digital recording, Patras, Greece, 2 March 2003. Hereafter cited as "Monk C."

Many of his spiritual children recalled similar first impressions. By the mid-1970s, a dedicated group of spiritual children arose around Meletios. After nearly every service at his church of St Eleftherios, the young men would follow the Archimandrite to his apartment to carry on the spiritual discussion.[32] His apartment became a lively center of spiritual discussion, with nary a free space on the floor being available on many afternoons due to the number of people.

With the blessing of the Archbishop of Athens Seraphim, Archimandrite Meletios began to tonsure some of his spiritual children as monks at the monastery adjacent to the Holy Synod, Moni Petraki. The assumption was that the burgeoning community would not stay in Athens but find a monastic community in "a quiet place," presumably on Mt Athos.[33] In 1979, Father Meletios with twelve of his spiritual children (five of whom were already tonsured monks) traveled to Mt Athos to find a permanent community. Two options were apparent: the Holy Monastery of the Grand Lavra, which had yet to be converted to a cenobium,[34] and the Holy Monastery of Dochiariou. Father Meletios let the abbots of Mt Athos, many of whom he knew personally, know that he intended to come to Mt Athos. Yet they would not rush a decision but wait for the Holy Spirit to guide them. In the words of one of his spiritual children, "We waited and what came to us . . . Preveza!"[35]

Archimandrite Meletios' election as bishop interrupted the plans of many and surprised many more. Meletios himself had privately possessed plans for retiring in a short while to Mt Athos, with or without his spiritual children.[36] But rather than retreating from the

---

[32]Archimandrite Meletios had many female spiritual children and he would meet with them at the church, but his female spiritual children were not allowed in his apartment.

[33]Monk B, interview by author, digital recording, Monastery of Prophet Elias, Flamboura, Greece, 11 February 2003. Hereafter cited as "Monk B."

[34]In Orthodox monasticism, there are numerous forms of monastic life. The most common is the cenobium in which the monks live in common under the direction of a spiritual elder. However, for historical reasons, many of the monasteries on Mt Athos had converted to an *idiorhythmic* form of monasticism where monks lived in common but without the direction of a spiritual elder.

[35]Monk B.

[36]Interview, SLM.

"worldly" life of the Church, he was placed into the heart of it as the leader of a scandal-plagued, disorganized Metropolis in Nikopolis/Preveza. And it was only with a heavy heart and mixed emotions that Meletios accepted this task. The reaction of his spiritual children was mixed, though nearly all would eventually join him in Preveza. With six young monks by his side, on February 26, 1980, Meletios began the next stage of his life as Metropolitan Bishop of Nikopolis and Preveza. The process of this event will be outlined in the next chapter.

†

The trajectory of Bishop Meletios' life could have been different. He could have not picked up the books he did at that book stand at the age of sixteen and instead dedicated his vast intellectual abilities to spreading the vision of Nietzsche rather than Christ. He could have entered a healthy monastery and never left, living a life of holy obscurity as I suspect he wishes. He could have been successful in his desire to "retire" to Mt Athos, becoming another one of the legendary charismatic abbots responsible for the recent Athonite renaissance. He could have done many different things. But never would he have planned or wanted to become bishop of a dispirited, scandal-ridden, poor Metropolis in provincial Western Greece. Only God, so they say, could plan such a twist in his life story.

The Church is always a mix of universal and timeless ideals meeting particular contexts and personalities. As will be apparent in the next chapter, Meletios in 1980 was entering into a context and engaging with personalities that could not be more challenging. He had witnessed many Church communities throughout Greece and the world by this time in his life, but Preveza was unique and, perhaps more worryingly, it was wholly his. He was now responsible not only for a handful of monks but the souls of nearly 100,000 people in his diocese. In a sense, nothing could have prepared to him to take on this task; but in another sense, his whole life had led to this moment.

CHAPTER THREE

The Dramatic Turn:
The Scandal of "Holy Preveza" and
the Arrival of Bishop Meletios

On the Friday before Palm Sunday in 1980, Bishop Meletios Kalamaran was installed as the thirteenth metropolitan of the new Metropolis of Nikopolis and Preveza. On the surface, the ritual proceeded like all those who had gone before him, a lineage that was inaugurated by the Apostle Paul himself. Yet this day was different from previous enthronements. Several pregnant subplots were converging just below the surface: Preveza/Nikopolis, once the spiritual crown of all of Epirus, was suffering from a prolonged scandal involving the previous bishop and years of spiritual neglect; the man chosen by the Holy Synod of the Church of Greece to be the town's savior was one step away from being an Athonite abbot but reluctantly accepted his call to be bishop; many of his spiritual children were torn between their loyalty to him and their dream of being monks on Mt Athos; and politically, the newly elected socialist ruling party was declaring civil war against the Church and its influence in society. Most people greeted the new bishop with guarded hope, but many were openly skeptical, waiting for him to prove himself. These conditions were widely known but never directly uttered on that day, when no one knew how they would conclude.

That night, the communist-leaning city government hosted a banquet for the new bishop. Despite being a traditional fast day and within Great Lent—both of which forbade meat, oil, and dairy—they served steak. No one thought twice about it until the new bishop asked for a bowl of lentil soup without oil. The times were changing in Preveza. The bishop himself was signaling this change, not by words but by his action.

"THE HOLY ONE OF PREVEZA"

The Greek island of Makronisos in the 1940s and 1950s was a fortress/prison where the right-wing military leaders placed their political opponents. The reform process carried out there was not just political; it was also spiritual. A priest was assigned to the island, which is not surprising given that throughout the second half of the twentieth century the Church of Greece was becoming increasingly tied to the right-leaning political parties. From 1948–1950, a priest named Stylianos held this position. He was a political as well as spiritual player. He stood for tradition, church, and state. His connections were at the highest level of the state and the church. His friends of that era would eventually form the now-dreaded military Junta that controlled Greece with an iron fist from 1967 to 1974. For his work on Makronisos, Stylianos was rewarded with a bishop's seat in the town of Preveza.

For nearly the next three decades, Bishop Stylianos led the Church of Preveza. His political connections proved fruitful for the town, especially during the era of the Junta. He was close personal friends with both the third-ranking person in the Junta, Oiannis Ladas, and also the leader, George Papadapoulos himself. Knowledge of these friendships was well known in Preveza. In the words of one local resident, "You could say that he was one of them. He was friends with all of them."[1] Bishop Stylianos' support of the Junta was very public: whenever members of the Junta or other high-ranking government officials came, he always treated them with great care and public celebration. He used these connections for the good of the town. He won for the town an important new port, which ensured the economic vitality of the region, as well as an advanced new hos-

---

[1]Lay Person, ΣT, interview by author, digital recording, Preveza, Greece, 18 May 2003. Hereafter cited as "Lay Person, ΣT."

pital, a new rest home, and innumerable individual acts of charity. He used state funds to rebuild many of the churches and monasteries in the region damaged during the wars, even if there were no monks in them. This link placed Bishop Stylianos in a position of tremendous power in the city. All *prospeti*[2] and economic privileges were made through him. He often provided jobs, government appointments, and economic activity through his connections. In the polite but telling words of one local resident, "Bishop Stylianos was involved in *every* aspect of life."[3] He was the deal-maker in town because of his political connections to those in power. However, his connection to the ultra right-wing also created spiritual turbulence, for Preveza itself was changing.

All over Greece, left-leaning opposition to the dominant right-wing parties would often automatically include some degree of antagonism toward the Church, who was seen as supporting or at least condoning their sometimes ruthless actions. It was "in fashion," particularly for intellectuals and artists, to be atheists or at least anti-church in modern Greece. The result was that significant segments of the country were indifferent or even hostile to the Church *quid pro quo* due to their alignment with certain political factions; anti-church became a *political* expression. This environment was even more pronounced in Preveza itself. The general populace of Preveza had always tended to be more left-leaning than most of Greece, with particularly strong socialist and communist sentiments.[4] This political outlook was particularly common for the large group of migrants who moved to the city of Preveza from the island of Lefkada during the 1950s and 1960s: from 1951–1990, the population of Preveza stayed constant around 10,000 persons but the demographics of that population shifted as locals from Preveza migrated to Athens and "immigrants" from nearby Lefkada

---

[2]Essentially bribes to government leaders in order to obtain something, such as a job for a son or daughter, a building permit, or a license to operate something. The amount of money was usually small, but depending on the situation, sometimes could become very large. This way of doing things was a holdover from the Turkish period.

[3]Lay Person, ΣΤ.

[4]One notable exception exists: for historical reasons stemming from the civil war, many in the Metropolis who lived near Arta were right-wing politically.

and Kephalonia filled their ranks.[5] This shift is important for our examination because Lefkada and Kephalonia had long been considered one of the strongholds of leftist, particularly Communist, political thought.[6] Therefore, as the population of Preveza became increasing dominated by people from the islands, the political character became increasing leftist and so with it attitudes toward the Church became more hostile. This trend was all the more exacerbated by Bishop Stylianos' identification with right-wing politics.

As a result, the spiritual state in Preveza in the 1970s was extremely poor. Basic Christian practices such as confession, fasting, prayer, chanting, preaching, and catechism had been allowed to fade or become impossibly warped. Discipline had broken down among the ranks of the clergy. Beyond two nuns running a school for poor girls and one hieromonk, there was no monastic life whatsoever. Few people went to church at all, and the few that did had very little insight as to why.[7] In short, the spiritual state of the Metropolis was unhealthy—there had been a slow gradual corrosion of faith of many years in Preveza.[8]

---

[5]Βαγγέλης Γρ. Αυδίκος, *Πρέβεζα: 1945–1990* (Πρέβεζα: Δήμος Πρέβεζας, 1991), 406.

[6]Not all "left wing" Kephalonians were anti-Church. A group of them reinvigorated St Nicholas, especially with the feast to St Gerasimos.

[7]In the words of one local resident, "We went to church but we did not really know why. It was just for tradition or habit." (Lay Person, NK, interview by author, digital recording, Preveza, Greece, 29 April 2003 and 1 May 2003. Hereafter cited as "Lay Person, NK.") As many interviewees noted, if anything, the poor spiritual state of Preveza during the era before Bishop Meletios arrived should be read as a condemnation of the contemporary Church in Greece in general. Several people pointed out that, sadly, the piety of the present Bishop Meletios was the exception rather than the rule for bishops in Greece during that era. Widespread indifference toward the Church and participation by only a dedicated few seemed to be the norm since at least the post-World-War-II era. Likewise, the clergy had long been of mixed quality and dedication. Thus while Preveza may have been home to more of the symptoms than other metropolises, the spiritual disease that infected it was common throughout Greece during the time.

[8]Recognizing this dynamic is instructive for understanding the next phase of the life of the Metropolis: just as the decline was gradual, so the renewal would be gradual. Regaining trust, re-educating the people, and restoring the sanctity and authority of the clergy could only occur over many years, and even then the renewal and restoration would only be partial.

As the shepherd of the flock for nearly three decades, Bishop Stylianos bears the responsibility for this neglect. Of course, some of the clergy, particularly his Protosingelos Filaretos, are remembered for their tireless devotion to improving the spiritual lives of their flock, but Bishop Stylianos seemed to have more worldly concerns. In the words of one resident, Bishop Stylianos "was rather a cosmopolite: he liked celebrations and festivals, appreciated good food, and admired pretty women."[9] Rumors of affairs with women had circulated since his first days in Preveza, and it was a widespread "public secret" that he often sought illicit relations with women. It was widely known that his favorite gift to women was intimate apparel.[10] However, the scandal that would make the Church of Preveza famous begins in 1975.

On November 19, 1975, the bishop's driver, a priest named Stavros Kaskanis, photographed the bishop in the midst of one of his illicit affairs, but this one was especially scurrilous: it was with the priest's own wife. As revenge, he blackmailed the bishop, asking for 300,000 drachmas at once and 10,000 drachmas per month so as to not make the photograph public. The authenticity of the photograph was questioned almost immediately and a conclusive determination has never been satisfactorily rendered. Nevertheless, the suggestion that it was authentic was damage enough. Some reporters caught on to the story and began to investigate the rumors themselves. The story "broke" in early 1978 as a remorseful Father Kaskanis told some of the other nearby bishops of his plan. By summer of 1975, the scandal was brewing as the Minister of Education sent a letter dated June 22 to the Holy Synod of the Church of Greece arguing for the authenticity of the picture and demanding action. The picture soon after appeared in some of the local papers. A criminal trial was then held, and while the photographs were determined to be authentic, Father Kaskanis was sentenced to jail for blackmailing the bishop. This determination of authenticity was later questioned once again, yet more articles

---

[9]Lay Person, IT, interview by author, unpublished written responses, Preveza, Greece, Spring 2003. Hereafter cited as "Lay Person, IT."

[10]Anonymous source.

appeared in the local newspapers most every day, as people continued to debate the authenticity of the photo and further details of the case arose. Reporters even produced secretly recorded phone conversations between the bishop and this priest's wife. As the reporters pressed the bishop for details and the scandal grew, the bishop fled rather than defend himself.

The local affair grew into a nationwide scandal as the national media picked up the story. Further allegations arose of other affairs, widespread corruption, and even of the murder of enemies—those later allegations were later found to be reckless and vindictive accusations with no substantive evidence to support them. Nevertheless, those in Bishop Stylianos' "inner circle" began to flee the city as well. Those priests that remained were embarrassed of their status as representatives of the Church, even to the point of avoiding going out into the streets due to the shame they felt.[11] Now embroiled in one of the legendary scandals in the Church, the Metropolis of Nikopolis and Preveza was unable to function. Bishop Stylianos resigned his position as Metropolitan of Nikopolis and Preveza.[12]

Eventually, a play and then a movie were made about the Church in Preveza. The title was "Agios Prevezis" or "The Holy One of Preveza." The movie in particular took certain liberties with the facts, symbolically condensing all Church corruption everywhere in Greece into the single figure of the bishop of Preveza. Yet regardless of the historicity of the presentations, the judgment by most Greeks had already been made: at a time when a demonstrably anti-Church ruling coalition was taking power, Preveza came to symbolize Church corruption, hypocrisy, and misplaced faith. This characterization became so implanted in the Greek psyche that, in some parts of Greece, "Prevezarian" came to have adjectival meaning in the Modern Greek parlance for corruption and hypocrisy. The Metropolis of Preveza came to symbolize everything that was wrong with the Church.

---

[11] An observation shared by a priest to Monk A.

[12] As several interviewees noted, Bishop Stylianos was never defrocked; he died as the "former" bishop of Preveza, performing liturgies and memorials with the full blessing of the Church.

Many people believe that the tremendous uproar caused by the scandal far exceeded the depravity of actual events. While acknowledging that the former bishop "saddened and scandalized the people," Bishop Meletios in an interview called it a "great journalistic tumult ... [that] was not, however, as ugly as the press presented it."[13] What caused the scandal to gain such notoriety so quickly? Beyond the perennial fascination of Church-related sex scandals, it seems that Bishop Stylianos was a victim of timing: the articles appeared at a time when the political sands of Greece were shifting. Newly invigorated left-wing parties were beginning to chip away at the long-standing right-wing rule, which, as noted above, was identified with the Church. Thus many people in Greece were seeking a way to discredit the Church in order to repudiate the previous governments. They found such a scandalizing symbol in Bishop Stylianos and manipulated this scandal for their own political ends. In the words of one Preveza resident, in many ways "he was the black sheep sacrificed for sins of many in the Church."[14] This analysis is not intended to condone the actions of Bishop Stylianos—scandalizing the Church in any way is the most grievous sin of a hierarch—but it does recognize that the uproar had a context that fed its growth and further dissemination. Bishop Stylianos became a political symbol—a sound bite—whose very name could swing votes.

Without question, the scandal had a destructive impact on the spiritual life of the people of the Metropolis. The precise nature of the impact depended on one's relationship to the Church. For the vast majority who were not active in the Church at all, the scandal was greeted locally with indifference and dismissal; it only affirmed their belief that the Church was an ancient, corrupt institution unsuited for the contemporary world. Those within the Church broke down into three groups: first, there were some believers who had largely disassociated themselves from Stylianos' Church previously by joining a local para-church youth group called ZOE; for them, the scandal reaffirmed their decision to seek spiritual growth outside the Church.

---

[13]*ΕΠΙΛΟΓΟΣ.*
[14]Lay Person, NK.

Second, there were those who blamed the events on a left-wing conspiracy and denied the basis of the claims altogether, supporting the bishop until the end. However, the scandal had the most significant impact on the common parishioner. One resident observed that in this group, many people stopped going to church altogether and they began to view all clergy with suspicion.[15] Many of these people no longer trusted the Church; they had lost faith in the ability of the clergy to represent Christ in purity.

The foundation of the Church had been compromised. This impact was clear to Bishop Meletios and his spiritual children.[16] One member of the clergy present during and after the scandal observed, "Holy Scripture says the worst thing is the scandals of the priests. It shoots the people in the hearts, especially the weak people. But who is not weak? Who is strong? Christ says that whoever scandalizes the people, it is better to throw a weight around their neck and drown."[17] Indeed, the hearts of the people—many of whom were already skeptical of the Church—were wounded by the scandal. The scandal was the culmination of years of spiritual neglect by the Metropolis. In the words of one monk, "The flock had been left unattended and uncultivated; then, the scandal was the final blow."[18] The Church leadership was absent, the faithful had become hostile, and the spirit of Christ seemed distant. The final years of the 1970s must be remembered as the nadir of the spiritual history of the Church in Preveza.

---

[15]Lay Person, IT.

[16]Bishop Meletios has never publicly commented on the scandal directly and has had only words of praise for the good that Bishop Stylianos did for the Metropolis. His only comment, which is oblique at best, was in an interview when he commented on scandals in general saying, "Christ was speaking about the scandals and said they are a catastrophe of the world. Every evil example of the clergy or far more of a bishop is a catastrophe of the world. . . . The rules of the Church have austere punishments for those who invite scandal into the people and it is necessary to do penance, unfrock them, and expel them from the Church. Unfortunately, these things sometimes do not occur, sometimes wrongly, because if a sin cannot be established, the Church cannot rely simply on an opinion and condemn innocent men" (ΕΠΙΛΟΓΟΣ).

[17]Monk C.

[18]Monk B.

A contemporary spiritual elder on Mt Athos, Father Paisius, is famous for once saying, "Where the devil tills, God sows the seed." The people of Preveza today see that the devil had been doing some tilling in the spiritual grounds of Preveza and by the winter of 1979–1980, the fields were as barren as they had ever been. However, as one monk explained, "The devil thought he was destroying everything, but God sends Meletios to make it even better."[19]

THE ELECTION OF ARCHIMANDRITE MELETIOS

The scandal and resignation of the bishop of Nikopolis and Preveza was national news in the winter of 1979–1980. The Holy Synod of the Church of Greece needed to elect a replacement quickly. With a very public scandal, the scrutiny of their choice would be particularly intense. In retrospect, the antidote to the problem was clear: in the words of one Church observer with whom I spoke, "With the Church scandal on all the headlines, the Church needed someone who was holy, ascetic, and above it all."[20] At the time, Archimandrite Meletios was not the obvious choice.

Within the Synod, Meletios was not seen as having a lifetime clerical career; he is not one who seemed to seek out honor or positions of authority. His reputation for asceticism and personal discipline was well established; however, he was mostly known as an intellectual who was writing at the time an extended academic treatise on the Fifth Ecumenical Council. Undoubtedly, it was the combination of these qualities that contributed to his eventual selection as bishop of Nikopolis and Preveza. In Archimandrite Meletios, they found someone "in" the Church but not perceived as "of" the Church; he had placed himself above the politics that then divided the people; and his personal holiness stood in stark opposition to the human frailty that caused the bishop's throne in Preveza

---

[19]Monk B.

[20]Personal conversation with Anastasios Karipidis in Thessaloniki, 23 January 2003.

to be empty in the first place. Archimandrite Meletios slowly emerged as the perfect antidote to heal the wounds of the Church of Nikopolis and Preveza.

The question was whether Meletios wanted such a position. Melitios himself was intent on "retiring" to Mt Athos with his spiritual children, not embarking on a challenging new stage in a clerical career. Rumors that began to spread about his candidacy were received with trepidation by his spiritual children, and many decided to leave him if he were elected bishop so they could pursue their intentions to go to Mt Athos. They had "plans" with their spiritual father that did not include Preveza. As a result, both Father Meletios and his spiritual children greeted the upcoming election with mixed feelings.

On February 26, 1980, the Holy Synod of the Church of Greece considered three candidates to become the new bishop of Preveza: Jacob Pachi (who would later become Metropolitan of Argolidos); the Protosingelos of Preveza, Filaretos Bitalis; and Archimandrite Meletios. Archimandrite Meletios received forty-eight votes, while seventeen voted for Archimandrite Jacob and one abstained. Archimandrite Meletios was proclaimed the next Metropolitan of the Metropolis of Nikopolis and Preveza. He was ordained on Saturday March 1 at his home parish of St Eleftherios in Athens, in the presence of eleven bishops from the Church of Greece, the Metropolitan of Nubia, and the Archbishop of Sinai.

After the ordination, the newly ordained bishop offered a homily of great rhetorical interest.[21] He begins by comparing his election as bishop to the Cross for Jesus, "the bitter cup," which Christ was called upon to drink for the salvation of the world.

> Our Lord and Savior Jesus Christ, when he was going to the Cross for us, responded to the pleas of those who had loved him earthily by saying: "This cup, which the Father gave to me, should I not drink of it?" And this cup was very bitter. So bitter. So that, in thought alone, He, who was all-God and all-powerful, knelt down, wept,

---

[21]The complete text with translation appears in Appendix A.

imploring with beseechful prayers, with cries, and mighty tears, per-spired drops of blood from the agony and was in need of his angels to come to strengthen him. Never has a man on earth experienced such pain or felt such contrition as our Lord in the garden of Geth-semane; but he did not retreat. Because the salvation of the world does not happen by proclamation but only with suffering and sacri-fice. For this reason, Christ not only did not avoid the Cross, but also he made it his desire, his aim, his glory. And so the Cross became the great glory of the super-glorified Lord of Glory, Jesus Christ, who is the great glory of the Holy Trinity.

Archimandrite Meletios notes that Christ did not retreat from his Cross, but welcomed it. So, likewise, he suggests that he too cannot deny his cross, the Metropolis of Preveza. By using this imagery, Bishop Meletios recognizes the challenging situation of the Metrop-olis of Preveza, the tempest into which he is being thrown. And implicitly, just as Jesus made the Cross his "desire, his aim, his glory," so Bishop Meletios welcomed the "cross" of Preveza with reserva-tions. In a recent interview, the bishop continued to reflect this sen-timent when he was asked about how his life would have been different if he had not been elected bishop but instead retired to Mt Athos as he had planned. He responded, "I never imagined myself as a savior of anyone. Neither a savior of a place nor of a man, not even one. The one Christ is the Savior of all. I was entrusted with this ministry."[22] Even now, one recognizes the same sentiment that he expressed at his ordination: he did not ask to be a "savior" but he was thrust into circumstances where he needed to seek a miracle of spir-itual transformation. He accepted this burden, this cross.

The ordination speech continues by imploring that Cross, recog-nizing that only by bearing it will he produce fruit. He says:

> O, Cross of Christ, all-holy, thrice-blessed, and life-giving, instru-ment of the mystical rites of Zion, the holy Altar for the service of our Great Archpriest, the blessing—the weapon—the strength of priests, our pride, our consolation, the light in our heart, our mind,

[22]Interview, SLM.

and our steps; Our Lord and Savior nailed to you revealed and instigated his priesthood for us. For this also, the priesthood saves and
glorifies only as a Cross; only the one who bears it radiates virtue,
which the Cross symbolizes and inspires, illumines and sanctifies;
only when it has something from God and the inexpressible beauty
of the virtues of our first and great priest, Christ.

Here he is inviting the Cross upon himself, willingly accepting it as a
blessing and a source of strength. The rhetorical dynamic is interesting at this point: after equating his assignment to Preveza as his cross,
he turns to the Cross of Christ to fortify him. In other words, only by
the Cross of Christ will he succeed in facing his personal cross, the
future work ahead in the Metropolis of Nikopolis and Preveza.

Then, Bishop Meletios, as if recognizing his extreme need for
the prayers of others, implores the prayers of the Theotokos, St Eleftherios, the saintly former bishops of Nikopolis and Preveza, the
hierarchs of the Church, his co-workers at the Holy Synod, and
finally "of my venerable mother, of my spiritual children in Christ,
and of all pious Christians, of parishioners of this holy Church." This
litany of prayer requests, which comprises more than three-quarters
of the homily, must have also sent a strong message: despite his qual-
ifications, which had been extolled by the Archbishop of Greece
immediately prior to his speech, the new bishop would rely not on his
own abilities to enact change but on the prayers of others and the
grace of God.

THE ARRIVAL IN PREVEZA OF THE
NEWLY ELECTED BISHOP MELETIOS

For the people of Preveza, a new chapter in their spiritual life was set
to begin, and they greeted the news with enthusiasm. In the words of
one resident, "That was a gift from heaven."[23] They knew little about
their new bishop, except that he was a very educated but humble cleric.
Word traveled from Athens that, according to one resident, "he was a

---

[23]Lay Person, IT.

saint and we are very fortunate to have him."[24] Yet they would greet him with caution. One of the priests from the pre-Meletios era recalled, "Justifiable, in the beginning, they had reservations. The people are so, I believe. They should not uncritically reveal their soul to someone who has not been tried. 'We shall see,' many said."[25] The people waited with cautious optimism for their new bishop to arrive.

On a bright, sunny morning, the Friday before Lazarus Saturday of 1980, Bishop Meletios arrived with his spiritual children to Preveza. He was greeted at the central square ny the local marching band playing, the army in formation, and local leaders welcoming him to his new town. To many in the crowd, he seemed surprisingly meek, quiet, and simple. He was accompanied by five of his spiritual children. After a welcoming ceremony, the group processed to the Episcopal Seat, St Haralambos Church. When Bishop Meletios entered the altar area for the first time, he knelt down, embraced the altar, and wept. He then offered his first liturgy as bishop of Nikopolis. At the end of the liturgy, he offered only a brief homily, but one of great rhetorical interest.[26]

While Bishop Meletios' election homily suggested some reservations about his appointment as bishop of Preveza, these misgivings were not apparent in his enthronement homily. He began with customary humility but clearly indicated his belief that his election is the will of God for him and the Metropolis. He stated:

> I feel very small in front of the greatness and the gravity of the responsibilities which the laying on of hands and the election by the Hierarchies has placed upon my feeble shoulders, and in front of our great Archpriest Jesus Christ, who is "over all, the eternally blessed God. Amen." "As the Father has sent me, so I send you."

In quoting John 20.21—when the disciples receive their original mission from Jesus—Bishop Meletios reminded the audience of the

---

[24]Lay Person, ΣΤ.

[25]Priest A, interview by author, digital recording, Preveza, Greece, 15 May 2003. Hereafter cited as "Priest A."

[26]The full text in English translation is in Appendix B.

source behind his election: ultimately Christ himself. Implicitly, his statement acted to reassure the audience that God was indeed still in control; He had not abandoned the Church and people of Preveza but rather had a plan for it, which included the arrival today of a new shepherd.

As the representative of Christ, Bishop Meletios then sought to set the stage for his ministry. He continued, "The mission of Christ was to save the world. Not to judge it. To save it. The mission of the representative of Christ, the bishop, is the same mission of Christ." The audience knew the context in which he was speaking. An atmosphere of accusations and condemnation reigned in Preveza: priests spying on fellow priests; a priest jailed for blackmailing his own bishop; reporters making sometimes wild allegations; and suspicions buzzing throughout the Metropolis. Bishop Meletios diffused this charged atmosphere with these words. He communicated to the people that he arrived not to point fingers and condemn but to heal and save. His focus would be future salvation, not the misdeeds of the past. A new era had arrived, one based solely on salvation.

Bishop Meletios then turned directly to the problems of the Church, both locally and nationally. He began by repeating the call of Christ in John 20.21, but it is important to note the new meaning it gains when placed in this new context: "'As My Father has sent me, so I send you.' But how great a difference! The height of the mission is hard to contemplate even more for the angels! And what an abyss of wretchedness are we!" The problems of the Church should be located within the wider understanding of sin itself; it is the personal sinfulness of specific individuals that underlies all problems within the Church. Just as all people are called, all are wretched and sinful. Thus in turning to the collective human condition, he implicated no one; or rather, he implicated all people.

If *all* people are sinful, including himself, Bishop Meletios was in rhetorical danger of leading those present into despair. However, he quickly provided his solution:

> I am very much aware of my smallness, bearing to my mind the
> problems with which our Church is confronted in its entirety and

especially the local Church which I am called to shepherd. How? In
the name of Christ. With Christ as the model. Imitating Christ.

At this point, Bishop Meletios conveyed his most deep-seated prin-
ciple: health and salvation will come only through individual devotion to and imitation of Christ himself. He would offer no strategic
plan or clever campaign, only Christ and the pledge to follow him
personally.

Bishop Meletios' call to imitate Christ was not a generic rhetorical device, however pious it sounded. Rather, he turned specifically to
the evidence for Christ's restorative powers. He began by quoting
Matthew 11.29: "Take my yoke upon you, and learn from me; for I am
gentle and humble in heart, and you will find rest for your souls." He
then explicated this verse, noting that the role of the bishop is to offer
such respite for the soul. He is to be the proclaimer of peace and the
one who gives rest through Christ. Bishop Meletios continued this
theme by recalling the biblical story of when Jesus and his disciples
were caught in a storm. Lacking faith, the disciples called out (as the
residents of Preveza might be tempted to, given the recent scandal):
"Master, save us, we are perishing!" Bishop Meletios then presented
the salvific response of Jesus as a message to those in the crowd who
might have been thinking along the same lines as the disciples. "And
then the Lord got up and 'rebuked the wind and the sea.' And tranquility was restored." The bishop, in this case Meletios himself, is the
bearer of that calm, a "messenger of peace, a fount of tranquility."
Christ will heal the city through his representative the bishop.

Bishop Meletios then reiterated his understanding of the manner
in which a bishop transmits this peace and healing. In this section,
which constituted nearly one-third of the overall speech, Meletios
sought to redefine for the people of Preveza the role and place of the
bishop. Given the notorious behavior of the previous bishop, these
characteristics seemed quite foreign to the people. He presented a list
of characteristics that were increasingly demanding. He began with
the passive command to "not seek out honors"; in the eyes of many
lay people, seeking honors was and is a favorite pastime of many bishops in Greece. Bishop Meletios then turned to seeking out *actively*

the forgiveness of others. The bishop must be willing to say "to those who hate us and have wronged us, forgive them, Lord; and give to them your rich mercy and Your Kingdom." However, he recognized that "for the mission of the clerics, this is little." In other words, the bishop must be expected to do more than (merely) remain humble and offer forgiveness. Herein lies the most important insight of his homily: the bishop is expected to suffer for his people:

> The chief mission of our Lord Jesus Christ, was to offer his soul, his entire self, as ransom on behalf of the world. And in this way of "mystagogy," the Lord taught his disciples saying, "Pay attention dear friends. Nothing separates you from me. For if I suffer, it is for the sake of the world. Therefore, if you are friends of mine, imitate me. . . ." The bishop sits in the place of Christ. His throne and glory is the Cross. His joy and jubilation are persecution and reproach from the men of this world, who live far from God.

The role of the bishop is to imitate Christ, not in his glory but in his suffering. The chief characteristic of the bishop, as Bishop Meletios presented it, was to suffer for his people for their salvation. The mark of the bishop, then, was not his scepter but his willful acceptance of the indignation shown to him by the world. Bishop Meletios announced on that day that he welcomed the "persecution and reproach" that came with his new position. His "cross," the Metropolis of Nikopolis and Preveza, would not be golden but marked by nails and marred by blood unto the salvation of all.

The effect of this section of the speech was to redefine the role and place of the bishop for the residents of Preveza—most of whom only knew the worldly example of the twenty-eight-year reign of the previous bishop, Stylianos. Thus Bishop Meletios was telling his faithful not *what* he would do, but *who* he would be. He would imitate Christ, even unto suffering for them and for their salvation. In return, "his comfort, his power, and his consolation" would be "the love and devotion of the faithful." The people were immediately aware that their new bishop was unlike any other in their age.

Having outlined the path to restoration, Bishop Meletios conveyed to the audience that it would not be achieved by him alone but only through collective struggle. He describes this struggle in stark military terms:

> Let us prepare ourselves. Work is necessary. Struggle. Battles. War. Tough war, merciless. Merciless for our own selves. Not for others. I, like a responsible father and your director, call upon you to stage an uprising. A glorious uprising. An uprising of Christ. For the good of all. For the bad of none.

By using war imagery, Bishop Meletios transmitted in clear terms the urgency with which he perceived the situation. He called for *jihad*, a collective spiritual war waged upon each person's own internal battle-fields so as to transform the character of the Church by all, for all. By each person urgently transforming him- or herself based on the model of Christ, the collective body of Christ—the Church—would be transformed. "And we, the lovers of Christ and Christified, who rally together and are united in one heart, one soul, one mind, one intellect, one will, one action, let us struggle for the glory of God and the salvation of his people." This call to arms represents the rhetorical pinnacle of the speech.

In light of the words above, Bishop Meletios then returned to his redefinition of the role and place of the bishop in society. For a Metropolis whose bishops had historically taken a significant political and economic role, he told them that the parameter of his mission was limited to their spiritual condition. His mission was clear: to imitate Christ in his role as the father of the Church in his area. He commented:

> This is my work! This and nothing else. Because I am a servant of Christ and nothing else! I am a priest, and nothing else. Nothing less; nothing more. Nothing higher; nothing lower. Nothing more to the right; nothing more to the left. Nothing more to the front; nothing more to the back. I am a priest and nothing else! I am a worker of the Kingdom of God.

Bishop Meletios accomplished a great deal in this rhetorical flurry. He implicitly rejected the political and economic roles that had arisen for bishops in Greece and that were particularly noted in the reign of his predecessor, Bishop Stylianos. He would not be (politically) left or right; he would not be an exalted figure who operates from on-high but "a worker of the Kingdom of God"; he would not do anything else but be a servant of Christ. Thus he communicated with these words that he was not only the new bishop in town but also a new kind of bishop.

Bishop Meletios concluded his enthronement speech by return- ing to his early theme of the peace of Christ. He ended, "And as a priest, a servant of Christ, I greet you all with the greeting of Christ, the greatest of all blessings: Peace unto you, peace unto all. And I pray, this is my greeting and my blessing, to find you all sons of peace.... Peace to you. Peace to all." While he previously spoke of uprising and war, he wanted the final message to be one of peace, love, and recon- ciliation. In doing so, he presented himself as an ambassador of Christ, restoring his peace to the town of Preveza and its people.

It is important to note how contrary this enthronement homily stands in comparison to most inaugural speeches, both within the Church and outside it. Bishop Meletios outlined no new programs; rather, he reiterated the basic Christian life. He offered no grandiose promises; rather, he promised future struggles and persecution. He offered no comments on the previous leadership, either positive or negative; rather, he redefined the position of bishop itself. Neverthe- less, by rejecting these rhetorical conventions, he made a significant impression upon the people of Preveza that day. He opened up a vision for them that was novel yet ancient, unfamiliar yet intuitive, realistic yet full of hope. He also established and communicated the vision by which his entire ministry would be guided.

His words were not the only significant impression made that day. His persona and actions, particularly his personal devoutness, made equally significant impressions on the people. In particular, his ascet- icism came as a shock to some. At the celebration of his inauguration, his quiet request for a bowl of lentil soup without oil instead of steak must have spoken volumes. The townsfolk were unaccustomed to such strictness on behalf of the clergy. In a similar vein, one resident recounts that in one of Bishop Meletios' first sermons at St Nicholas' Church, he said forcefully in his homily, "It is a sin to eat oil on

Wednesday and Friday!" A murmur swept over the crowd as they began to look at each other in astonishment—could he really be serious?[27] Such a level of asceticism and devoutness had been rare for the previous generation in Preveza. Yet as easily as the people noted Bishop Meletios' personal strictness, they also noted his compassion. One resident recalled, "I came to respect him the most because while he is very strict with himself, with others he is lenient."[28] Thus he quickly came to be known not only for his personal ascetic regime but also for the love with which he embraced the people.

Most of the clergy embraced the new bishop because they (as much as the people) were hoping to put the scandal behind them and move on. Some members of the clergy, however, were openly skeptical. Two priests were overheard at the enthronement service saying, "He thinks he is going to change us. He will see."[29] These two priests, and many others, did change over time. The story of this change constitutes the subject of the next chapter.

[27]Lay Person, NK.

[28]Lay Person LS, interview by author, digital recording, Preveza, Greece, 15 May 2003. Hereafter cited as "Lay Person, LS."

[29]Monk A.

CHAPTER FOUR

The Drama: The Religious Re-orientation of Preveza

On February 10, 1817, the feast day of the patron saint of Preveza, St Haralambos, was celebrated with great fanfare for the first time. The previous year the town had faced a great plague and believed they were saved by continually praying "St Haralambos save us!" A year later, the people stayed in the church that held his relics all night in psalm and prayer. Bishop Porfirios of Arta and the Protosingelos Joseph led the procession of Haralambos' relics throughout the town. When the procession passed under the house of the local Turkish ruler, his curious wife leaned out her window. Seeing the icon, she shouted that now the "unfaithful" were publicly honoring a piece of wood! She immediately fainted, fell from her window, and died. Everyone said that it was another miracle of St Haralambos, and the vigil in his honor was continued for another night.[1]

In 1981, the Metropolis prepared to celebrate the feast of their patron saint once again. There were no longer Turkish overlords or all-night vigils, and miracles had long ceased being expected. Bishop Meletios gathered his monks to begin vespers in honor of the St Haralambos. They were nearly all alone in the church of the episcopal seat. The church itself seemed tired and worn. The next day the same church would fill with local government officials and other dignitaries and a procession would once again occur, but the commemoration had lost much of its spiritual import. There was great pomp and circumstance, but seemingly little interest in the religious meaning of

---

[1]This account was written by a priest named Evangelos in the front cover the February Menian published in 1799.

the occasion. The continual petitions of the people from 175 years prior were now but a distant, faint echo.

On a blistery cold February evening twenty-two years later, Bishop Meletios, flanked by many of his spiritual children, commenced the service on the eve of St Haralambos' day. They were not alone. The church and the courtyard outside were filled nearly throughout the five-hour vigil. The next morning the crowds of faithful spilled onto the streets. In a spirited homily, the bishop extolled the value of St Haralambos and his meaning for the people of Preveza today. Despite the blistering cold, the procession extended almost the whole length of the town's commercial area. All received blessed bread from the bishop. That night, the people would gather again as a religious and civic community in the Spiritual Center for a celebration of St Haralambos and a concert of music and Byzantine chant. The bishop presided over the whole affair. The religious meaning of St Haralambos' day had been restored, at least in part.

This chapter recounts the process of religious transformation that occurred in Preveza from the arrival of Bishop Meletios in 1980 to the present. The change in the character of the celebration of St Haralambos' day is indicative of this transformation. As with the feast day itself, Bishop Meletios stands at the center of the renewal. In an image that he himself employs often, he has been the shepherd of the spiritual life of the people of Preveza. This chapter is a description of how he has used this role to inspire change in the Church and lives of the people of Preveza.

BISHOP MELETIOS' PROGRAM OF SPIRITUAL TRANSFORMATION

In 1980, Bishop Meletios was at the ecclesial center stage for Greece, and many, I suspect, wanted him to fail. He was a throwback to an ancient era of the church—one not tainted by left-right political ideological battles, generational conflicts, and the social ills that came with modernity. For many of the intelligentsia in Greece, the scandal of Preveza proved what they had recognized all along: the church is out of tune with modernity and unsuited for leadership in a modern

Greek society. Despite Meletios' personal sanctity and intelligence, the problem was deeper than the personal weaknesses and hypocrisy of a few hierarchs; Meletios' mission would fail because this ancient faith had no place in a modern world. All eyes were on him, curious to see his strategic plan for turning around the faith of Preveza.

Bishop Meletios disappointed all those who wanted a strategic plan laid out in his first years. In fact, he has deliberately avoided applying any boilerplate solutions, saying that he tries to carry out his mission "peacefully without calculation, without plans, without programs."[2] For Meletios, strategic plans are human-derived attempts to solve problems. But "the Church is not of man. The Church is of God. And whenever God is present, the human element ought to be extinguished. When it is not only not destroyed but also validated, the Church does not go well. Anthropocentrism kills the Church and its life."[3] Not surprisingly, then, Bishop Meletios promises that he never had a "program" for Preveza. Nevertheless, with hindsight, we can deconstruct how Preveza was transformed; we can identify goals toward which Meletios steered the institution of the Church; we can identify concrete actions that were taken; at times, we can even note which activities seem to have the most impact. However, in doing so, we are artificially reverse engineering a "program" that never existed in the first place.

While some actions of the bishop undoubtedly worked toward multiple ends, his actions can be grouped into five goals: 1) Restore the spiritual integrity and authority of the clergy; 2) Restore the Church experience to its spiritual, traditional, and aesthetic glory; 3) Construct forums for the Church to interact with the people; 4) (Re)educate the people; 5) Develop monasticism in the region.

---

[2]Interview, SLM.
[3]Metropolitan Meletios in Διονύση Μακρή, "Κλήρος καριέρας με ενδοκόσμια φρονήματα," *ΣΤΥΛΟΣ ΟΡΘΟΔΟΞΙΑΣ* (January 2001). Translated by author. Hereafter cited as "*ΣΤΥΛΟΣ ΟΡΘΟΔΟΞΙΑΣ.*"

GOAL 1: RESTORE THE SPIRITUAL INTEGRITY AND AUTHORITY OF THE CLERGY

Years of restrictions by the Ottoman Turks had led to a long-standing culture in Preveza whereby many of the priests, particularly in rural areas, were uneducated, undisciplined, and unresponsive to the people. Superstitions and misunderstandings often crept into Church life and teachings, with the priests unable or unwilling to correct. Ashamed of their connection to the Church after the scandal, many priests eschewed public gatherings altogether. The people looked at the clergy with "a guarded eye," with suspicion, with shame, and with sadness.[4]

Upon his arrival, Bishop Meletios set his first goal as the restoration of the clergy's spiritual authority. He told a local magazine, "Knowing about the problems which existed, I made one and only one prayer when I came: calling to Christ to make me worthy to help the clergy to attain spiritual authority through becoming teachers of the people which would withstand my death."[5] This decision was based on the recognition that the clergy practically speaking are an extension of the bishop himself; change can thereby only occur through the cultivation of the clergy. Bishop Meletios noted this when he wrote recently:

My first goal, when I assumed the shepherd's role of the Metropolis of Nikopolis, was the elevation of the clergy; in other words, the cultivation of the clerics so as to become and to be that which Christ wants them to be: his instrument for the sanctification and salvation of the world. Moreover, they are shepherds of the people of God. The clergy are the body, the eyes, the ears, the hands of the bishop—who is the "father" of the ecclesial metropolis. Without them, the bishop CANNOT do anything, even though he may have noble ambitions and even though he has faculties and virtues.[6]

---

[4]Monk B.
[5]ΕΠΙΛΟΓΟΣ.
[6]Interview, SLM.

The clergy are the mouthpieces and the tools of the bishop. Bishop Meletios did not see them, however, as employees executing a strategy developed on high. Rather, they are the earthly representatives of Christ; as such, the foundation of their spiritual authority must be the personal sanctity of the clergy themselves. Bishop Meletios said in a recent interview, "The chief characteristic of the cleric is piety—fear of God—that is, to have as his first priority the application of the commandments of God to himself. The priest must teach by his example. If his personal life does not speak, then his words will convince no one."[7] Bishop Meletios' goal was not to turn them into better instruments of the Metropolis—that is, better employees—but rather better Christians. Thus, in the early days of Preveza, Bishop Meletios made this focus clear to his clergy: he did not want effective programs or fiery oratory but rather personal holiness.

This personal holiness began with himself: unlike other bishops in Greece, he would not be clothed in fancy vestments, have a personal chauffer, or claim a bishop's exemption from monastic fasting obligations; on the contrary, while he stressed tolerance and forgiveness for others, he was extremely strict with himself. Despite his exalted title of "Apostolic Bishop of Nikopolis and Preveza," he stressed from the beginning that he would remain a simple priest. He was, as his enthronement speech declared, a simple "worker for the Kingdom of God."[8] The bishop preached first and foremost by his own example. And people listened. As every person interviewed noted, the example of the bishop himself was the single most important factor in transforming the clergy. The character of his Christian life inspired the religious change in the people. The question remains, though, how?

The bishop began this process by pressing the clergy to follow his own example. He told them that "they must have pain for their parish. And the people should be drawn to the Church due to this."[9] As bishop, Meletios would devote himself to the clergy with his whole

---

[7] *ΣΤΥΛΟΣ ΟΡΘΟΔΟΞΙΑΣ.*
[8] Enthronement Homily, see Appendix B.
[9] Monk B.

heart if they would dedicate themselves to the spiritual lives of their parishes. He told the clergy in one of their first meetings together, "I will be your servant if you live the spiritual life."[10] In other words, the bishop placed his energies in the clergy themselves. He recognized that if he devoted himself to their spiritual well-being, they in turn would devote themselves to the spiritual advancement of their parishioners. This devotion to the spiritual development of the priests has not waned in the three decades of his tenure. When I asked a local priest whether he spent the early months outlining for them the qualities of the good priest, he responded, "He has never stopped talking about it!"[11] Yet the good priest is not a bureaucrat for the Church, but one who has personal holiness, humility, kindness, and love.[12]

Bishop Meletios spoke about these things in religious education classes, not for the people but for the clergy. The diocese priests met monthly not primarily to deal with the Metropolis' administrative details but more to bolster the clergy's personal spiritual dedication. The bishop would often talk about some spiritual theme; speakers were brought in to discuss particular spiritual topics; specialized books were suggested; and priests were given the opportunity to talk privately with the bishop. He modeled his vision for the church in his personal relationship with the clergy. But he also established new rules for the clergy, particularly regarding the worldly elements of money, politics, and sex.

Bishop Meletios often notes that in the biblical story where Jesus asks to see the Caesar's coin, he does not touch the coin himself. This distance from money is the ideal for the clergy, who must concentrate on spiritual rather than material concerns. The bishop often mentions that his spiritual father in Kalamata, Father Joel Yiannakopoulos, never carried any money with him. When he needed something, God usually provided it. While such absolute monetary abstinence may not always be possible, Bishop Meletios has striven to minimize money's role. Money is necessary for the Church to operate, especially

---

[10]Monk C.
[11]Priest A.
[12]Monk C.

in the construction of churches, but it is a part of the worldly realm and thus holds no ultimate importance. Toward this goal, the previous practice of setting public tariffs for baptisms, weddings, and funerals—which is still widespread outside the Metropolis and was the norm in Preveza before Bishop Meletios—was forbidden in one of his earliest encyclicals. Married clergy can still accept money if it is offered, but they can never ask for it. Furthermore, Bishop Meletios also forbade the "special" donations that many clergy asked of parishioners during the great feasts in order to provide some extra funds for their families. This detachment from monetary motives does not mean that the clergy should show no concern for money; the Church must be able and reliable stewards of the donations of others. The attitude that the bishop has tried to inculcate might be described as "disinterested care." The result has been that the Metropolis has been not only free of financial scandals but also trusted in its finances.

Bishop Meletios recognizes and respects that each person, especially Greeks, will have his own opinion regarding political issues. He once told me that all Greeks have three political opinions: one in the morning, one at midday, and one in the evening. However, he stresses that as representatives of the Church and Christ, priests should be very careful in expressing these opinions and should do so only on very rare occasions. The clergy must be independent from any political structure. As one person recalled, "From the beginning, Father Meletios told the clergy that they should not express political views. Before, there was a bias here: if you are religious here you have to be the extreme right. That is not the case with Father Meletios, who says they all belong to our folk. Whatever their political views, they all belong to Christ. They are people who Christ was crucified for, so who are we to divide them into different groups?"[13] This independence from politics represents a marked change from the situation previously in Preveza, where the clergy were almost exclusively identified with right-wing political factions. Yet with the arrival of Bishop Meletios, the clergy in Preveza did not switch political persuasions

---

[13]Nun E.

but rather became nonpolitical altogether. Individual priests may (and will) have private political opinions, but as representatives of the Church, these opinions should not surface in their public lives. The priest must attend to the spiritual needs of all people—the political left and the political right and everyone between—without bias or favoritism.

The fruits of this practice have been quite noticeable, particularly in persuading communist and other left-wing individuals back into the Church. As one layperson in Preveza noted, "Many of the people I have seen return to Church in recent years have been former communists and people of the left wing."[14] The most noted example of this trend is the formerly staunchly communist Mayor of Preveza, Nikos Gionnulis, who through discussions with the bishop and monks has "converted" to become a dedicated member of the Church. But, it is important to note, the left-leaning "converts" to the Church do not find support for their positions in the clergy of Preveza but rather a nonpolitical clergy who, as representatives of Christ to all people, do not express their political views.

This apolitical character was readily apparent during the nationwide political debate beginning around the year 2000 that concerned placing the individual's religion on the national identity cards. The European Union required new identity cards for each of its member states but allowed them some freedom of design and content. Among the decisions that each country could decide for themselves was whether the religion of the citizen would be on the card. The left-leaning political party in power did not want to place religion (99 percent of whom would be Orthodox) on the national identity card, while the right-leaning opposition party supported placing religion on the card. The Archbishop of Athens and all of Greece Christodoulos campaigned to have religion included, including organizing protests and asking the Metropolis for the people to "vote" in the parishes on whether they wanted the identity cards. Bishop Meletios was one of the few bishops who spoke privately to the Holy Synod against such a public political position by the Church. He

---

[14]Lay Person, NK.

argued that it would divide the Church. He refused to attend any of the organized protests nor did he promote the campaign. In the end, he allowed a vote to be taken in the parishes but only voluntarily and without the encyclical from the Archbishop being read. The result of the nationwide parish "vote" was destructive as he predicted. One hieromonk from the Metropolis recalls:

> The bad thing is that the vote functioned as a division. For example, the leaders of the political parties would sometimes go to the parish president and ask how many people voted to support it and sometimes even the names of the people who voted. . . . Also, we have many faithful in the villages from the liberal party who had family connections with the communists, etc., . . . who, after seeing the new Archbishop and especially our bishop, were beginning to become closer to the Church because they saw that the Church was not only for the New Democracy and Mr Karamanlis but the Church is for all the faithful. When they saw this initiative by the Archbishop, they said that it shows that the Church is only for the right party. Some even came to me and said that they cannot come to Church again. This was very bad for the pastoral work of the Church. It was a great fault of the archbishop since in the beginning even professors of the university and great personalities were saying what a good archbishop [he is] and wanted to help him. And then they went away.[15]

The result of involving themselves in a political issue was to create divisions within the Church and between the Church and those whom it seeks to reach for Christ.[16] By focusing on these worldly affairs, the Church forgot its universal and unifying purpose. For Bishop Meletios, this incident once again provided proof of the need for the Church to disentangle itself from worldly politics as much as possible.

---

[15]Monk A.

[16]Bishop Meletios has in the past supported "political" positions that have a direct *spiritual* bearing on the Church itself. For example, in the early 1980s he spoke out against the government confiscating Church property and seeking to influence the governance of the Church.

Given the nature of the previous scandal in Preveza, Bishop Meletios was particularly careful for the clergy to not invite any scandal into the Church due to improper sexual relations. He stressed to the clergy that their restoration would only come about by their personal sanctity, which required not only personal holiness but also avoidance of any *chance* for scandal to arise.[17] Toward this end, he immediately dismissed the female cleaning staff at the bishop's house and the metropolitan's office, raising the ire of many because these particular women had been supporting their poor families by this job.[18] He also reminded the clergy of the need to not even give off the appearance of any sexual impropriety. For some, this noticeable caution with the opposite sex branded the bishop and his monks as misogynists. Two women with whom I spoke noted with chagrin that even now Bishop Meletios treats the male population of Preveza differently than the female. Another resident noted: "I will ask you a question, 'Have you ever seen Bishop Meletios even standing next to a woman, especially in photographs?' "[19] Most women reported that they felt comfortable around the bishop; *much* more comfortable around him than with the previous bishop. Yet his reputation of prudence around women is widespread. This reputation has served him well in restoring the trust of the people. The air is free from even the hint of scandal in Preveza. Given the conduct of the previous bishop, cultivating this environment has been critical to restoring the trust of the people.

The internal spiritual transformation of the clergy sought for by the bishop was to be mirrored by external reforms that would restore the dignity and distinctiveness of the clerical class. Regarding their personal appearance, it had been commonplace to trim the beard and hair, especially for feast days. However, for Bishop Meletios, any attempt to conform to the styles of the world was discouraged. Many

---

[17]This carefulness regarding intersexual relations was a long-standing practice for the bishop: while the bishop was an Archimandrite in Athens, even his female spiritual children were not allowed in his apartment for any reason.

[18]Over time, women were once again hired to assist in the cleaning duties in the metropolitan offices and the bishop's residence, but only after several years and then only women of known good repute.

[19]Lay Person, NK.

of the clergy throughout Greece had also become sloppy with their dress, unbuttoning their *rason* and frequently failing to wear their *skoufos* in public. Bishop Meletios made it clear: when in public, the *rason* should be properly worn and the *skoufos* aligned.[20] One priest remembers what Bishop Meletios said in one meeting: "He told us to be careful with our cassocks; we must teach with our external elements. When you see a priest with a cassock and *kalimavhi*, his appearance must be a kerygma [proclamation of Christ]."[21] In other words, a priest's appearance is not arbitrary or subject to the whims of the world; rather, it is a sign of the sanctity of the priesthood itself and their role in spreading the message of Christ.

Moreover, priests were to be disciplined in their behavior: no longer were they to live worldly lives, noisily supporting their favorite team at the local football stadium, smoking in public, or drinking at the local café.[22] Their status as a person dedicated to God was to extend to every part of their life, including their "spare" time. Occasionally in the monthly meeting of the clerics, Bishop Meletios was pointed in his criticism of a particular cleric's behavior. He would say to him: "Father, how can you scandalize the Church? How come people don't come to services? Why do you smoke, sit in the café, drink wine. . . . Be serious about your spiritual life. All your life is to be a light."[23] Bishop Meletios' message was clear: their priestly functions were not to be considered a job akin to other jobs but a way of life. As such, the priestly vocation had to extend to every part of their life so that even their external actions witnessed to the Gospel.

These external reforms were not the central element of the bishop's hope for restoring the spiritual authority of the clergy; however, we should not be tempted to trivialize them. For Bishop Mele-

---

[20]Monk A tells a humorous story: Once the bishop stopped him as he was getting into his car so as to make an appointment. The bishop told him, "Are you going out for a fight?" The puzzled monk inquired what he meant. The bishop explained, "Only people looking for a fight would wear their *skoufos* crooked like that."

[21]Monk C.

[22]Under the previous bishop, Father Panagiotis of the Church of John Chrysostom was a frequent and animated supporter of the local sports teams.

[23]Reported by Monk C.

tios, internal discipline is often a result of external discipline. More-over, these expectations sent a message to the people of the Metrop-olis, many of whom had come to disrespect the clergy: the spiritual life was of utmost importance now. The priests would demonstrate with their outward appearance and behavior their inner devotion, dedication, and resolve. As respect grew for the clergy, so would their spiritual authority.

Not all the clergy in the diocese embraced these reforms. One hieromonk recalls that at the inauguration celebrations, two priests were overheard saying to one another, "This is a joke; he cannot change us."[24] Bishop Meletios made a point to identify those who refused to change and reward those who did.[25] This process entailed realigning resources to maximize the spiritual good for the people. He had to be, in the words of one of the early hieromonks, a "very good general . . . putting the right person, at the right place, at the right time."[26] The basis was always the degree to which their personal sanc-tity informed their priestly life, not their administrative effectiveness or education. For example, in one of his first moves, Meletios made an uneducated, but by all accounts pious and gifted priest of a small rural village, the lead priest in a region of the diocese known as Philip-piada. This move demonstrated in concrete terms Meletios' values.

Bishop Meletios also placed his monks—who without exception were young, educated, and zealous—as secondary priests in churches with the most need.[27] To continue the military analogy introduced by one of the hieromonks, the monks became a sort of "special forces" who were sent to particular hot spots to quell disturbances and win the peace. The primary priest would perform many of the daily func-tions of the parish, such as house blessings and administrative duties,

---

[24]Monk A. This same monk went on to note, however, that these two priests did change after great persistence by the bishop and today are very good priests.

[25]"Bishop Meletios was very quick in identifying the problem parishes and doing something about them." Lay Person, NK.

[26]Monk C.

[27]For example, Father Vasileos Bakoyiannis became the assistant of Father Con-standinos at St Nicholas parish in Preveza and Father Ioannikius Bilias came to assist Father Spyridon at St Constantine's church.

while the hieromonk would preach on Sundays, hear confessions, and coordinate the catechism instruction for the young. Although this practice was certainly never presented as such, the placement of monks in particular parishes was widely seen as an attempt by the bishop to inculcate his ethos into a parish when the existing clergy were either unwilling or unable to change. By placing close confidants in oversight roles, the bishop solved one of the inevitable problems of new bishops: how to influence the entire Metropolis as a single person from the Metropolis city. As one monk stated, "In many other Metropolises, the bishop comes in and he is alone and as a result nothing happens. You need people to do the work. Here, he could divide up the Metropolis."[28] The monks thus became the eyes, ears, and mouthpiece of the bishop. In doing so, the bishop could functionally "be" in more than one place at a time, and very quickly the "presence" of the bishop could be felt throughout the Metropolis.

At times, tensions arose between the young hieromonks and the incumbent priests, especially as the former received more honor in the liturgy due to their hieromonk status and when the monks were perceived as "supervisors." However, in most cases, mutually beneficial relationships developed so that they learned to work together for the good of the parish. The results have been dramatic: even in parishes where the resident clergy have been unwilling or unable to support the reformed spiritual goals of the Metropolis, the presence of the hieromonk usually has led to the spiritual reformation of the parish.[29] However, this practice was also strategically astute: Bishop Meletios could peacefully and diplomatically mend unhealthy situations or invigorate stale environments without demeaning the incumbent priest.

---

[28]Monk B. One should also note that as the bishop divided up the Metropolis geographically among his monks, he also divided up informally some of the administrative and pastoral duties: to those who had the charisma to write, he had them write; for those who had the charisma to preach, he had them preach constantly; for those who had administrative skills, he asked them to work in the Metropolis offices. In other words, he maximized the value of each person that he had unto the betterment of the Metropolis.

[29]The most recognized example of this phenomenon is the success of the long-standing presence of Father Ioannikios at St Constantine's church, whose resident married cleric, Father Spyridon, had alienated many parishioners.

When new vacancies arose in parishes, Bishop Meletios filled them with trusted spiritual children. Occasionally, these were hieromonks, but they were often married clergy, some of whom transferred from other areas of Greece to help the bishop. After only three years, five of the eight largest parishes in the Metropolis had priests who were long-standing spiritual children of Bishop Meletios.[30] The result was that the spiritual ethos of the bishop spread remarkably quickly.

One should not get the impression that this change was absolute or happened overnight. Rather, the transformation took place gradually and still continues today. The bishop does feel some degree of satisfaction in the state of the clergy. He credits the clergy with this change:

> I suppose that the greatest success of my episcopal ministry is the elevation of the authority of the clergy of our Metropolis in the consciousness of all the people in our area. This I placed as my first goal. I have the satisfaction that it was blessed in all respects. However, regarding this success, praise is not due to me, who am nothing, but to the fertile soil of the hearts of the priests that caused the word of Christ to germinate and to bear fruit. Let God have glory. Whatever good happened or becomes in our Metropolis, it is in debt to the willingness of the priests to listen to and realize the commandments of the Gospel with their soul.[31]

However, the change was not merely "prayed" into existence. While we should not discount the prayers of the bishop and the clergy, the restoration of the spirituality authority of the clergy in the eyes of the people was due to a combination of spiritual and strategic factors. The bishop was very astute in using the resources available to him—particularly his monks—to create the spiritual ethos that he recognized as foundational to the spiritual elevation of the people of the Metropolis.

---

[30]St Basil's in Preveza, St Nicholas in Preveza, St Constantine's, St Visarion's in Filippiada, St Dimitrios in Neochori.

[31]Interview, SLM.

Dialogue and oversight, however, are not enough to create a common ethos. The consistent example of the leader is the critical ingredient. A common vision for the Christian life is shared by nearly all in Preveza because it is embodied in the bishop. He sets himself as the example and opens his life for scrutiny. One must grant that Bishop Meletios is unique. His ability to be simple yet erudite, strict with himself yet compassionate with others, apolitical yet politically astute—these are rare qualities to put together in a single person. But as he himself notes, the specifics of any spiritual "personality" are not as important as the continual struggle for virtue, self-denial, humility, and love. This struggle is what should be emulated—and it is contagious. As one of the early monks observed:

> St John Chrysostom said that if your works are evil, whatever you say to the people, they will not believe you. . . . [In Preveza] they saw the fathers fasting, working, changing; they saw the new fathers who were educated and monks, who were preaching to them; they saw their goodness. In a few words, they saw their spirituality and virtue . . . over time, the people saw that Bishop Meletios and his company of fathers were not actors: they fast, they pray, etc. . . . When the people see something genuine, they appreciate it. Keep in mind, these things are like a magnet.[32]

As Bishop Meletios emptied himself for his flock, so did his representatives and this became apparent to all. However, this struggle for holiness was not achieved by a force of will but by losing their will. Bishop Meletios reminds the clergy often that the work of the Church is the work of Christ, not of men. Any effort done for human ends is ultimately in vain, no matter how successful it appears. The clergy must "do" nothing but allow Christ to do things through them. This requires them to "be" something: vessels of God, servants of Christ, the least among men—for the good of all.

---

[32]Monk C.

GOAL 2: RESTORE THE CHURCH EXPERIENCE TO ITS SPIRITUAL, TRADITIONAL, AND AESTHETIC GLORY

The town of Preveza arose almost completely under foreign occupation, either Ottoman Turk or Venetian. As a result, the churches often reflected the influences of these foreign powers and the stifling conditions of occupation. They were built in rectangular, basilica style rather than with central domes and often with canvas paintings of Italian renaissance style rather than Byzantine iconographic frescoes. Ornate golden decorations on the altar that were foreign to the traditions of the Orthodox Church also had become the norm. They were also usually small, with none of the churches able to accommodate more than a couple of hundred people. They were unfit for the liturgical traditions that had such a rich history in Orthodoxy. Bishop Meletios came to argue that the holy traditions—especially Byzantine ones—could communicate the message of the Gospel and put a new face, sometimes literally, on the Church. Thus the reclamation of the authentic Church traditions and forms was not sought for sentimental reasons but rather for spiritual ones: they lead people to Christ. This belief is not grounded in blind dedication to tradition but in an important evangelical insight. Lasting change in people does not derive from chastisement, psychological guilt manipulation, or shallow missionary "techniques." Even social or familial pressures will not produce sustained spiritual growth. Rather, the people must want change themselves. So, the Church must transform itself into something of which people themselves *want* to be a part. For Meletios, this need meant transforming the liturgical experience into something the people would seek out.

This effort to restore traditions took place at numerous different levels: in the physical structures of the building, the organization of the liturgical year, the liturgical rubrics, the musical style, and the role of the spiritual father. It is important to keep in mind at this point that these changes were not made instantaneously. On the contrary, they were introduced gradually over many years and still continue today. Moreover, they were coordinated with the educational programs that will be discussed in the next section. By coordinating the changes with catechetical efforts, the changes were not seen as arbitrary, but rather the people (usually) understood the motivations for change.

The Church Buildings of the Metropolis: The twentieth century had not seen a single church built within Preveza itself, while three had been destroyed in the wars.[33] Those that remained were small, decaying, and often structurally unsound.[34] Some churches were torn down and new ones, built in Byzantine style, took their place.[35] Other churches were remodeled on a Byzantine style. However, the most important, and controversial, was the decision to replace the historic Church of Sts Constantine and Helen in central Preveza. The church was built in the eighteenth century and was venerated by some because it was also the site where St Kosmas had preached to the people of Preveza in 1779. Its parish, while historically not particularly active, was large. In 1985, the decision was made to demolish the old church to build a grand basilica in the Byzantine style. The foundation was laid on March 21, 1987, and the structure finished in 1992.[36] The furniture and iconography from the original church were preserved by building a basement chapel to St Kosmas. The main church, whose iconography is still not completed, is Byzantine in style. Nearly twenty-one meters high and with a capacity of nearly 1000 individuals, it is far and away the largest church in the Metropolis. While some do not appreciate it aesthetically,[37] it has come to fulfill the needs of the Metropolis for a large church. For some feasts, such as the Annunciation, all the people of Preveza gather in St Constantine's to celebrate the feast

---

[33]St Demetrius, St John Chrysostom, and The Church of the Apostles.

[34]Preveza suffered extensive bombardment during World War II due to its strategic position. The Italians, the Germans, and finally the British mercilessly bombed the city. After the war, the city was honored with a commendation stating that Preveza was the most bombarded city in all of Greece during World War II.

[35]The first church torn down was the Church of St Paraskevi in Preveza, which was structurally unsound by the time Bishop Meletios arrived. Soon, in other areas throughout the Metropolis, churches were either replaced or razed. St Prophet Elias and St Christos in Preveza and St Thomas in Agios Thomas are a few examples of many throughout the Metropolis.

[36]Κόλλια, 82.

[37]One interviewee simple stated, "St Constantine's is not a church to me."

together as one Metropolis. Such events would be impossible without such a grand church.

It is important to note, once again, that such attention to the physical structures of the Metropolis did not occur because they carry value in and of themselves. Rather, they contribute to the people's spiritual advancement by creating an environment in which the spiritual goals and values can be experienced and communicated. Externals—in this case edifices, frescoes, and iconography—contribute to the internal spiritual development of the people. The bishop encouraged this dynamic by encouraging the people to take pride in their churches. One of the early hieromonks recalled, "There was also very much a focus to look after the churches; to make them a pleasant place to be. They had not been looked after, seemingly abandoned, full of dirt."[38] This call led to a great number of volunteers—mostly older women—who devote themselves to the maintenance and beautification of the churches of the Metropolis. They were returned to their ancient status as valued houses of God amidst an increasingly secular world.

The Liturgical Calendar: The liturgical calendar in Orthodoxy is premised on the notion that church is not just relegated to Sunday mornings. The year rides in cycles of fasting and celebration in which the person is reformed, educated, and inspired as the year unfolds. Each sunrise brings a service to welcome the day; each new day brings a saint to emulate; each new season brings a new feast; each year brings a new step on the sacramental life. The church becomes intertwined with one's daily routine. According to Bishop Meletios, "The liturgical year is the worship of God with human garb. With its great fluctuations due to such different feasts, the liturgical year becomes joyful, the amusement of the people of the Church; tied with their life."[39] The aim, then, of designing the liturgical life was for the Church to become an integral part of the individual's life. This connection was missing when Bishop Meletios arrived in 1980. The Church calendar was largely relegated to Sunday liturgy alone. The

---

[38]Monk B.
[39]Interview, SLM.

meat of the liturgical life—morning matins, afternoon vespers, feasts, fasting periods, and occasional vigils—were nowhere to be found and had little meaning for most people. As one Prevezian remembered, "Before [Meletios], it [Lent] was probably only for the priests and not the people. . . . Lent before did not mean anything except going to the services of Holy Week and having it as a feast."[40] Bishop Meletios sought to establish a rich liturgical life out of nothing.

He began by encouraging the priests to hold daily services, especially morning matins and afternoon vespers. At first few people attended these daily services and even now the churches are rarely full. However, the practice demonstrates to the people that the priests are serious about their faith and the Church is dedicated to living a full liturgical life. He also encouraged the parish priests to add occasional vigils to their liturgical calendar so that today nearly every major feast has at least one vigil connected with it somewhere in the Metropolis. Most parishes today have four vigils a year in addition to the Christmas and Pascha vigils. Furthermore, the primary monastery of the region has a monthly vigil that people are encouraged to attend. These are moments of particular concentration in the faith.

The liturgical practices introduced by Bishop Meletios were not novel; rather they represented a return toward an ancient rhythm of worship. However, Meletios has adjusted them for modern life. As one of the hieromonks noted, "For the liturgical program, effort was made to take in mind the way in which people live today and make it easier for them to participate. . . . . We changed hours, chanters, the atmosphere of the Church. . . . ."[41] Accessibility without compromise became the key. For example, the vigils, known for being sometimes ten hours long in the monasteries, are not long—three or four hours—and they begin at a reasonable hour (at least for Greeks) so that even families can attend.

The Lenten season—the highlight of the liturgical year—became a particular focus of the bishop. Participation had been very limited,

[40]Lay Person, NK.
[41]Monk A.

but Bishop Meletios realized that in order for people to embrace all the Lent, he needed to make it more accessible, without compromising its purpose. Previously, all services occurred in the morning, if at all. Bishop Meletios inaugurated daily vespers, evening presanctified liturgy on Wednesday evening, and Friday evening services to the Panagia. He changed the "Agape vespers" of Pascha Sunday from a midday event to an early evening event, so that more people could attend. He also inaugurated a forgiveness vespers in the main cathedral every Sunday. He has even tried to make the services themselves more accessible. For example, the prophecies on Pascha night are read now in demotic Greek rather than ecclesial Greek so that more people will understand them. The result is that Great Lent has become a central element in the spiritual lives of some people of Preveza.[42] It has been restored to its original place of the highlight of the liturgical rhythm of the year. It has been altered in order to retain the same role it has played in the lives of Orthodox Christians for generations.

---

[42]It is important to note that this appreciation is not felt by all. In a country where religion and ethnicity exist side-by-side—intermingling and cross-fertilizing one another—the ethnic traditions are paramount for many. "Clean Monday," which traditionally entails abstinence from all food, has become a feast in which the people gather in the central square of their village and partake of sumptuously prepared vegetarian and seafood dishes, keeping to the letter of the fasting tradition, but not the spirit. "Clean Monday" is supposedly dedicated to recalling one's sinful state (which should not be difficult to do given the revelry with which carnival is celebrated the previous week) but has become for many the occasion for dancing, flying kites, and celebration. For many, Great Lent is then forgotten until Holy Week, when another series of celebrations occur. These culminate in Pascha night, when the people gather fifteen minutes before midnight in order to "rush" the priest as he emerges from the altar with the unwaning light. Many of the children hold fresh candles with Barbie doll and action figures attached, since religious holidays have become big business in Greece. After the stampede subsides, the "illumined" group goes outside to chat while the priest reads the Gospel, which culminates in his proclamation that "Christ is Risen!" The traditional response of "Truly, he has risen" is drowned out in most parishes by the sound of firecrackers and bombs that "celebrate" the event, to the particular dismay of the infant of a particular foreign researcher. A second stampede then follows as most people depart before the liturgy begins in order to eat the traditional soup comprised mainly of lamb innards. The highlight of the Lenten season for most occurs the next day when the lamb is turned on the spit and the people partake together.

The Liturgy: Communion is the pinnacle of the week in a traditional Orthodox society. It is the moment when the bread and the wine—mystically transformed into the body and blood of Christ—are offered to the parishioner to transform him or her from within. All the magnificent prayers, all the melodious hymns, and all the rich rituals lead to this holiest moment in the most important service. When Bishop Meletios arrived, while the clergy partook of the sacred elements, two plates came out from the hidden altar. They did not offer communion but directly asked for money. Instead of preparing the people for communion, the Church found itself seeking funds at the most holy time in the service. "Even as a child, it reminded me of Judas," recalls one local resident.[43] Bishop Meletios quickly stopped this practice and publicly rebuked it in an encyclical to the people. The mark of Caesar would be separate from worship.[44]

Disrupting the communion process in actuality had little effect on the people because very few of them actually took communion on a weekly basis. Most people only received communion once a year, the Saturday morning before Pascha night.[45] Bishop Meletios encouraged more frequent communion. The people's deepening connection to the liturgy was not only through communion but also in other areas. The liturgy occurs in ecclesiastical Greek, which is closer to ancient Greek than to modern Greek. For many, it felt like a foreign language, particularly during the parts of the service that fluctuated each week. Often, the Epistle reading began to be read in demotic Greek, since few people could understand the ecclesial Greek. One layperson noticed, "I have seen people stare at the person reading in modern Greek because it was the first time he understood the read-

---

[43]Lay Person, NK.

[44]To accentuate this point, Bishop Meletios also removed the "price lists" that were often found at the candle stands. He realized that this pocket change did not affect greatly the income of the Church yet alienated many. Now, if the Metropolis needs to ask for special donations—for example, if the Holy Synod asks money for Jerusalem—the priest leaves a plate at the back of the Church so that people can contribute if they choose. Liturgy is for worship, not fund raising.

[45]In popular practice, receiving communion at this time is preferred so as to not have to wait through the liturgy after the midnight service.

[46]Lay Person, NK.

ing."[46] The use of modern Greek in a service was novel, but true to the ancient practice: ecclesiastical Greek was the language of the day and the people would have had no problems in understanding it. Thus to stay true to the spirit of the ancient Church, Meletios needed to change the modern one.

The liturgical music also was reformed. Music in Orthodoxy is supposed to bring the spirit to the brink of the divine. It echoes, on earth, the praising of God in heaven. This purpose was not always apparent in Preveza before Bishop Meletios. Reflecting its struggle between East and West, the local style of religious music sounded quite Western with its polyphonic tones, but employed classically Byzantine notations. However, most chanters saw the liturgy as an opportunity to demonstrate their own artistic spirit, regardless of talent. In the words of one resident, "most of them [chanters] were not very good and sang just how they felt. They were singing according to their own inspiration."[47] Few in the "audience," however, felt the divine echo.

For Bishop Meletios, there was theological and practical value to establishing Byzantine chant in the diocese. Theologically, it restored music to its traditional place as an earthly vehicle to the divine, but practically, it also brought people to church. As a result, upon his arrival, he immediately organized lessons in Byzantine chant, which eventually turned into Byzantine music schools complete with concert choirs. Thus while still not yet ubiquitous throughout the Metropolis, the chanting is restored to its primary role

Spiritual Fathers and Confession: One of the residents of Preveza told me that as a boy, when the time for confession arose, he would go into a room with a priest, who would then list a series of sins, usually from the Ten Commandments, and then request a nod or denial from the sinful child. Confession for adults was rare, but of similar format. While expedient, this rigidity rarely fostered spiritual growth. Bishop Meletios recognized, however, that most spiritual development occurred through direct relationships between those of spiritual maturity and those seeking to grow.

---

[47]Lay Person, ΣΤ.

The first task was to establish a group of spiritual fathers from the most mature of the priesthood. He trained them specifically for their task, holding special meetings in which he would address them personally or bring in speakers from outside the Metropolis to assist them.[48] He often suggested specialized books for the spiritual fathers to read. More important than the training, however, was the desire to inculcate into the relationship a spirit of love rather than judgment. One of these spiritual elders told me, "A bodily father decides himself if and when and how much his children will acquire. The spiritual children choose their spiritual father. And his debt is to love them as also a bodily child."[49] Their task was spiritual counseling, not just offering formalistic forgiveness. This goal dramatically transformed the context of confession. Regarding his discussions with his spiritual father, one local resident noted, "It becomes a general discussion . . . you confess and at the same time you learn about what things mean. . . . Confession is informal, talkative, and probably solved many problems in addition to major ones. But everything is about Christ, who Christ is, and how he should be part of one's life."[50]

The goal of confession and the wider relationship with a spiritual father is the development of the spiritual life. It is based on mutual trust and love, not on condemnation and berating.

†

The church experience is inevitably modern in so far as it is the experience of individuals dwelling in and shaped by the contemporary scene; however, especially in Orthodox Christianity, it is also consciously ancient, or at least Byzantine. The tension between these two poles shaped Bishop Meletios' reformation of the Church practices in Preveza. The success of the Metropolis of Nikopolis and Preveza is the way in which they found means to accomplish both at the same

---

[48]Monk B.

[49]Abbot Ephraim, interview by author, unpublished written responses, Monastery of Prophet Elias, Flamboura, Greece, Spring 2003. Translated by author. Hereafter cited as "Abbot Ephraim."

[50]Lay Person, NK.

time.[51] For Bishop Meletios, it was not a choice—ancient *or* modern—but always both together: ancient in modern. At times, this meant adjusting the ancient traditions due to modern constraints; at other times, this meant inspiring the people to see the beauty and value of the ancient. Yet this fine tuning did not mean compromise but rather the recapturing of the spirit that inspired the traditions in the first place.

For Meletios, the church is the place where the individual should feel most at home, for it is closest to one's divine origin. In Orthodoxy, a church is the place where people are sanctified. It may just be a building composed of the most lifeless of external elements—mud, water, and wood—but they have the capacity to bring life to the individual. So, while many of the efforts in this goal dealt with "externals"—the design of building, the type of singing, the order of worship—they should not be rejected as "spiritual" people might be tempted to reject them. In our fallen world, there is a symbiotic relationship between the external and the internal. Bishop Meletios showed great discernment for balancing and building up in parallel the external and the internal elements. He did not allow one to jump ahead without the other. As a result, they mutually reinforced each other so that as the spiritual life deepened, the traditions of the Church were kept more faithfully. And as the traditions and other externals of the Church were faithfully kept, the inner spiritual life deepened. This spiral is one engine of spiritual growth. The job of the clergy and in particular the bishop is to cultivate it.

---

[51]Success in this area was also due to the careful manner in which change was introduced. While some elements were changed immediately to signal the fresh attitude of the Metropolis, most were introduced slowly over time. Recognizing the correct moment—when the clergy and parishioners are ready to change—took and takes discernment. Such discernment comes only from experience.

Bishop Meletios

The Bishop of Preveza accepts the truce of the Turks in 1912.

Bishop Meletios and his spiritual children on Mt Athos on their scouting mission to find a monastery in 1979.

Bishop Meletios with one of his spiritual heros, Father Joel Yiannakopoulos in Kalamata in the 1960s.

Bishop Meletios as a young hieromonk in Kalamata in the 1960s.

The 5th century mosaic from the cathedral of Nikopolis.

Another 5th century mosaic from the cathedral of Nikopolis.

Bishop Meletios on the day of his
ordination as bishop in 1980.

Bishop Meletios with the nuns
of Zalongo.

Bishop Meletios leads an epiphany procession during the early years in Preveza. Note how
everyone has an umbrella except the bishop and the monks.

A current picture
of Bishop Meletios.

Monastery of Prophet Elias surrounded by the Greek countryside.

The courtyard of the Monastery of Prophet Elias today.

Stephen Lloyd-Moffett with his son and Father Barnava

Goal 3: Concretely Forge the Community of Christ, the Church

In Greek, the word for Church, ἐκκλησία, derives from the ancient words for those who are "called out." The Church is the community of the those set aside for Christ. As a result, there is no salvation in Orthodoxy apart from community. The fierce individualism that dominates so many forms of Protestant thought is absent in Orthodoxy. Living in authentic communities is the very condition for human spiritual development. The path of salvation runs through and alongside others.

Bishop Meletios came to realize that this shared community of faith is not created in churches alone. New forums needed to be developed in which the people of faith could gather and the leadership could reach out to the people as fellow Christians. This identification of the one body of the church—clergy and laity alike—was central to his vision. Bishop Meletios states that his goal is to "search out more easily the lost sheep. Many, hearing and recognizing that the characterization 'lost sheep' applies to them, perhaps are hurt by it. But we, when we chant 'I am the lost sheep,' understand it means ourselves. And we beseech Christ to gather together his flock."[52] Underlying this statement is a missionary zeal for community, for "the people of God to be gathered, to commune with one another, to experience the love and holiness of the faith."[53] This communion has been the vessel of spiritual growth from the beginning of Christianity. However, it has been increasingly rare in the modern world, even in rural Greece. People tend to isolate themselves, separated by walls with television and computers filling the space. Bishop Meletios realized that the community needed a new physical center that could bind the people of faith together; a place that could focus the spiritual life of the city;[54] a place where the spirit of Christ could take concrete form in the modern world. This place would be a new spiritual center for Preveza.

---

[52] *Orthodox Globe.*
[53] Interview, SLM.
[54] Monk B.

Work on the Spiritual Center began soon after Bishop Meletios' arrival in Preveza. He chose a piece of land that was already in possession of the Metropolis, the former bishop's house, which had been abandoned after being destroyed in World War II. He hired a respected architect to draw up a design. He dispatched the young monks to promote it. The government, the Church of Greece, and the World Council of Churches all offered small amounts of assistance. However, the bulk of the funding would come through private donations. While several families in Preveza were very supportive of the endeavor, many of the donations came from outside of Preveza, through the personal contacts of the bishop. After several years of fund raising and construction, the Spiritual Center was functioning in 1986.

The Spiritual Center sought to become the spiritual hub of Preveza. Its primary use would be as a large forum where the Church could interact with the people. Every Monday, the bishop, hieromonk, or visiting speaker offers a homily in the grand hall of the Center. These lectures are quite popular, especially with the devoted faithful. Likewise, smaller group sessions with the bishop, protosingelos, or other lecturers are held every Tuesday. Twice a week, the Byzantine music school has classes at the Center. Children's catechism classes occur every other week. Every month, classes and discussions occur regarding Christian parenting. A Christmas pageant is held each year at the Center as well as the official celebrations for the patron saint of Preveza, St Haralambos. It has become a spiritual hub.

Community is formed not just during formal Church events, however. Bishop Meletios wanted the Center to become part of the "everyday life of the people."[55] As a result, groups not directly affiliated with the Church, such as social groups, school groups, recovery groups, and others, hold their regular meetings at the Center. Only political groups and unions are forbidden to use the facilities, because the Church does not want to give the impression of supporting one faction over another. Secular events also happen at the Center, such

---

[55]Monk D, interview by author, digital recording, Preveza, Greece, 19 March 2003. Hereafter cited as "Monk D."

as graduations, festival events, special conferences or lectures, recitals, and concerts. During these events, many people unaffiliated with the Church visit the Center. On a daily basis, the top floor provides a children's playroom that opens every afternoon in order to provide a positive environment for children to have fun. Today, there are around 18,000–20,000 visits to Preveza's Spiritual Center each year.[56] The Church is the people gathering, not merely the buildings made of stone.[57]

If the Church is one as the body of Christ, the individual parishes all represent smaller manifestations of this community. Yet because most parishes began as private chapels for wealthy individuals, public meeting spaces were not considered. Thus nearly every parish has built or has rented a space to act as a sort of small Spiritual Center for the parish. These parish halls are also used for multiple parish needs, such as parish council meetings and confession. Most of them have a small library of religious books and religious music. The parish priest usually goes to the parish hall after the services and has coffee and a sweet with his parishioners. Often, a discussion about the Gospel reading of the day or some issue of faith ensues. Sometimes these discussions go on for hours. As with the Spiritual Centers, the goal is to create an environment whereby the Church can easily interact with the people. The parish halls provide a more intimate forum for these contacts to occur.

Over time, relationships with the parish and with the parish priest have flourished. They are often cemented through shared religious excursions that usually happen once or twice a year in most parishes in the diocese. Sometimes these are close, for example day trips to an ancient church or monastery. However, occasionally they are extended pilgrimages to holy places in Greece, Italy, Constantinople,

---

[56]Interview by author with the director, Lazarus Synesios, digital recording, Preveza, Greece, 16 May 2003.

[57]"These secular purposes also had spiritual benefits. Inevitably these groups had contact with the priests and it was a good chance to get to know these people. Of course, it helped very much to make them trust us and to show them that we did not have a problem with them. There was nothing separating us. The bishop was not narrow-minded and only concerned about spiritual things, for example." Monk A.

or the Holy Lands. The aim of these trips is partly educational, partly fellowship, and partly vacation. They have the effect of tightening the bond of the parish priest with his parish. As such, the fruits of these excursions extend beyond the length of the trip. Although popular throughout Greece, they began in Preveza with Bishop Meletios as part of the campaign to create opportunities for the Church to move close to the people.

The bond among parishioners and between parishioners and the clergy is also strengthened through volunteer and charitable opportunities. The Metropolis has sought to be a leader in this regard, focusing the natural goodwill of the people of Preveza. The volunteer spirit of Prevezians made a stark impression on Bishop Meletios after his arrival. He said in one interview:

> Let me explain to you: when I was first handed the Metropolis, an acquaintance of mine told me, "And now, when you go over there (then there had been various incidents a little before I came) to these savages, be careful!" I crossed myself and told him, "Are you sure that they are savages over there?" He told me, "Look, I am telling you so! Be careful, because they are savages and bishop-eaters!"
>
> . . . Last of all, I came here and made an impression myself. After a little time, I went down to Athens—and here is the funny part—and met that same man, who told me, "How are you doing with those savages?" I said to him, "Which savages?" He replied, "I told you something the other time etc. . . . ." I said to him, "Listen when I tell you that I am a priest but in certain relationships of mine, I am completely devoted to the natural sciences; I do neither theology nor philology, and philosophy—areas which I studied—but I do math. $1 + 1 = 2$. And I will judge the people of my Metropolis by math. He told me, "And what does your math say?" I replied to him, "The city of Preveza is almost 15,000 inhabitants and we have an institution, the rest home, which accommodates twenty-five people. We do not have any resources from elsewhere, except the voluntary donations of the residents of the city. What donations would you expect from a city of 15,000 residents each month?" He answered, "Don't tell me that you collect 100,000 drachmas?" I told him, "Do you think an

institution with twenty-five old people and a staff can survive on 100,000 drachmas per month? In winter, that is not enough for heat, for the old people want it all day long." "And how much do you raise?" "500,000, not a penny less!" The same thing I was told by another priest. I told him, "How much do you collect for charitable funds each month?" He told me 50,000 drachmas. When I told him, "We collect 500,000 drachmas each month only for the nursing home. And the charitable contributions from the Parish Councils and parishes are another source."

Consequently, the number, as is shown via mathematics, reveals that the people have more depth than some of us imagine. And they are a very blessed people, very generous, with great love and faith— for faith is shown in works, and does not appear in perceptions that anyone has, and in portrayals that anyone might make.[58]

Bishop Meletios wanted to encourage this work, so he renovated the rooms and improved the facilities of the rest home. Yet he also recognized the opportunity for the rest home to become another forum through which the Church might reach out not only materially but also spiritually. Toward that end, he organized a group of women that largely replaced the rest home's paid staff. While the motives were partly financial, it created an opportunity for the Christians of the city to give of themselves. Bishop Meletios recalled, "Here [Preveza], I see a spirit of sacrifice which I have not encountered elsewhere. Such a disposition and willingness to voluntarily offer themselves and sacrifice. Wherever we say something, wherever we ask or something, we always discover the willingness for voluntary work. And not only voluntary work but literally hard work."[59] The goal is not only individual spiritual development but also the development of a community of faith.[60] Christ is made present through these actions, the people

---

[58] *Orthodox Globe.*

[59] *Orthodox Globe.*

[60] A similar dynamic is at work in the Metropolis' efforts at the regional hospital in Preveza. The hospital had been built in large part due to the efforts of the previous bishop, Stylianos. It served the material needs of the people greatly, but it lacked an organized spiritual presence. This changed under Bishop Meletios through the efforts of Father Alexander Tzimas. Father Alexander began to bring

are brought together, and the Church is reconstituted in each moment of shared sacrifice for others.

†

Many churches identify missionary work with far off lands and distant peoples. Upon his arrival, Bishop Meletios defined the mission field within. He recognized the need for more opportunities for the Church to interact with the people; "missionary" opportunities needed to be created. Yet these forums were also important in fortifying the faithful in the face of the secular challenges of the contemporary world. Bishop Meletios explained:

> All of us, we are in danger of becoming lost sheep. And for this reason, we are obliged to take hold, hand in hand, and to discuss between us, not only politics, not only soccer, not only about what we will eat or drink or how we will amuse ourselves, not only how we bathed ourselves or how we chatted or gossiped in the café or whatever else . . . but to have discussions about spiritual things, with a basis in the Holy Gospel, and to do some more serious work. This is the work of the Church: to help man to become aware of his eternal vocation, to draw near through a higher power, to Christ our Savior.[61]

The places created by these efforts serve as beacons that bring Christians together. They are "escapes" from the world where thought and discussion are directed toward Christ. In previous generations, perhaps, these discussions occurred in the cafés and street corners. Per-

---

communion and offer confession to the sick and infirm in the hospital in 1983. In 1985–1986, he began a campaign to build a chapel on the site of the hospital. The hospital itself offered no material assistance, but many of its doctors were a part of the council responsible for guiding its construction. All the funds used were from private donations. It was completed in 1993 and dedicated to the great healer, St Panteleimonos. Now, each Thursday a liturgy occurs and communion is brought to patients if they want to partake. Confession and spiritual guidance are also offered. The goal of these efforts is to bring the Church to the people, in this case quite literally. Along with the rest home, the hospital provides another forum for the Church to reach out to a demographic that is in need.

[61] *Orthodox Globe.*

haps in the ancient world, spiritual centers and parish halls were not needed. However, in the modern world, they recapture the spirit that once came naturally. They draw the people into the body of Christ, not only through spiritual programs but also through common causes and shared experiences. They are contemporary missionary centers in a land officially already Christian.

Goal 4: (Re-)educate the People

Orthodox Christianity is grounded in ancient traditions, preserved in symbolic rituals, mysterious theology, and shared lore. The original intent is often lost, frequently shifted, and often made more colorful. The law of *yiayiaology* among theologians is that every *yiayia* (grandmother) in Greece knows precisely why everything is done in the Church although her explanations are almost never historically accurate and almost always more lively. Yet there is a danger in all ancient faiths that their practice becomes routinized to such an extent that they lose their relevance. In generations past, the social pressure to preserve ancient practices even without understanding them was formidable. In the contemporary world, even in rural Greece, these pressures have waned. As a result, in a world where faith has often trumped education, the lack of the latter has become a spiritual crisis. Tradition is no longer enough to warrant practice, at least it was not in Preveza; in 1980, even the few that attended church knew little as to why.

In response, Bishop Meletios began to teach: two homilies a week for nearly three decades and more than sixty books and articles. For him, this process of nearly continuous preaching across formats is the primary role of the bishop. "The servant of Christ [the bishop] must have a mixture of all things. However, his work, his work par excellence, is to preach the Gospel of salvation, to have vigilance in the ministry of the word."[62] The goal is to create Christians who have both faith and knowledge of their faith. In the words of one local res-

---

[62]Interview, SLM.

ident, "Meletios gave to the people the meaning of going to Church. To know why you should want to go not just because it is Sunday or some holy day. That is the big difference."[63] Numbers are thus not an adequate measure of the faith of the diocese. It is better, I was told, to have one person attending a liturgy who knows why he or she is there than ten who do not. The goal is to create informed Christians who believe in knowledge, not merely habit.

The homily at the liturgy became one of the primary vehicles for this educational project. Although it seems strange to many Protestants who are used to sermons being the highlight of a service, prior to Bishop Meletios, a homily was often not given, or relegated to a few general words at the end of the service. All this changed with Bishop Meletios, who restored the ancient form of the homily as the primary vehicle for education. Each week, he and each of his hieromonks would fan out from the bishop's residence (sometimes by public bus before they had cars) in order to preach in parishes around the diocese. The hieromonks spent many hours preparing these sermons, often in consultation with one another and with the bishop himself. The minutes of the homily were not time to fill, but precious moments to grasp the mind and heart of the parishioners and lead them to insight. After the homily on their way out the door, the parishioners would be given a flyer about a lecture the following night in the Spiritual Center.

The Monday night lecture series—which has been going since 1980—is a more formal lecture that occurs in the Spiritual Center in Preveza. The topics are usually practical in nature: loneliness, relationships, volunteering, though they are also sometimes dedicated to particular saints or theological doctrines. Some of the attendees return the next day for a more intimate discussion about spiritual topics. Over time, this setting has emerged as a men's group, many of whom originally attended secretly because they were liberals and communists who did not want to be seen at liturgies or larger events.

---

[63]Lay Person, IT. Another local resident, NK, commented similarly: "The greatest change brought about by Bishop Meletios and his followers is that people know and understand why they go to Church; we know more what Christ means to us."

Six times a year, the parents of the town are invited for religious education on parenting as a Christian. Taught usually by outside experts, these are often practically oriented but from a Christian perspective.[64]

Of particular interest for the Bishop is the education of the youth. Before the arrival of Bishop Meletios, the Metropolis had few organized interactions with the youth of Preveza. There were only a few classes for small children in a few of the parishes; now, nearly every parish in the Metropolis has some form of youth religious education, often led by local monks. In many ways, such a "program" is not unique; however, the approach is. While it is fashionable for older generations to blame the younger ones, Bishop Meletios turns the table on this analysis:

> The older generations, although they lost the correct conviction, they maintained a compulsory surface of decency, but one which could not be imposed upon the youth. Because the youth want authenticity! And when looking at the inauthenticity of their elders, they rebel. Truly, they rebel! Truly! We, as Christians, and I, as a priest and spiritual father and bishop, do nothing else in all my life than to speak to all of them: "Attain authenticity, internal authenticity because only this will help you attain all others. Not a façade, not a mask." The young always have something deeper. They seek authenticity. And it is a shame that they have been found without a guide.

Bishop Meletios here switches the burden of responsibility. The whole Church needs restoration and repentance, not just the young. Characteristically, this condemnation includes the clergy's education of the youth, which has often failed in Greece. He comments:

> It is not up to scratch. This is for many reasons. And because it is our fault—the clergy—the responsibility is ours, since we do not do the best and the most we can! But it is also not our responsibility since some of the groups are tragically difficult for clergy to

---

[64]Some recent topics include, "Preconditions for a happy family," "The use of anger in child-parent relations," "From frog to prince—Can character be magically transformed?"

approach and do a responsible "job." However, the interests of the
shepherds must not be confined to the ninety-nine sheep who are
found within the "yard": those who are under our influence. We must
seek out the "one" who strayed, who today is not only "one" unfortunately. And he does not stray to the mountain, but into conditions
three times worse. It is not enough for the shepherd to "find" this
one. He must also take him onto his shoulders; that is, he must take
him by the scruff of the neck and place him above his head. It is necessary, in other words, to bear him with humility, with kindness, with
affection, and with love.[65]

The goal of youth education cannot be merely to give them facts
about the Church; "catechism" should not mean simply memorizing
prepared statements. It is necessary first and foremost to love the
young person, to "take him by the scruff of the neck and place him
above his head." This call to love is the central component of Bishop
Meletios' youth education program.

    Not all people will attend lectures or youth catechism. Thus, while
Meletios had been a frequent publisher during his years in the Holy
Synod (he published seven books during this time), the content and
style of his authorship shifted upon coming to Preveza.[66] As one of
the hieromonks noted, "The goal was to write short books with spiritual themes that were understandable to the people. We did not want
to write just to write."[67] The writing style of these books is simple.
The issues are always clear. The Metropolis has not lost sight of its
goal: to educate the people about their faith. But the bishop is also
aware of the danger of the written word and is careful to avoid creating any problems by the works of the Metropolis. He reflected:

> The books which our Holy Metropolis publishes, mine or other
> authors, are chosen always with one criteria: to help their readers to

---

[65]ΣΤΥΛΟΣ ΟΡΘΟΔΟΞΙΑΣ.

[66]The bishop was awarded a distinction from the Athens Theological Academy
for an introduction, translation, and commentary on the Fifth Ecumenical Council.
This book was already in progress when he was elected bishop and thus reflects the
Athens audience more than his Preveza flock.

[67]Monk B.

see the essence of faith and to not attach to the reader details which disorientate him, stimulating misguided fanaticism and fundamentalistic inclinations which would do double the harm to our work, that is, the spiritual work of the Church. Before we make a decision regarding the publication of a book, we look into not only if it responds to some demand—a pastoral problem of the sheep—but particularly how it might create problems rather than solve them.[68]

Bishop Meletios recognizes that "spiritual" books can cause as much harm as good. By and large, he avoids taking any extreme positions, but this does not mean that he shies away from controversial topics.[69] During the debate about legalizing abortion in the mid-1980s, Bishop Meletios wrote a series of articles and small books regarding the Church's position on the matter. Likewise, during the uproar in Greece about bar codes as the sign of the devil and the meaning of the number 666, Bishop Meletios wrote a series of books and articles that sought to clarify the authentic teaching of the Church. Most of his writings are inspirational in tone. He has translated and published a series of writings and lives of saints, particularly Russian saints. His translations of five books filled with wisdom from the Russian *staretzs* have proved particularly popular. He has also authored himself five books on lives of contemporary saints. These are inspirational tales, including the lives of his two most important spiritual influences, Father Joel Yiannakopoulos and Father Agathangelos Michaelidis. Yet most of his works are inspiring tales of faith, written simply. The most popular of these is simply titled, *What Is Christ?*, which is in its sixth printing and has been translated into several languages, including English, as seen in the appendix. Eventually, the educational program through publishing became so extensive that in 1986 they began their own publishing wing, which has since published more than eighty books. Widespread dissemination of the books is encouraged by the low price for which they are sold. The vast majority sell for the

---

[68]Interview, SLM.

[69]The only qualification one might make is the decision to translate in the 1980s an anti-evolution book written by an American evangelical of questionable repute, Dr. Duane T. Gish.

equivalent of only two dollars while many of them are given away by the clergy to their spiritual children in response to questions about the faith. The goal is education, not fund raising.

From the first month of Bishop Meletios' tenure, the Metropolis has also published a monthly newsletter, which is a common practice in Greece.[70] However, usually these Metropolis newsletters are polished publicity statements, filled almost entirely with information about the metropolis, for example, where the bishop went, with whom he celebrated the liturgy, requests for donations, and so forth. Without doubt, these efforts often border on self-promotion and are masked under the guise of Church promotion. The spiritual aims are not erased in this effort but rather overshadowed, muted by their parallel placement alongside other aims of the metropolis. From the beginning, Bishop Meletios rejected this model. He insisted that the newsletter must be totally dedicated to spiritual matters.

The diocesan newsletter is called *Lychnia*, which means "The Lamp." Its goal has been to live up to its title by being a spiritual light for its readers. For over three hundred editions, distributed each month, there has been a spiritual theme expressed on the cover. Page one is dedicated to an exposition of this theme by the Church Fathers. Sometimes, this page is a translation into demotic Greek of writings from the Church Fathers. A second page is an exposition of biblical views on the theme. A third page comprises a modern reflection upon the theme in light of the tradition of the Church. Throughout, there are small sayings of Church Fathers or even religious poetry. They are monthly opportunities to learn through print—and not only in Pre-

---

[70]As with most metropolises in Greece, the Metropolis also produces a calendar to give to the faithful and to donors. Many metropolises turn this into another occasion for publicity—filling it with pictures of the bishop, its priests, or its churches. The Metropolis of Nikopolis uses it as an opportunity to instruct the people about a given theme each year. For example, the calendar for 2003 is dedicated to understanding baptism. Throughout the calendar there are excerpts from the Bible, Church Fathers and contemporary Church thinkers about the meaning of baptism within the Orthodox Church. Included are some of the excerpts from the baptismal service and prayers with baptismal themes. Each year, a different theme is chosen. In the end, it represents another opportunity for the Metropolis to educate people through yet another medium.

veza. Today, more than 3,500 people outside the Metropolis—many of them international—subscribe to the newsletter and it is the only Metropolis newsletter to have a significant following outside its region.[71]

†

In the ancient world, the mediums through which one could educate the people were few: books were rare and public forums aroused suspicions in the era of persecution. One of the values of modernity is the diversity of forums to education and the relative ease of their dissemination. The Metropolis of Preveza has taken advantage of all of them since the arrival of Bishop Meletios in 1980. It has been a monumental task to educate—and sometime re-educate—the people about their faith. Their result was not an initial explosion of interest in the Church. But change is evident, even if its internal character makes it hard to recognize. One resident observed:

> If there were one hundred people going to Church before Bishop Meletios, now it is only one hundred and twenty. . . . But there are sixty to seventy who know *why* they are there. A certain number— little or great—are now into the Church and they know why they are there. . . . [My priest] is always saying, "What I want are ten, but ten who know why they are here and to know what Christ means to their life." . . . And I think they have succeeded in that goal: to get a small percentage of the population to know why they go to Church and what Christ means to them. For that reason alone, Bishop Meletios is already successful.[72]

If the metric is numbers in the pews, the achievement has been slight. "Success" for Bishop Meletios is measured by the *depth* of the spiritual lives of the people of Preveza. The fruit of creating this knowledgeable core group of dedicated Christians will be recognized only

---

[71]Sixteen thousand copies are published each month. As one monk stated, "The magazine, *Lychnia*, is the only magazine that is read by the people all over Greece. They wait to receive their copy." Monk C.

[72]Lay Person, NK.

after many, many years. Holiness may beget holiness but only slowly and all the while the forces built up against it grow stronger. Just as the spiritual decline of the region was gradual, so will its ascent be gradual and arduous. And for this long-term goal, the bishop and clergy have been continually writing and speaking.

GOAL 5: ESTABLISH MONASTIC EXAMPLES

Monastics, monks and nuns, play very little role in the lives of contemporary Christians in the West, even among Catholics. Their lives, often sequestered from society and seemingly unproductive in terms of the creation of tangible goods, seems almost uniquely unsuited for the hustle and bustle of the modern world. They are often seen as antiquated relics of a bygone year whose chubby caricatures might be useful for advertisements but seem irrelevant to the average parishioner.

In 1980, there had been no functioning monasticism for at least a generation in the region of Preveza. It had not always been that way. A century prior, there were ten active monasteries in the Metropolis with hundreds of monks. However, as the modern world crept into the region, monasticism disappeared. Bishop Meletios recognized the need for monasteries in the region. In part, this was a practical consideration: he had numerous monastic spiritual children who had no functioning home in which to reside. But beyond the practical need for a monastery, Bishop Meletios recognized the value of the monastery to inspire the people. He reflected on this purpose:

> The presence of young monks was and remains a dynamic stimulation for all the people. Even when they don't realize it. Their [the monks'] ethos and their education (they come from different subject backgrounds: theology, philology, physics, mathematics, astronomy, law, music, technical college, for example) establish unobjectionably that the monastic quality is the fruit of a wholehearted internal dedication, which is expressed also in their ascetic life. Their contribution is immense.[73]

[73]Interview, SLM.

The contribution of the monks is not primarily what they do for the diocese but rather the example they set. The monks embodied the Christian ideals and manifested the love of Christ through their action to the people of Preveza. They inspire the people to see the world in new ways, much like an artist can transform others through a painting. Their goal, according to Bishop Meletios, is "to radiate light. Not to act. . . . As much as he conscientiously keeps his vows and promises, the more he becomes a light for the people and hence a guide to eternal life."[74] For the monks to be a light to the people, the monastery must be, and be perceived by others as being, part of the Metropolis. If the monastery is too remote or too detached, this light will never be seen. Yet the light can only be cultivated separated from the pressures and temptations of society, in an environment of total dedication to Christ. Seeking this balance has been the struggle and achievement of developing monasticism in the region. One resident noted, "They do not seclude themselves in the monastery like at other monasteries. But in Flamboura, the monks go out according to the bishop's program and help the people . . . , this is a very good thing. They maintain their spiritual life within the monastery, but they go out into the world, even if that is not the central focus of their life."[75] Their presence in the community also gives a sense of spiritual protection to the people. As one resident noted, "Although I do not go often [to the monastery], I feel close to them. I feel like I always have a relation to them. . . . I like very much just that it is there."[76] The presence of the monastery and the monks in the community seems to give the community some sense of spiritual security.

Yet they have become the supporting actors in the Passion Play that has emerged in Preveza. As such, they will be analyzed in depth in the following chapter.

†

---

[74]Interview, SLM.
[75]Lay Person, ΣT.
[76]Lay Person, LS.

In the spring of 2003, Bishop Meletios preached incessantly about the meaning of Easter, the importance of fasting and confession, and the worthy celebration that will mark the midnight moment of Sunday morn when he will declare to his people with a single candle in hand: "Christ is Risen!" He spoke to crowds day after day with the same message. On Good Friday, the whole town seemed present in the central square and he exhorted them to uphold the faith. After weeks of preparation, the night of Pascha arrived. For as long as anyone could remember, the people of Preveza, as with most people in Greece today, arrive in droves for the moment when the Resurrection is declared but then leave equally swiftly, skipping the most profound moment of the year: the liturgy of the resurrection. Perhaps tonight would be different. Perhaps people have changed and now know why they celebrate with such joy. Perhaps tonight they will embrace the resurrected Christ.

In the metropolitan church of St Haralambos as they prepare for the midnight moment, Bishop Meletios comes to a part of the service where it is sung, "Let the enemies of Christ depart." He stops the service to remind them explicitly that *they* are not the enemies of Christ; do not depart but stay and partake of the resurrected body of Christ. The hall is filled to the rafters, with government and military officials filling the first few rows in full regalia. Near midnight, the hall darkens until it is pitch black and eerily silent. Bishop Meletios emerges out of the altar area with a single candle, whose rays shoot out through the darkness like lasers. The congregation takes the light in a moment of solidarity in Christ. These are Meletios' people and he is their shepherd. They walk outside and after a few prayers, the hierarch declares, "Christos Anesti!" "Christ is Risen!" A commotion breaks out. Fireworks go off. Hugs are exchanged. Children, woken up by the din, begin to cry. Dogs all over town bark. It is the highlight of the year. Then, the people leave. Only a few return to the church to celebrate the resurrection liturgy. The bishop only watches. The joy in his face, still glowing from the candlelight, is not mixed with measured sadness. As he returns to the altar, the deacon notices tears welling up. He recognized that the religious transformation of Preveza is still far from complete.

Preveza today is one of the most devout areas in all of Greece, but one should not gain the impression from this chapter that the spiritual life in Preveza has been perfected and the work is done. Progress has been made, without a doubt; however, very real problems still exist. The five goals of this chapter have not been achieved. Not all the clergy are personally holy. Many parishes still lack participation. With a few noted exceptions, the young—especially the university students of the town—are nearly entirely absent from the Church. Superstitions still supersede authentic knowledge of the Orthodox tradition for many, especially in the villages. People still walk away from Pascha before its culmination. Indeed, the spiritual transformation of Preveza is far from complete. But it has begun.

Bishop Meletios never established public goals to guide his work. Quite the contrary; he publically rejected the idea of any such program. However, his actions were not haphazard or wanton. On the contrary, Bishop Meletios repeatedly made very astute and diplomatic choices in directing the activities of the Metropolis. But we should not ascribe his success to the cleverness of his "program." Rather, as one person recognized, "There were no great spectacular programs, but rather slowly, slowly, changes occurred. . . . [Because of] the example of the bishop himself: his words, his way of life."[77] By eschewing programs and concentrating on encouraging holiness in the representatives of the Church, Bishop Meletios was allowing God to act through them. In other words, he was creating an environment where the Church's representatives would be more finely tuned to a divine plan and was rejecting human ones. This sensitivity embodies Bishop Meletios' alternative to common practice of developing clever programs to win the people for Christ.

I have talked with hundreds of people in Preveza about the spiritual transformation that is occurring. When queried about the most important factor, not a single person responded with *anything* the Metropolis did during the past twenty-three years. Without exception, they all said the exact same thing: the character of the bishop and the example he sets. This is not to say that actions are unimpor-

---

[77]Monk B.

tant, but rather without support of genuine holiness, they will ultimately be ineffective. He once said, "For me, then, according to the
words of Christ, my service to the Holy Metropolis of Nikopolis and
Preveza is a debt to render every day the peace of Christ to all men
with whom I come into contact."[78] This decision—to "render every
day the peace of Christ to all men with whom I come into contact"—
is the single most important concrete action that the Metropolis has
undertaken since Bishop Meletios' arrival. The lesson is that personal
holiness, as demonstrated first by the bishop and then by the clergy,
ultimately attracts people to the Church and through the Church to
Christ. Holiness begets holiness.

Bishop Meletios' "program" (or perhaps "anti-program") hinges
on the single belief that lasting change in an individual follows from
an encounter with genuine holiness. Clever promotions may fill
churches; dynamic oratory may bring people to the altar; institutional
discipline may make the Church appear more effective. However, all
these things do not produce the lasting change within an individual
compared to one moment with a genuinely holy individual. The
clergy, and especially the monks, must seek to become these lights.
The value of the representative of the Church is measured by his holiness or at least his continual struggle to become a pure vessel of God.
Bishop Meletios has never sought "effective employees" for the
Metropolis or the most educated, self-confident workers. He has
sought one thing: holiness that will beget more holiness.

This emphasis on holiness does not mean that the Metropolis
must not "do" things; on the contrary. The Metropolis must be constantly doing things to bring the people to Christ; it must be acting
all the time. Authentic holiness allows the cleric to be sensitive to
God's plan for Church rather than rely on his own abilities or desires,
however noble they may be. For Bishop Meletios, any "program" is an
imposition of a human-derived scheme on the work of God. It is destined to fail, no matter how successful it may appear. The "anti-program" of the Church is to *actively seek to be passive*; that is, to
continually strive to allow Christ to work through the Church with-

[78] *Orthodox Globe.*

out self-will interfering. For this reason, one cannot measure the success of this "anti-program" with any metric; I or anyone else cannot judge it in the end. It will be judged, I have been reminded, but only by souls entering heaven.

CHAPTER FIVE

The Supporting Actors:
The Monastery of Prophet Elias

The "monastery" of Prophet Elias appeared like many other half-finished multi-family dwellings dotting the landscape of rural Greece when I first visited it in the fall of 1994. The central fount was a cement mixer and the only church was a basement with white-washed walls. It bore none of the distinguishing marks of a Greek monastery: no high protective walls, no revered relics, no miracle-working icons, no antiquated wine presses, no surly old monks, and no impossibly uncomfortable old beds. The monks showered in individual bathrooms with radiant-heated floors. They cooked in industrial kitchens equipped with German appliances. They zoomed in and out in speedy cars and seemed to be coming and going as much as the visitors did. It was a far cry from the ancient isolated monastic communities on the revered Mt Athos.

After my first evening meal, the monks congregated in the kitchen for their *pankoina*, common work. Everyone was there, including the abbot, though they treated him no differently from the others. The task was to clean octopus, the next day's meal. I expected the atmosphere to be like Mt Athos, where common work is done in silence as one monk recites, "Jesus Christ, Son of God, have mercy upon me, a sinner." I kept my head down and concentrated on my task. No one else had such solemnity. An octopus eye came whizzing by my head. Laughter. A tentacle slid across the table into someone's lap. More laughter. Finally, an octopus became a hand-puppet for a mini-play whose content I failed to grasp but knew from others' reactions must have been hilarious. I knew that I had walked into a family—true brothers—but was it also a monastery?

Later in the week, the same brothers who slept on comfortable beds and threw octopus eyes held a vigil to celebrate a saint I did not know. Their little basement church was utterly transformed, so as for a moment to transcend its earthly ties. Their sound was unified and melodic; their movements precise; and their total devotion evident to all. They were not alone. Local villagers, young and old, came to participate. One young girl clumsily crossed herself when the time came for communion. The service lasted long into the night. Having observed many Athonite vigils, few could compare.

This chapter is dedicated to the story of this unique monastery and its development from a group of college friends to a vibrant monastery. Very seldom can one reliably tell the story of a monastery from its inception since across generations details are forgotten and legends created. This story was compiled from the oral histories of those who were there. The story is far from over and undoubtedly will change as generations become more removed from the founders. Nevertheless, the story is instructive for us now to examine not only the specifics surrounding this context but also the place of monasticism in the modern world.

MONASTICISM IN MODERN GREECE

Greeks call Mt Athos the Holy Mountain. Set up on an isolated peninsula in Northern Greece, it is the Jerusalem of the Hellenic world. Since the tenth century, it has been the center of the monastic world in Orthodoxy, with tens of thousands of monks in two dozen large monasteries and hundreds of smaller dwellings. A hike around the mountain was a journey around the Orthodox world. The Russians, Bulgarians, Serbians, and Romanians all had monasteries alongside the numerous Greek ones. It was a place set apart from the world, and seemingly from time. However, as the modern world encroached all around it, the number of monks began to decline in the twentieth century. The millennium of monastic life on the Holy Mountain was celebrated in 1964, but it felt more like a funeral than a birthday. There were hardly more than a thousand monks left on the peninsula, and most who remained were old and uneducated. Of the two dozen monasteries, only one truly functioned as a traditional Orthodox monastery. The word murmuring around Orthodox circles was that monasticism had fallen victim to modernity.

Inside the cities of Greece, however, the spiritual life was beginning to experience a renaissance among the youth. Youth groups with clever acronyms such as ZOE (life) and SOTIR (salvation) arose that attracted the faction of the young that were not drawn to the hippy lifestyle being exported from Western Europe. Although they were not directly controlled by the Church and were often perceived as anti-monastic, these movements produced a series of fervent, educated young Greeks. At the same time, new charismatic spiritual fathers arose in the monastic world: Elder Aimilianos (later Abbot of the famous Monastery of Simonopetra on Mt Athos) and Elder George (later Abbot of I.M. Gregoriou on Mt Athos) both had communities that began on the startling pinnacles of Meteora in central Greece but eventually moved to Mt Athos as they grew. On Mt Athos itself, the spiritual children of Elder Joseph, Ephraim, and Joseph the younger began to enliven other parts of the Holy Mountain. To the surprise of all, by the late 1970s, all throughout the Holy Mountain were signs of vitality and new life. Monasticism was experiencing a renaissance in Greece, led by an army of young, educated, and pious Greeks who rejected the modern world so as to embrace their ancient faith.

The group that would one day form the nucleus of the Monastery of Prophet Elias were part of this movement. In the late 1970s, they were mostly from the same dorm at the University of Athens. The dorm was sponsored by the religious youth group SOTIR, although they were not active in it. Word spread that there was a charismatic monk who lived alone in an apartment near his parish in central Athens, St Eleftherios. They travelede to meet him, and there were already many young men gathered around him (as a monk, he did not allow women in his apartment). They sat on the floor. On the table were the classics of Orthodox monastic spirituality: *The Life of St Antony the Great, The Ladder of Divine Ascent* by St John Climacas, *The Ascetical Homilies* of St Isaac the Syrian, and the teachings of St

Dorotheos of Gaza. Over the next few years, they would read these books together and discuss them. There was indeed something different about this man who had a speckled beard and a sparkling eye; he was wise beyond his years, holy but not pretentious, and compassionate but stern. He became their confessor and spiritual father.

Under Meletios' influence, the trajectory of their lives began to shift. Some of these young men decided to emulate the vocation of their spiritual father by dedicating themselves fully to God. Father Meletios has always been very careful to allow individuals to choose the monastic life by their own volition and without pressure. As one of his female spiritual children recalled:

> He never told me to become a nun. I kept asking him whether it was the will of God for me to become a nun because before when I was in my teens I never thought about it. So, I kept asking him. He never encouraged me exactly but told me just to pray and wait; pray and wait to see whether it is the will of God or not. . . . It was my decision 100 percent. Sometimes I was even a little disappointed because he would never say "Do this" or "Do that;" Always, I had to make the decision.[1]

With the blessing of the Archbishop of Athens Seraphim, Bishop Meletios tonsured his first monks in 1977 at Moni Petraki, the monastery connected to the Holy Synod. Within three years, their number would grow. However, Athens was no place to be a monk. Instead, they dreamt of Mt Athos and of becoming part of the spiritual rebirth of the Holy Mountain.

In 1979, Archimandrite Meletios gathered a group of about twelve of his spiritual children and traveled to Mt Athos to find a monastery in which to live. Two possibilities emerged: the Monastery of the Great Lavra—the oldest, most remote, and probably the most famous despite falling on hard times in recent centuries—and the Monastery of Dochiariou. Neither had an abbot at the time and the few old monks that inhabited them had little discipline or vitality. The chance to revitalize the Grand Lavra of Mt Athos is the Olympic moment of monasticism: the single moment to enter into the most revered site

---

[1]Nun E.

in Orthodox monasticism with the whole world watching and show what you are made of. For Meletios, it would be the capstone of his life; for the young and eager students, it would be the beginning of a fantastic journey in one of the holiest and most beautiful sites in the Orthodox world. It was their dream.

It is important to appreciate the degree to which Mt Athos is different. It is called the Garden of the Panagia (the all-holy one), and it is guarded, it is said, by Jesus' mother herself. Many of the great relics in the world reside in her ancient chapels; the finest and most ancient manuscripts appear in her libraries; miracles are common, as testified by the numerous stories surrounding her miraculous icons; its caves and huts hold numerous spiritual elders, renowned and obscure, who represent a living continuity to the holy fathers of yesteryear. While monasticism aims to separate itself from earthly concerns, Mt Athos is unique in its protections. It lies outside all practical ecclesial authority, reporting sometimes nominally to the Ecumenical Patriarch. However, there are no bishops eager to harness the resources of the monks to assist them; no non-monastics nearby whose spiritual needs the monks could attend; no encounters with other faiths, new social trends, or modern technology. At this time, there was one road, one telephone, and one ferry linking it to the mainland.[2] Its isolation allowed contact with the "world" to be carefully controlled and monitored, with only a handful of visitors allowed at any time. It was a timeless oasis in the midst of a rapidly changing world. It was a direct link to the purity of an imagined lost monastic glory of the Orthodoxy of antiquity. For Meletios and his spiritual children, it was going to be their Eden, the beginning of their communal ascent to God literally on the banks of the Holy Mountain.

Then, a scandal in the Church unrelated to them and in a largely unknown land disrupted these plans. The future Athonite abbot, the

---

[2]More recent times have shown, however, that the "world" has made inroads into Mt Athos. With the coming of roads, telecommunications, mass tourism, European Union grants, and other worldly elements, the peace of the Holy Mountain has been disturbed. Many of the monasteries seems to have become seduced by the world: with their spiritual focus being distracted by the number of pilgrims, marketing products, developing financial resources, and seeking worldly audiences for their ideas.

spiritual father of these men, was suddenly elected bishop.[3] For most, the change of circumstances came as a shock. In the words of one monk, "Of course we had heard of Preveza because of the scandal, but we could not find it on a map."[4] After imagining the rest of their lives in the peace and solitude of Mt Athos, the busy life of urban Preveza did not sound appealing. Instead of joining the blossoming rebirth of Mt Athos, the new bishop and his spiritual children were called upon to lead a spiritual rebirth in a metropolis plagued by spiritual neglect and scandals. Instead of finding solace and peace in an ancient, isolated monastery, they would live in cramped apartments in the center of a bustling town. Instead of dedicating themselves to the monastic life, their attention would be necessarily shared with priestly and administrative duties. The two lives could not be more different.

It is no surprise that some of Bishop Meletios' spiritual children sought to go to Mt Athos without him. Later, some more would leave Preveza, unable to forgo permanently the appeal of the Holy Mountain. Nearly all the monks struggled with the dilemma of where to locate. For those who were torn, Meletios "encouraged them to see things in a spiritual light about what is the meaning of obedience, what is the meaning of the Church, etc."[5] In the end, most of them— especially the "core group" who populated the Archmandrite Meletios' apartment in Athens—chose to join the new bishop in his work in Preveza.

Underlying the decision to stay with Meletios or leave for the Holy Mountain were not just issues of loyalty or serenity. Monasticism outside of Mt Athos in Greece was very different. These areas lacked the natural "protection" of the Holy Mountain. More often than not, problems arose, especially between the local ecclesiastical authority and the brotherhood. The local bishops frequently had mixed feelings toward vibrant brotherhoods within their metropolis. Some embraced the new or newly rejuvenated monasteries, but many

---

[3] As one of the early monks recalled, "We were in a state of uncertainty because suddenly he was elected bishop." Monk B.

[4] Monk A.

[5] Monk A.

feared their influence, especially because they perceived the monks as "meddling" in various Church programs. Fearful bishops wanted the monasteries to remain isolated and secluded. On the other extreme, many bishops sought to use the monks for the ministerial tasks in their metropolises by ordaining the monks and asking them to serve in local churches. Sometimes, these requests compromised the monastic life, draining the monasteries of hieromonks. Due to these various problems, there are numerous examples of whole monasteries sometimes leaving their metropolis and relocating on Mt Athos where they could essentially avoid all of these issues. Other monasteries merely became stagnant from the strife with the local Church and competing claims stifling their spiritual development. There were few, if any, good contemporary examples of monasteries operating healthfully within dioceses.

Of course, the monks of Prophet Elias were different. Their charismatic "near-Athonite" leader was also their bishop. Presumably, he would recognize and respect the boundaries and goals of the monastic life. But the Metropolis had uniquely pressing needs after the scandal and there were few people the bishop could trust other than them. They would be the best sorts of lieutenants, demonstrating the Christian life to the forlorn faithful of Preveza. The dream of the Holy Mountain was now gone, but the shape of the monasticism in Preveza had yet to take form.

THE PREVEZA PERIOD

After the enthronement of Meletios on March 28, 1980, the bishop and the five young monks moved into the bishop's house. Although not as they imagined, they now shared a "common" life—they were a monastic community without a monastery. They selected an abbot, the one of them a bit older who was already ordained a priest, but his duties would only be organizational. Bishop Meletios would still be their spiritual father. Within a few months, the five were eight, and then more, so that some were even sleeping in the small private chapel. Their monastic plans had taken a detour, Bishop Meletios observed, but it was by the will of God. They would have to do their best to live a monastic life within the constraints of a modern Greek town.

They awoke at 5:30 in the morning with those sleeping in the chapel rolling up their beds so that prayers could begin. For two hours, they performed Orthros or Matins. Then the monks would begin their duties. Each monk was given tasks consistent with their abilities and temperament. Two or three helped out in the offices of the Metropolis, which after years of total neglect were in need of significant reorganization. Several of the monks developed religious education programs for the young. Another monk developed the bookstore while several monks developed the publications, including writing a column to a local paper. One monk was dedicated to developing the Spiritual Center and the various construction projects. All of them also had liturgical duties in the parishes. When there were no priests, they would become the head priest but more often they were secondary priests responsible for confession and preaching. In the end, each monk had multiple duties. The days only became longer and more arduous as the needs of the Metropolis were recognized. They kept a common meal, *trapeza,* at midday before they would return to work. In the evening, they would gather again as a group for the service of vespers, which was followed by dinner and the compline service. After compline, the fathers usually congregated on the stairs to speak with the bishop. All the fathers interviewed for this study recalled this custom fondly. One recalled, "After compline, we would sit around the stairs and have spiritual discussions. He would usually begin with a joke or something and then he would turn the speech to spiritual things, asking and joking. It was a very nice gathering there."[6] Throughout the day in town, the monks' responsibilities put them in close contact with the people of the Metropolis, but their friends were found on the staircase in the evenings. These were their friends since the university, but now they had become a family, with Bishop Meletios as their common father.

---

[6]Monk A.

Constructing a modern monastery

The brotherhood grew quickly. By the end of 1983, Bishop Meletios had tonsured more than twenty monks, with many living together in various apartments spread throughout the city. Bishop Meletios gathered the brotherhood together to talk about finding a permanent monastery for their community. He asked each person to write an open and personal report about how they saw their future monastic life and, particularly, how they imagined their future monastery. One monk recalled, "Bishop Meletios was very polite and very spiritual in saying that whoever wanted to go to the monastery, he may go; whoever does not want to go, don't go. Think for yourself. Think seriously. What do you want?"[7] Two monks, including the abbot, decided that their temperament was not suited for a monastery and eventually they would leave to join other Metropolises.[8] The brothers then elected Abbot Ephraim to oversee the design, construction, and fund raising necessary for the construction of their monastery.

Abbot Ephraim continually solicited the advice of the brotherhood in deciding the shape of their future home. Their deliberations included reflecting not only on the specific circumstances that could affect their life (proximity to the bishop, continued work in the Metropolis, climate and geography, and so forth) but also on the nature of monasticism in the modern world. Should they be near to the people they serve since they will not be totally separated from ecclesial duties as most monks were in the past? Or do the modern conveniences of cars and telephones allow them to be more isolated and still have connections to the town? Should they emulate Mt Athos with its fortress-like designs, thus symbolizing their rejection of the world, or create a more open and inviting form, knowing that they will have many visitors? As they began to reflect upon these

---

[7] Monk C.

[8] The former abbot Vasileos departed to serve the Metropolis of Patras, which did not have any hieromonks in its service and therefore offered new opportunities. Archimandrite Vasileos is still close to the bishop and the monastery. He became a prolific writer, authoring more than thirty books in Greek and English.

issues, they came to rethink the meaning of isolation itself. Bishop Meletios remarked:

> Today, with the means of transportation and information, the "world" is very near. It comes "within" the grounds of the monastery. The monasteries today have one struggle: to remain "spiritually" "outside" and "far" from the world. The "world" in this sense does not only enter in the grounds of the monastery, with the presence of lay people in the monastery, but also enters into the hearts of the monks as individuals. And it makes them human-centered, self-promoting, men of impression and action.[9]

Separation from the world would be first and foremost spiritual in nature. Distance would help this separation, however, and so they decided the monastery should be at least twenty-five kilometers from Preveza: close enough for the bishop to visit easily and the fathers to continue their work in their parishes but distant enough to not court the influence of the world. One option was the old monastery of Prophet Elias, which was on a mountain near the town of Stefani about thirty-five kilometers from Preveza. This monastery, built in the eighteenth century, had been almost totally destroyed by the Germans in World War II. Miraculously, the central church survived unscathed. However, the church needed extensive repairs and the distance would have required significant travel time for the monks. After analyzing the matter, Abbot Ephraim convinced the brotherhood that it would not be feasible given these drawbacks. In 1986, the monks bought a piece of land twelve kilometers from Preveza near Flamboura, a small village that they did not know well. The advantageous location was quite central in the Metropolis and close to Preveza; yet it lay in a quiet village. The location also possessed a view of both the mountains and the sea below.

The monks developed the design of the monastery with a local architect. Again, while there were geographic constraints, much of the discussion centered around the meaning of monasticism in the modern world. In particular, how the monks would regulate the

---

[9]Interview, SLM.

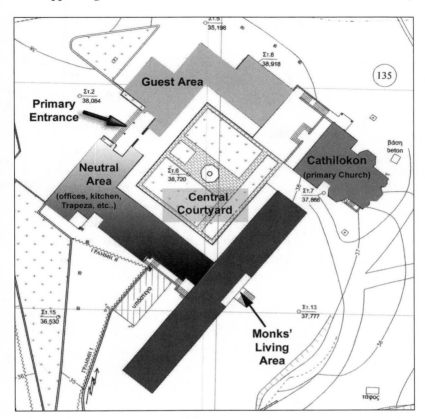

The Design of the Monastery of Prophet Elias, Preveza

inevitable interactions with the world governed their decisions. Knowing that they would have many visitors, especially spiritual children, the monks wanted to design the monastery so that visitors could be welcomed "without them destroying the crucial *hesychia* of the monks."[10] They wanted to create an environment whereby the "spiritual separation" from worldly things could be fostered without physical inconvenience. At first, the plan was to create guest quarters and a welcome center in a separate building outside the central part of the monastery. Consistent with this plan, the central church (the *cathilokon*) was placed on the outside edge of the monastery rather

---

[10]Abbot Ephraim.

than in its central courtyard, as is common in many monasteries. This positioning allowed access directly from the outside and left the monastery proper to the monks alone. Over time, however, this plan seemed impractical. Instead, they incorporated the guest house and welcome center into one corner of the monastery. The end result was two "pods" of activity: one exclusively for the monks and one for the interaction with the "world." Separating the two worlds would be the work areas: the kitchen and the offices. The central courtyard would be the zone where the worlds most often interacted.

In style, the monks decided that the Athonite fortress look was not only expensive but also unnecessary today. As the abbot noted, "Today, we do not have pirates."[11] They ended up with a simple but elegant design of a square courtyard with a central fount flanked with a broad marble peristyle. The structure would be built mainly out of inexpensive concrete painted white. Wood and marble highlights would give it touches of class. Careful landscaping within the central courtyard would add to the peace and serenity of the monastery. Once many of these decisions were made, the architect created a mock-up of the final design. The funds then needed to be procured.

Since the government offered little support, nearly all of the money for the monastery needed to come from private donations. The fathers obtained lists of people who subscribed to various religious magazines in Greece. They sent to each subscriber a simple letter detailing their plans and including a picture of the mock-up. Of the 25,000 letters sent out, about 6,000 people responded with a donation.[12] Most of them were small in amount. One of the monks recalled, "It was very moving that many of the contributors were pious old people who were very poor and sent something like 1000 drachmas [about three dollars]. They would write that I know that it is very little money—perhaps just a small candle in the monastery—but it was very moving to witness their devotion."[13]

---

[11]Abbot Ephraim.

[12]I have been told by a fund raiser for religious causes in America that this response rate is extremely high.

[13]Monk A.

There were also some large individual donations that contributed greatly to the cause.

One unexpected source of long-term income came as the new monastery inherited the property of the defunct and destroyed Monastery of Prophet Elias in the mountains. Among their holdings was a a significant piece of land on the Ambracian gulf, which comprised a series of lakes and wetlands. The brotherhood has developed it since 1998 in two ways. First, they created a joint company to fish the waters to provide income.[14] The second use has been the development of an ecological preserve catered toward both tourists and locals. Included in this endeavor has been the opening of a Visitor's Center in 2002 that is filled with explanations of the ecological value of the area as well as the Orthodox Church's ecological position. Tours are offered of the wetlands by small boat, which also include a tour of an old monastery constructed on the shores. In its first year, more than 1,500 visitors came to the preserve. Income from this endeavor will continue to fund expansion of the monastery.

The monastery did not wait to raise all the funds before beginning construction. Rather, when they raised enough funds for the next phase of the building, they would begin. However, as one phase was completed, the funds for the next phase always arrived. One monk recalled, "It was a miracle, you could say, that the money arrived always when we were just in need. We did not have all the money from the beginning but God helped us. As soon as we finished one part, the money would come to continue the project."[15] Construction started in November 1987 and, exactly four year later, the monks moved in. More than eleven years after arriving in Preveza, the brotherhood finally had a permanent home.

Although initially rather primitive, the monastery has matured greatly in the ensuing years. The main church eventually gained frescoes; relics were donated by a close friend of the bishop's, including

---

[14]While this commercial enterprise assists in the financial security of the monastery, it has also created problems as it has been embroiled in a series of lawsuits with the government and poachers.

[15]Monk A.

an ornate frame containing small pieces of the relics of St Peter and St Paul, as well as St Linus, St Laurent, St Blaise, St Lucia, and St Barbara; the library grew to some 27,000 volumes and 7,000 periodicals, including a complete original edition of the great cataloger of Greek patristic sources, Migne. It will never be Mt Athos, but there is the widespread feeling in Greece that something unique is emerging in this unlikely location.

MONASTIC LIFE AT PROPHET ELIAS

The building, however, is ultimately just a shell for the life that happens therein. As with any structure, the monastery can be more or less protective of the monastic life within. Yet the quality of the monastic life within creates sanctity, not the building itself. In fact, every monastery is different—different location, different design, churches dedicated to different saints—however the monastic fathers stress that the monastic life is everywhere one and the same. For this reason, there are no "orders" in Orthodox monasticism. The goal of all monasteries everywhere throughout time has always been the spiritual perfection of the monks. The monastic tradition is composed of common tools to assist the monk toward this goal; for example, the monastic *typikon* (corporate prayer rule), private prayer rule, obediences (essentially jobs), common work, fasting, *synaxes*, and so forth. Each monastery pursues the same goal with the same tools, yet each monastery also has its own character, its own way of localizing the common tradition to the specifics of their situation. In this sense, for the Orthodox Church, every monastery embodies the same monastic tradition yet is unique in form at the same time.

When the brotherhood moved into the monastery in November of 1991, Bishop Meletios, in conjunction with the abbot and the abbot's council, needed to develop a monastic program that would fit the "Flamboura" era. As with the physical construction of the monastery, this process began with a commitment to the long-standing canons of the monastic tradition; they did not set out to create a "new" or "updated" model of the monastic life. "On the contrary, they sought to identify what adaptation of the classical tools was needed in light of their particular circumstances to keep the monastery focused on the unchanging goal of the spiritual perfection of the monks. Proper reflection required not only recognition of local factors (parish assignments, availability of the spiritual elder, personalities of the monks, and so forth) but also reflection about the role and future role of monasticism in modern Greece. Thus the development of the monastic program was as much a self-reflective exercise about who they wanted to be as it was a question of organizing their time and resources.

From the beginning, the bishop always sought, by historical standards of monasticism, a moderate program. This accommodation should not be read as a judgment on more strict programs. On the contrary, Bishop Meletios reflected:

> The Orthodox tradition is one; common to all the monasteries. Therefore, if one attributes *idiorhythmacy* to us, we should respond: unfortunately, we are! This derives not from excessiveness of virtue but from weakness. We follow a bit of a moderate way of the monastic life, which is condescension for our weakness. If one ascribes our *idiorhythmacy* to our supposed virtue, they have made a mistake. I am naked, bankrupt, and destitute. God help me.[16]

Spiritual weakness, not virtue, is the source of the more moderate program. Retrospectively, we can see that this decision to create a moderate program and the form it would take was motivated by three factors. The first one was a desire to follow the classical monastic canons as much as possible. Bishop Meletios always stressed the ancient tradition of which the monastery is a part. The second factor, however, in part counterbalanced the first: a recognition that the monks would not "disengage" fully from the work of the Church as long as there were unmet spiritual needs and the bishop sought their activity. The people of Preveza had grown attached to many of them and likewise the hearts of the monks were devoted to their spiritual welfare. Some of the monks would continue to have parishes, teach

---

[16]Interview, SLM.

catechism, and offer frequent homilies. The monks therefore needed a program that was moderate and flexible enough to allow them opportunities to fulfill the needs of the people. The third factor was the individual temperaments, biorhythms, and spiritual states of the monks of the brotherhood. Among the various factors here, one stands out: the group was and is by and large social in nature and compassionate toward other people. Moreover, many of them began their cenobitic life as long-standing friends and had come to value the Christian fellowship they shared. While they would not compromise the traditional monastic pursuit of hesychia and continual prayer, near-absolute silence and individual isolation from others would not work for this community. The monastic program was developed with these three factors in mind, although perhaps not consciously.

The monastic program has seven parts. First, and perhaps most important, is the monastic *typikon*, the schedule of corporate prayer and worship. The traditional monastic *typikon* was reduced and adjusted to be more flexible and individualized compared to the classical models. After some degree of experimentation, the following program was developed: around 5 a.m., the monks leave their cells and proceed to the central church, at which time the "midnight" office is read. The midnight office is followed by Orthros (Matins). On Tuesday, Thursday, Saturday, and Sunday, Orthros is followed by the Divine Liturgy. On these days, the midnight office is shortened by excluding the reading of the psalms. The monks receive communion twice a week: on Tuesday and Saturday.[17] During Lent, however, they receive communion on Wednesday, Friday, and Sunday instead. The morning services usually end around 7:30 in the morning. After the dismissal, the monks have a light, informal breakfast. After breakfast, they return to their cells for rest, prayer, or quiet work. Most begin their *diakonima* (obediences or tasks) around 9–9:30 a.m. They work until 1 p.m. when the *talanton* (a carved board that is rhythmically hit

---

[17]The lack of communion on Sunday seems strange at first glance. The bishop decided that fasting on Saturday would be burdensome for the monks. However, it is also a bit misleading. Since many of the fathers are sent out to villages on Sundays to perform the liturgy and preach, over half the brotherhood has communion on Sunday.

as a sort of alarm clock) indicates *trapeza* (mealtime). *Trapeza* begins with a prayer and, during the meal, a reading occurs. Beyond the standard for Lent, *The Ladder of Divine Ascent*, the readings usually consist of monastic treatises, lives of saints, or theological texts. *Trapeza* concludes with a prayer. After *trapeza*, the monks rest for a couple of hours during the heat of the day. At 5 p.m., the vespers service begins, which usually takes about one hour. The monks are free after vespers until 8 p.m., when the evening *trapeza* begins. During this free time, the library is open and oftentimes there are guests who need attention. *Trapeza* is immediately followed by *apodeirno* (compline). After church, the formal day is finished.

Second, each of the monks has a private prayer rule that they carry out in their cells. The rule is worked out individually based on the monk's preference and biorhythms. Some perform their prayers before bed while others finish it before the morning services. The goal is four to five hours a day of common prayers and ample time for private prayers in their cells. Unlike some monasteries, the prayer life of the monastery does not openly center on the Jesus Prayer, which is common in some Athonite monasteries. It is a tool that the monks use but it is not exalted as the only or even highest tool of the monk. There is little mention of it in the daily lives of the monks, and *komboskinia* (prayer ropes) are rare.

Third, in designing the liturgical calendar, several considerations were taken into account. The monastery attempted to balance the desire for hesychia and the desire to show hospitality and provide counsel for its spiritual children. The monastery receives a great number of visitors daily, so the bishop decided to "close" the monastery periodically to protect the hesychia of the place. The monastery is currently closed to outsiders two days a week, Monday and Thursday. During these days, the phones are not answered at all. In extreme cases, the monks are available, but normally these days are dedicated to the hesychia upon which monasticism is predicated. In regards to fasting, the monastery tends to the traditional fasting regime with a slight accommodation to their weaknesses. In accordance with monastic tradition, fasting occurs on Monday, Wednesday, and Friday. However, there is no fasting on Saturday night, which means that most of the monks do not take communion on Sunday morning. Because the monastery is closed on Thursdays, the monks take advantage of that time to regularly schedule a common meeting or *synaxis* with the bishop. These occur every other week and are most often led by the bishop, though occasionally the abbot or an older monk will officiate. They take the form of an open conversation wherein spiritual topics and struggles are discussed. The monastery also holds periodic vigils, usually once a month. The vigils normally begin at around 7:45 in the evening and last five to six hours. The calendar of feasts celebrated with all-night vigils changes year after year so that the monks gain broad exposure to the lives of the saints. They usually do not have all-night vigils on major feasts, because they have many pilgrims during these times.

Fourth, usually once a day there is *pankoina* or common work, where the monks come together to engage in some large project that would be too time consuming for a single monk to undertake. Sometimes this involves kitchen work, such as peeling potatoes or cleaning fish for the next meal. Other times it involves office work, such as placing mailing labels on copies of the Metropolis newsletter or counting the money from the candle stand. Other times, it involves physical labor, such as tending to the garden or bringing in the bee hives. In each case, all the monks (including the abbot) are expected to participate, unless a blessing is provided to do some alternate task. There is no preferentiality in these common tasks—the youngest novice and the most mature monk are equal during these tasks. A common spirit is cultivated during these sessions—in many ways as much or more than during the common liturgical rites. Usually, they are jocular affairs, with the monks talking and joking while they work, which stands in stark contrast to the *pankoinas* at many other monasteries.[18] A warm, familial bond is readily apparent. New members of the community are welcomed into this "family" as much through these moments as any formal consecration.

---

[18] I have been in *pankoinia* on Mt Athos, which are somber affairs, where a single monk recites the Jesus Prayer as the monks work. This is not the case here.

Fifth, the *diakonima* or obediences that the monks perform during the day are mostly centered on the tasks necessary for the monastery to function, for example, cooking, cleaning, welcoming guests, gardening, attending to the church, and so forth. The monks are also responsible for archiving the history of the monastery and tending to the publications of the monastery and Metropolis. These obediences change every year, except when a monk possesses a unique skill, such as knowledge of computers. Two monks and a lay assistant work in the garden each day, which supplements the food for the kitchen (most of which is purchased from suppliers in Preveza). Fourteen of the monks are priest-confessors and serve the local community in addition to their obediences. Especially during Advent and Great Lent, they spend much of their time tending to the spiritual needs of their flock. Their salaries as priests are paid by the Greek government and are one of the most consistent forms of income for the monastery. Without this money, in the words of one of the monks, we "would have to find some sort of handicraft to sell or paint icons or something."[19] While the monastery is not wealthy compared to many, it has enough funds for a comfortable existence.

Sixth, short-term travel away from the monastery is frequent for many monks due to their duties in the Metropolis and the procurement of the material needs for the monastery. In general, extended absence from the monastery is discouraged. It occurs under a few conditions, primarily if a monk is deeply involved in a parish and they want him to accompany them on a spiritual excursion or if they are offering a lecture. Monks can also obtain blessings to see family, officiate weddings, and take care of other familial obligations. These are rare but are based on the fundamental recognition that some familial obligations still exist even after becoming a monk.[20] Fourth and finally, some monks have responded to a call by the bishop of Central

---

[19]Monk A.

[20]The monks keep strong relations with their family, usually having a blessing to speak with them at least twice a month. Other monks, such as one older monk who has twelve grandchildren in the area, receive family quite regularly at the monastery. Thus there is not a sense that monastic tonsure severs all ties with family, as is the case in some monasteries.

Africa to assist him. One monk has decided to reside on a semi-permanent basis in Africa. Likewise, a monk from the Congo has spent some time in this monastery. In sum, extended periods away from the monastery are rare but not forbidden.

Seventh, during the early period of the brotherhood, confession was always offered to the bishop rather than the abbot, who had a more organizational role. Historically, such a separation of the roles of the spiritual elder and abbot of a monastery has led to difficulties; for that reason, most of the Church Fathers discourage it. However, this split in roles was inevitable with Meletios' election to bishop since he could not devote himself fully to both the monks and the flock of Preveza. The separation of roles did not create many problems while the brotherhood was in Preveza, as the bishop was a constant spiritual presence. However, since moving into the monastery, the bishop has asked the abbot to take a more prominent spiritual role in his leadership of the community. In part, this was a practical consideration since the bishop could no longer be there all the time as he was while they all lived adjacent to the Metropolis. It was also, I believe, a realization that the monastery would live beyond the life of the bishop and it would be wise to graduate to this autonomy over time.

For some in the community, especially for those who had long been close friends with Father Ephraim, this shift has been a difficult transition at times. While patterns of confession and obedience have developed, the situation is still very fluid. Most of the older monks only go to confession with the bishop, while the youngest have confession almost exclusively with the abbot. Many of the monks seek counsel from both. The current situation lacks definition and has caused uneasiness for many monks. Open division over the split in spiritual authority, however, has been avoided so far because of the congruency of thought between the abbot and bishop: the abbot has been trained in the spiritual life only by the bishop and tends to reflect his spirit when offering advice to the community.

Each of these seven elements of the life of the monastery—the daily *typikon*, the private rule of prayer, the liturgical calendar, common work, obediences, absences from the monastery, and confession—has been developed to foster an environment for spiritual growth within the circumstantial constraints. The seven elements evolved over time; they were not selected from the beginning and held onto rigidly ever since. Rather, they reflect the ongoing self-discovery of the Monastery of Prophet Elias' own unique take on the common, ancient Orthodox monastic life. As conditions change, the life will undoubtedly adjust. But these adjustments represent mere tinkering with the means toward an unchanging, higher goal.

THE PERSONALITY OF THE COMMUNITY

A monastery is more than the sum of its buildings and its monastic "program." Ultimately, these are the tools that are used to protect and shape the individual monks, guiding them in "the struggle for purity from the passions and acquisition of virtues, which is everywhere the work of the monk."[21] This struggle is made easier by being within the monastery. Abbot Ephraim notes:

> The struggles for perfection in Christ comprise the singular goal of the monks. This struggle exists and justifies our life. It becomes better, in other words, more effective, in the monastery. In hesychia, in other words, removed from the disturbances of life and in harmony with the spiritual ethic that the Orthodox Church and the ascetics of tradition delimit.[22]

All the externalities of monasticism—the buildings, the monastic program, the dress, and so forth—serve only to shape the monk into a more-perfect vessel for God. As Abbot Ephraim has stated, monasteries are intense training grounds for Christian athletes: the monks.

As a result, it is not the antiquity of the buildings or the quality of the frescos or the presence of relics that indicate great monasteries. Great monasteries are composed of people who have arduously struggled in the spiritual life and share the fruits of this struggle with those around them. As one monk said, "Buildings do nothing. The

---

[21]Abbot Ephraim.
[22]Abbot Ephraim.

fathers give life to the monasteries."[23] The fathers are the life and the blood of the monastery. The twenty-five fathers of the Monastery of Prophet Elias are a diverse group.[24] Nearly all the brotherhood is educated, including several Masters degrees and one Ph.D. Although many studied theology, some studied physics, economics, chemistry, philosophy, and philology. Among them are two sets of natural brothers from Cyprus: a set of two brothers and a set of four brothers.[25] The presence of other non-Greek born monks gives the monastery a more international flavor. There is one American monk and a Scottish monk, as well as frequent visiting monks from Africa, the West Indies, and other places in the West. Only two of the monks are from the local region Epirus; almost half of them are from the Peloponnese, the birthplace of Bishop Meletios. Their ages range from twenty-eight to seventy-two.

Despite this diversity, the Fathers of the monastery are bound by their common affiliation to Bishop Meletios. As with the religious life of the people of Preveza, Bishop Meletios stands at the center of the life in the Monastery of Prophet Elias, even when he is physically removed. Without exception, his presence initially attracted the fathers to monastic life in Preveza. As a result, the fathers have come to reflect the bishop in many ways: their "style" of confession, how they serve the liturgy, their way of interacting with others, and their general theological perspective directly mirror the bishop's. Some say that his strict asceticism is not evident in the waistlines of some of the monks, but by and large, his imprint is everywhere.

Over time, Bishop Meletios' influence will wane and the monastery will develop its own independent personality.[26] At its center will be the common life, the *cenobium*, which has formed after years of experi-

---

[23]Monk C.

[24]The monastery has twenty-eight cells, with one housing a novice and another held for the protosingelos, who is still a member of the brotherhood. Therefore, the monastery is about at capacity.

[25]The Theofanous family had seven children, four of whom are monks here, one nun in Cyprus, one Presbytera, and one business woman who must feel like the black sheep!

[26]Metropolitan of Silibria Aimilianos Timiadas, a frequent visitor to the monastery, is strongly advocating for the necessity of this independence.

mentation. This common existence is one of the great mysteries of the monastic life. The community somehow becomes greater than the collection of its individuals and it lives beyond any of the fathers themselves. Struggling as a group toward a common goal becomes more worthwhile than if each struggled independently. The monastery's ultimate value lies in the ability for this group to inspire spiritual growth in the individual. This is the "end" for which all these men have come together, but upon which I as a researcher cannot pass final judgment.

Over time, each monastery also develops its own corporate personality. This personality is the intangible "spirit" of a community, an attitude that is exuded in the monks' every action. After spending time in a monastery, this personality usually becomes readily apparent. Perhaps it can be cultivated, but it cannot be consciously constructed or artificially promoted. It is usually the unspoken manner by which the community exists; the way in which the monks interact with each other and with visitors. Most often, it is a reflection of the spiritual elder or founder of the monastery. In a way, this corporate personality is the individualized face of a monastery within the ancient lineage of Orthodox monasticism. Herein lies the uniqueness of the Monastery of Prophet Elias.

The Monastery of Prophet Elias has a unique personality which balances the extremes that often occur elsewhere. It is not unduly somber and serious, with the monks so immersed in their own perceived sinfulness that fellowship with others and compassion for all is forgotten. Yet neither does it fall for the opposite extreme: a sort of undisciplined levity where the overriding sense is of a summer camp for immature older men with a façade of dedication to the Church. Rather, in interpersonal affairs, the monastery appears most often jovial—the monks joke continually with each other and frequently are engaged in casual conversation.[27] Showing tolerance for all, they

---

[27]One pilgrim tells the story of his first encounter with the monastery in 1996. He was in the guest quarters when he heard hollering and shouting like as in a soccer match. He ran downstairs to the central courtyard to find almost the entire brotherhood lining the peristyle. The visitor went to the monks to find out the source of all the noise. In the courtyard was a cat chasing a mouse, with all the brotherhood cheering it on.

enthusiastically embrace visitors, no matter the physical or spiritual state in which they arrive. However, just under the surface there is a continual sense of absolute dedication to the spiritual life. Conversations switch fluidly from jokes to the Sayings of the Desert Fathers and back again. The same monk that laughs and plays with a visiting child in the courtyard one hour prostrates himself in the church the next. After playing a practical joke on his brother, a monk may sit down to write a treatise on fasting for the Metropolis newsletter. The same group that cheers a cat chasing the mouse chants praises in unison to the Theotokos an hour later. It is this blend of "jovial seriousness" that defines the personality of the monastery.[28] The monks always keep their goal in mind, but they never lose sight of others in their pursuit of it. As one monk here noticed, the monks here do not take themselves too seriously but they take the spiritual life very seriously.

An event which transpired during the writing of this chapter provides a characteristic example. In 1993, Father Haralambos, a very old man with a warm disposition and a friendly smile, became a monk at the monastery. He would live only a little more than a year longer, becoming the first monk of the brotherhood to die. He was buried behind the monastery because no cemetery or place of internment had been constructed. In 2003, the monks exhumed his body to place his bones in the crypt of the Chapel of St Anthony, which was constructed in a garden adjacent to the monastery. All the brotherhood attended. There was a due degree of seriousness for the exhumation of a loved-brother of the monastery, but, at the same time, there was also a degree of levity. As they dug to the proper depth, the fathers prodded each other about the varying degrees of fitness of those wielding the shovel. When I arrived, they asked if I had come to interview Father Haralambos since I had interviewed everyone else. The monk who discovered his dentures immediately called for the oldest monk to see if he needed another pair. Someone commented

---

[28]Webster's Dictionary defines jovial as: "endowed with or characterized by hearty, joyous humor or a spirit of good-fellowship." Seriousness is a state of dedication or sincerity in regard to an intention, purpose, or thought.

that the socks and shoes found in the coffin were in better shape than his own. Another monk suggested that this monk switch shoes with the corpse. Yet throughout these times of levity, there was also seriousness. The process commenced with a series of prayers. As the diggers moved closer to the body, one could notice the monks crossing themselves and saying prayers. They took utmost care with the bones. Afterwards, the monks reflected upon the spiritual significance of such an event. The brotherhood managed to balance both the jovialness that comes from authentic fellowship with the spiritual gravity that must accompany contact with death.

This personality of "jovial seriousness" is directly connected to the bishop's influence and personality. He, too, is known for his jokes *and* his spiritual wisdom. It is hard to know whether the monks have come to emulate him in this regard or whether similar personalities attracted one another from the start. In any case, the presence of this "jovial seriousness" at the monastery represents the preservation of the experience around the stairs in the Metropolis after evening services during the early Preveza years that so many of the older monks remember so fondly. As such, this spiritually edifying environment from the past is able to be shared with new generations of monks and those who come to the monastery only for a visit.

†

To witness the development of a monastery from its beginnings as a few friends seeking a spiritual father to the forming of a cenobium and the construction of a fully functioning monastery is rare in the modern period. The story of the development of the Monastery of Prophet Elias is of interest not only because such a story can be told but also because of the continual adjustments that were required in light of shifting realities. In many ways, this story is more instructive than the Athonite ones that so often tell of the rejuvenation of a monastery from near collapse. In Preveza, the monks began from nothing. They had to consciously consider the long-term nature of the relationship the brotherhood would have with the local Church representatives. They had to plan for a world that would inevitably encroach into their monastery, regardless of how quiet a village or

how remote a mountain they would choose to livein . They had to
build a monastery from the ground up, rather than remodel an ancient
one. All these decisions—even the most trivial ones, such as whether
to put phones in the room or whether the rooms should have individual bathrooms—would impact the style of their monastic witness.
While some of these decisions would be dictated by money, time, or
some other outside influence, most decisions required reflection upon
how to tailor the canons of traditional monasticism to the situation
in which they found themselves. This called for continual reflection
on the monastic tradition itself, its place in the modern world, and its
relationship to the Church.

As with any grand endeavor, the ascent has not always been
smooth: there have been monks who came and later left, deciding this
brotherhood was not for them. There have been fights and legal battles with neighbors and the government. There are repeated challenges to the unity and peace of the brotherhood. There have been
miscues, as would be expected. As Abbot Ephraim reflected:

> They say that the first building that is built, one sells; the second,
> one rents out; and the third, one lives in. The latter is better than the
> others, in other words. And it is so, because anyone in every new
> effort of him or her, gains experience. This is true of us as well: if we
> would build again some monastery, we would have done different
> things than what has happened here. However, something as such is
> not very probable. A monastery is not a house.[29]

With the completion of the monastery, some permanence has been
added to the brotherhood. But it will not stand still because the
nature of the world is always changing, perhaps now more than ever.
Abbot Ephraim noted about the future of the monastery:

> The chief characteristic of our era and more of the era to come,
> appears to be the fluidity in not only social, political, and cultural
> things but also religious, perhaps even in Church affairs. The static,
> stationary, secure have been replaced by new, continually unsettled

---

[29]Abbot Ephraim.

elements. This involves a continual change of the form of difficulties that the Christian will encounter in the modern world, but also the monk. Overcoming these difficulties perhaps demands new practices, corresponding to circumstances. And then we will not hesitate to use them. Nothing is going to change, however, the common denominator of all of our problems was, is, and will be the veneration of the prince of this age; in other words, slavery to our passions. And nothing will ever change regarding the way of our salvation, which requires upholding the commands of Christ, within the Church.[30]

This statement represents a keen observation by Abbot Ephraim: to remain unchanging in their otherworldly goals, it may be necessary to continually change vis-à-vis a changing world. For example, a hundred years ago, visitors to an isolated monastery would be rare, so the monastery could welcome pilgrims on any day of the week. However, with advances in the ease of transport, a visit to the monastery is less of a burden for people so many more people come, threatening the hesychia upon which traditional monasticism is predicated. As a result, the monastery might choose to "close" for several days of the week (as Prophet Elias does) in order to protect at least in part the hesychia. These new practices will not represent attempts to adapt to the world but rather attempts to keep from changing with it. In other words, remaining monolithically unchanging in its relationship with the divine may require it to change vis-à-vis the world.

---

[30]Abbot Ephraim.

CHAPTER SIX

The Church and Modern Society

In early 1980, "The Holy One of Preveza" was a phrase with solely ironic and malicious meaning. The ecclesiastical situation in Preveza symbolized everything that was wrong with the Church. Over the past quarter-century, the situation has transformed so as to become a fount of spiritual good for all of Christianity. The writing of this book is part of this process. The change has occurred slowly and deliberately and is far from complete. Preveza is not yet holy. The monastery is not full of saints. The bishop is not infallible. But the Metropolis and the monastery are walking the path toward holiness each day; they strive for it, never giving into despair for not yet attaining it. This continual struggle for the Kingdom of God is what has always made people holy across time.

In some ways, the story told here has been nothing extraordinary; the bishop and the monks of Prophet Elias have sought only personal holiness and to follow the will of God. This is nothing other than the Christian life as it has been practiced since its inception. Perhaps what is so extraordinary is that this success story is so rare in today's world. Yet the better history of the Church is always the tale of how saints apply a timeless message to particular times and contexts; their struggle to shape society without being shaped by it. The value of the story of Preveza is not then found in elucidating the elements of the timeless message of the Gospel or by analyzing the specifics of this particular context: the former has been done many times by people more qualified than myself; the latter is not really relevant as there is no place where the specifics of Preveza have been repeated. The value is found in elucidating principles by which one may think about applying the message of the Gospel to different contexts, for this is the task of the Church. Bishop Meletios once noted:

The Church must be near to man and to society; it must not be detached. This does not mean that the Church must be a continuously transforming body . . . transforming in ideas and in principles because it conveys the truth of God which is one and will always remain one. In this sense, it is necessary to be monolithically unchanging. The adaptation of the Church to the world is that it must be accommodating to human limitations. And those who lead the Church must be eager to show such consideration and to bear the message of Christ, which is the life-giving word of God, to the modern world. Some men conjecture that we must slightly alter the message of Christ in order to come closer to the people. This must not be, because the truth is not the property or figment of man, so that every time in history the best and brightest can change it.[1]

The goal seems to be *monolithically unchanging* in the constant adaption of the faith to particular eras, particular places, and particular personalities. Bishop Meletios' greatest gift is his ability to hold onto and apply his ancient faith to a modern context without hiding from it. He does not wish that our world would return to a pre-modern age; in this sense, he is thoroughly a modern man. However, he also does not wish that Christianity would become modern by adjusting itself to contemporary conditions or worldviews; in this sense, his faith is thoroughly ancient. His genius lies in his ability to carry the ancient faith into a modern world without violating either.

My wish is that this genius could be elucidated, but Meletios is not a systematic theologian. In fact, he is skeptical of any human attempt to put categories around any area of the Gospel and its message. Yet having observed him and read many of his writings, four underlying principles tend to drive his actions in the Church. While the themes may be familiar to him, the articulation in this form will not, so I offer them as propositional principles rather than laws. They are as much my own, in this sense, as they are his. However, they represent an attempt to systematize a dynamic process in which his ancient faith finds its home in the modern world.[2]

---

[1] *ΕΠΙΛΟΓΟΣ.*

[2] Despite their presentation here, these principles of his "ecclesiology" cannot and

Principle i: The Church is and must remain "of God" and not "of man."

The "work" of the Church is often measured in what it does: the programs it initiates, the buildings it constructs, and the people it impacts. The leaders of the Church are considered effective when their actions are perceived as bearing much fruit. These "fruits" can be measured, marked, and publicized in terms of attendance, donations, and vocations. As a result, whole publications arise in places regarding the "work" of the leaders of the Church: their activities, their successes, and the challenges that they foresee facing. Bishop Meletios wholeheartedly rejects this paradigm. For him, any human attempt to alter the course of the Church is a failure from the beginning, for it loses sight of the fundamental relationship of the Church to its leaders. The Church is and must remain "of God" and not "of man." That is, humans were not placed in stewardship of the Church in order to invoke their will for where *they* see the Church going but rather to guide the Church into the will of God. Anything else—any human-derived effort—is ultimately harmful and perhaps sinful for it places human will over and above divine will. Bishop Meletios describes this problem when responding to the problems of religious education in the Church of Greece:

> First and foremost, it is necessary to have an ethos, an ecclesial mindset, and inspiration from the Holy Spirit. Without these things, ecclesiastical zeal according to God for salvation and life will not be created. And the efforts which occur are only of man. However, the Church is not of man. The Church is of God. And whenever God is present, the human element ought to be extinguished. When not only is it not destroyed but also validated, the Church does not go well. Anthropocentrism kills the Church and its life. When it becomes evident that both the bishops and the priests have mindsets "each unto himself," the world turns cold. Because every

must not be separated from his wider considerations of the Gospel of Christ and its place in the contemporary world; the four "pillars" cannot stand alone yet they point to the shelter that supports them, which is Christ himself.

man does the same. He operates on the same interior pattern. The Church sets itself straight, gets up on its feet, and goes on the right path when it does not forget that it is of God; that is, when it rejects human activity.[3]

Strictly speaking, the Church of God should "do" nothing, if "doing" something is at the directive of the human will. This goal requires a complete shift in mindset. Rather than seeking to create industriously, those entrusted with the Church must stop and listen. Rather than be active, leaders are to actively remain passive. Rather than assert their will on the Church, they are to obliterate their will for the Church. Rather than seek to be first, they seek first to be last. This realization means that success does not come from design:

> Design means the effort to impose something upon the world. We do not seek such an imposition. The more a person bases himself on designs that he himself devised, the more he becomes human-centered, the more he becomes secularized, and the more God withdraws his grace and his blessing. Why? God does not work with someone who is self-centered, ego-centric, and who "trust in themselves and see themselves as the experts." (Isaiah 2.21) Not only does God not work with them, but he is opposed to them. And without His blessing, nothing happens. *It* [his blessing] is needed, not our noble ambitions.[4]

Underlying all programs, Meletios is arguing, is human arrogance, the desire to play God. Good intentions are not enough if those intentions are attached to a personal agenda. The challenge is to eliminate one's will; or rather, align one's will with the will of God. The purpose of the Church leaders should be to act as a conduit or vessel of the divine, not a marketing arm of God.

This mindset requires that we no longer view the Church as an institution. Commonly, the definition of the Church is often pre-

---

[3]ΣΤΥΛΟΣ ΟΡΘΟΔΟΞΙΑΣ.
[4]Interview, SLM.

sented as a divine institution sent by God to represent Him in the world. In so far as it is blessed by God and has divine ends, it is unique in the world; however, in so far as it is an institution, it is like any other human institution. As such, the laws and paradigms that govern such human institutions apply equally so to the Church. Bishop Meletios rejects this viewpoint. The conception of the Church as an institution represents the hijacking of the Church by humans for their own end. Bishop Meletios notes, "The beginning and end of every act of God is the salvation of the world. We must place the weight of our attention on this, not in the work of institutions."[5] The hope of humanity cannot be placed in the Church but only in God. If the Church is only an institution that acts like any other institution and can be evaluated like any other institution, then it will fail.

There are three indications that the Church is acting as an institution and thus in danger of becoming another earthly vessel destined to fail. First, it functions by human-conceived plans and agendas. Despite the grave problems facing Bishop Meletios upon his arrival in Preveza, he refused to articulate either publicly or privately any plan or program for change. Commenting on this fact, he said:

> I believe in the message of St James the brother of Christ who announced that "programs" are not compatible with the ethos of the Gospel. I never made a program for myself. Always, I await the possibility, at some point completely unforeseen, of my ministry to the Metropolis of Nikopolis being cut off. I have one noble ambition: I don't want to bequeath half-finished works, troubles, or situations leading to anguish to my successor. I want to proceed with boldness at the beginning of every good work, but I do not want to create and I have never created a debt for the Metropolis for work as "*I*" merely envisioned it for myself. I count as good only work that Christ advances. I wished to do many other things as well by own inspiration and noble ambition. But in spite of all of my attempts to realize them after many years, they were a complete failure. So, I believe that the Lord is in this way generous to us and rescues us from hard

---

[5]Interview, SLM.

to solve future problems, which would alter the character of the Church of Christ in our local metropolis.[6]

In this sense, God saves us and his Church from ourselves. By creating no plans or programs, the leader of the Church is open to the will of God. The importance of this stance is demonstrated clearly in the repeated observation that Bishop Meletios makes that he does not know how long he will be in this position as leader of the Metropolis and thus does not want to bequeath half-finished work to his successor. This observation is not made out of practical concern for the administration of the Metropolis; it is an ecclesiological statement. That is, the leader of any metropolis must be continually open to the will of God, even if He wills the cessation of his ministry. Such "radical" openness is hard to swallow for many Church leaders.

The second sign that the Church is acting as merely a human institution is that its leaders hold on stubbornly to their plans and programs. In any human institution, it is the persistence and the will of its leaders to see through their vision that leads to success. In this context, persistence constitutes "strong leadership" and is usually considered a virtue. Yet the Church represents a different environment from any human institution. Bishop Meletios commented on this in response to a question about "new currents" that threaten the Church:

> You spoke about new currents. They are but gnats in the horns of a bull. They are powerless. They do not constitute threats. For our Church, the threat is something else: the wretched state of her representatives. Every clergyman is stubborn in regard to his opinion and his own particular viewpoint. The mystery of the Church has been forgotten. The clergy and the laity see the Church as an institution. And due to this, they do not have the disposition to dislodge even an iota from their individual viewpoints.[7]

---

[6]Interview, SLM.

[7]Metropolitan Meletios in Δημήτρη Φερούση, "Απειλή για την Εκκλήσια η αθλιότητα των εκπροσώπων της," Ορθοδοξία (April 1998). Translated by author. Hereafter cited as "ΟΡΘΟΔΟΞΙΑ."

Bishop Meletios is saying that the stubbornness of the clergy is more threatening than even hostile worldviews for society. Why? Because the stubbornness of the clergy is an indication that they are seeking to impose their own will upon the Church. The virtues of the Holy Spirit and the naked receptivity to the will of God have been abandoned in this case. These representatives of the Church may be able to "push through" their agenda by their own power but then it is not of "God."

The third indication of the Church being viewed as a human institution is the inevitable despair that arises when approaching its outlook in today's world. As an institution, the Church cannot overcome the inertia of moral decline, subjectivism, and hedonism in our society. As an institution, the Church can never train all the priests to be educated, holy vessels of God. As an institution, the Church will not preserve the Truth of God and the purity of His altar unblemished. If the Church was only a human institution, despair would be entirely justified. Bishop Meletios wants to remind people that, fortunately, the Church is not merely a human institution.

> Our Church comprises about ten million people. A drop within the ocean of the people of Europe. A droplet within the vast ocean of the people of the earth, who today live all very close to one another. Some tremble in front of these correlations. The voices of anxiety are heard. That we will scatter. They are not right. Once a glowing ember of men [the apostles] played an active role unrivalled in the world. They re-created the inhabited world. Beginning without any support from anyone. Because they had within them the power of imperishable life. Today, we are not energized by the power of this imperishable life. We do not take it—this strength—seriously. Today, we see all things institutionally. And from this viewpoint, they are correct. Institutionally, we can do hardly anything. We are but a drop in the ocean. Spiritually, however—that is, with the power of the imperishable life of Jesus—if we have it, if we feel it, if we experience it, we can achieve all things. And more precisely, because this is the hope of the world, that is why it is manifested— even more from those more strange places—an incomprehensible

obsession with this underestimated factor. With the following result: We become all the more worldly. We become "within the world." And we think spiritually, not ecclesially. Not according to Christ and we experience a spiritual decline. The spiritual ghetto. The essence of faith—Christ and the salvation of the world—does not occupy us. The institutions occupy us. And their promotion. . . . Our presence in the modern world cannot be an institutional presence. We need to make another sort of presence. Not institutional. Not organizational. Not monetary. Not slick methods, which others did not discover until now. But in order to start off, the spiritual presence and campaign, we need to first make a reorganization. A spiritual reorganization. Let us pray quickly to search to find our spiritual aims. With the framework of the true spirit of Christ and of Orthodoxy. And by sealing it. Whatever you intend to do, do it quickly. Nightfall comes and nobody will be able to work anymore.[8]

For Bishop Meletios, our hope does not lie in the effectiveness of leaders. Our hope does not lie in trendy charismatic revivals, clever programs, or well-designed worldly motivators. Our hope is not placed in a human institution. Our hope is in God. As long as the true nature of the Church is not forgotten, we will never lose hope and fall into despair no matter what the circumstances we face. Yet this hope is predicated upon an understanding of the Church as the mystical vessel of God's grace and will. It is not an institution that we run, but a mystery in which we dwell. Only then will we be energized by the imperishable Life of Jesus Christ.

PRINCIPLE 2: THE BISHOP AND CLERGY MUST LEAD AND WITNESS BY THEIR OWN EXAMPLE.

For many of the clergy, the problems of the Church and the wretchedness of its state are seen as the work of the evil forces in the universe, or hostile sociological trends, or lazy and ungrateful people. While not denying these as contributing factors, Bishop Meletios

---

[8]*ΟΡΘΟΔΟΞΙΑ.*

places the blame squarely on the shoulders of the clergy themselves. From his perspective, the hope of the Church is not found in properly allocating responsibility but in the spiritual transformation of its leaders. This goal requires the leaders to take up the Cross of Christ themselves. Bishop Meletios said in his ordination speech:

> O, Cross of Christ, all-holy, thrice-blessed, and life-giving, instrument of the mystical rites of Zion, the holy Altar for the service of our Great Archpriest, the blessing—the weapon—the strength of priests, our pride, our consolation, the light in our heart, our mind, and our steps; Our Lord and Savior nailed to you revealed and instigated his priesthood for us. For this also, the priesthood saves and glorifies only as a Cross; only the one who bears it radiates virtue, which the Cross symbolizes and inspires, illumines and sanctifies; only when it has something from God and the inexpressible beauty of the virtues of our first and great priest, Christ.

The glory and hope of the clergy is the Cross. This statement is not merely rhetorical artistry but founded upon a deep-seated ecclesial position of Bishop Meletios: the hope of the Church is found in each of its representatives living within the imperishable Life of Christ. That is, the clergy and even more so the bishop must lead and witness by their own example. It is not enough for their words to preach; so must their lives. It is not enough for the clergy to tell the people to go to Church; by their own virtue, they must provide a reason for the people to go. It is not enough for them to speak about the Cross; they must bear it themselves every day.

The ideal characteristics of the clergy then are neither education nor knowledge of God, but rather piety and fear of God. Bishop Meletios commented upon this when he was asked about the common practice of ordaining less-qualified priests to fill rural parishes that are in great need of clergy. He said:

> Neither education nor scientific knowledge is the first characteristic of a cleric. The chief characteristic of the cleric is piety—fear of God—that is, to have as his first priority the application of the commandments of God to himself. The priest must teach by his exam-

ple. If his personal life does not speak, then his words will convince no one. The first priority in the clergy is his spiritual profundity. If this does not exist, deplorable incidents are a foregone conclusion. And all of these will increase. No matter how much education, they will exist. There are clerics with lesser aptitudes (equal to graduates of primary school) who shine as one of the luminaries. This does not mean that we do not need education. "Be patient with earthly things and then seek out higher things." It is best to have expectations, set boundaries, for the admission into the clergy of "young" men (why not also old in age?) but with depth, not in exterior attitudes but in the "inner man." And these are: a) to have Christ indwell in his heart; b) to be rooted and grounded in love; c) to comprehend what is the breadth, the length, the height, and the depth along with all the saints and not as an independent thinker; d) to live the love of Christ, which is 1000 times greater than all knowledge; and e) to be filled with all the fullness of God (Ephesians 3.16, 19). If a priest is impoverished in these things, he has the need for a Good Samaritan and he cannot be that very Good Samaritan.[9]

The chief sign of a cleric is not his cloak or his *skoufa* (priest's hat) but rather his disposition and his zeal for God. As such, authentic priests cannot be trained to be effective leaders of their parish or metropolis through leadership programs or organizational seminars but rather by repentance, humbleness, and compassion. If the priest is himself not full of the Holy Spirit then he will never be able to share it with others.

The hope for change in a metropolis does not then come from inspired programs but from inspired clergy, that is, when the clergy are truly aspiring to become useful vessels of God. The fate of the Church lies primarily in *who* the clergy are becoming rather than *what* they do. Bishop Meletios recognizes this when he states:

Because of us [the clergy], the people have been alienated; "because of us, the name of Christ is blasphemed." The main problem to which our attention must be directed if we want to see a recovery is:

---

[9]*ΣΤΥΛΟΣ ΟΡΘΟΔΟΞΙΑΣ.*

the quality of our clergy. The Alpha and the Omega in the work of the Church is the reputation of the clergy, which in general might be good, but not as it should be.[10]

The Alpha and the Omega of the renewal of the Church lies in the quality of the clergy. Herein should lie the focus of a bishop. So, while the activity par excellence of the bishop is preaching the Gospel, the bulk of his efforts must be located in the spiritual development of his clergy. When Bishop Meletios was asked about what advice he would give to a new bishop of a metropolis in need, he said, "I would say to him to occupy himself as much as he can with the deep cultivation of his clerics. Nothing else."[11] When Bishop Meletios took over the shepherd's role in the Metropolis of Nikopolis and Preveza, he followed this advice and placed as his first goal the development of the clergy. The goal of leading and witnessing by example began with the bishop himself. Every person interviewed for this study mentioned the example of the bishop as the primary impetus for any change in Preveza. In the words of one of the monks, his example was "like a magnet" attracting people to the Church.[12] His faith, his ascetic life, and his devotion to the Church became the model for first his clergy and then the people. This does not mean, however, that he expects each person in Preveza to live with the same discipline as he does. Quite the contrary. He writes:

> He must avoid the air of the public prosecutor. And when such an air is necessary, he has to use it for those within. Only for those who accept his message, "For what have I to do with judging those outside? Is it not those who are inside that you are to judge? God will judge those who are outside." (1 Corinthians 5.12) The shepherd reproaches only those "within," toward the faithful; to the alienated, he must direct his message of conciliation and counsel.[13]

---

[10]*ΣΤΥΛΟΣ ΟΡΘΟΔΟΞΙΑΣ.*
[11]Interview, SLM.
[12]Monk C.
[13]Interview, SLM.

Bishop Meletios is very strict with himself and compassionate with others. His witness then is not seen as condemnation but inspiration. He demonstrates the life of the Gospel and allows this example to speak to the people individually. As a result, the people who come into the Church do so out of a desire to share in this life in the Spirit, not out of guilt or fear. As a result, the depth of their spiritual life and the level of their commitment are more profound. Herein lies the ultimate benefit of this "evangelical" program.

Principle 3: The Church must be universal in scope and uniting in action.

In the history of Greek society, particularly since independence, the Church has as often been divisive and the cause of discord as it has been the source of unity. During different periods of history, the Church has formally or more often informally aligned itself with one political party over another, one social group over another, or one intellectual class over another. Likewise, its message has seemed to be directed more to one crowd than another. Bishop Meletios has argued in many different forums against such division and derision. For Meletios, the Church must not forget that because all persons are sinners, Jesus died for all. Thus the Church must be for all. This fact does not mean that the Church must become whatever the people want or need; he repeatedly stresses that the Church must maintain the purity of its altar while being accommodating to the people. Rather, Bishop Meletios stresses that the Church must be universal in scope and unifying in action.

As a result, Bishop Meletios has consistently sought to keep himself and the Church free from all political entanglements. The moment that the Church takes a political position, it is identifying itself with one group of people who support one party and alienating a second group. One monk described Bishop Meletios' position:

> From the beginning, Father Meletios told the clergy that they should not express political views. Before there was a bias here: if you

are religious here you have to be the extreme right. That is not the case with Father Meletios, who says they all belong to our folk. Whatever their political views, they all belong to Christ. They are people who Christ was crucified for, so who are we to divide them into different groups?[14]

Christ did not die for the politically left or the politically right but for all people. As the body of Christ, the Church must be the instrument of God for all people, regardless of political persuasion. Politics, as with everything "of the world," leads only to temptation and sin, especially if one places his or her hope in it.

Thus as something that divides and concerns primarily the world, it should be avoided. Bishop Meletios commented:

We avoid mingling in politics. "Politics" for every individual is a preference of certain viewpoints about the governance of the world. It gives rise to profits and passion. It stimulates antagonism and fanaticism. The cleric who is tangled up in politics, ceases to have the correct communion with the opposite party. And so he does harm to the Gospel. His duty is to love. And like a father, he has to counsel all the leaders without bias. And also he has to counsel even to the leaders who have anti-ecclesiastical attitudes.[15]

Bishop Meletios also recognizes the practical aspect of the mission of the Church: if the Church is to be a light in a darkened world and this light is to enlighten all, especially the leaders, the conduits of this light must place themselves in a position to spread it. That is, if the Church has relations with only one group of leaders, its capacity to spread the light of Christ is compromised. Bishop Meletios addressed this when he was accused by a local journalist of supporting the dictatorial Junta. In his response he stated:

I was never aligned with men who had selfish aspirations. I never became a member of any faction. Neither of the right nor of the left; neither of clerics nor of lay people. I was never enslaved to expedi-

---

[14]Nun E.
[15]Interview, SLM.

ency. And even more, I never served my own interests above those of the Church. I boast that in this world *I have nothing* except my *rason* (monastic cloak), which is of minimal value, and a few books. My most valuable treasure is *my pure conscience* and *my freedom.* I boast that I am *absolutely free* from worldly attachments. My target and my aim is to be and to remain always such: absolutely free from men—absolutely and completely a servant of Christ.[16]

By striving to be free of all men, he is free to counsel all men. For Bishop Meletios, this should be the position of the Church. By disentangling itself as much as possible from political pressures, it gains the freedom to be completely a servant of Christ. Only when it is completely free from worldly attachments is it completely free to speak to the world.

The importance of preserving the unity of the universal Church is apparent in Bishop Meletios' approach during inter-faith dialogues. Both in his former role as Secretary of Inter-Orthodox and Inter-Church relations and as bishop, he has striven to play a role in mending the divisions that have arisen in the universal Church. As one of the lead representatives in the dialogue with the Egyptian Coptic Christians, he negotiated an important common statement of belief that theologically overcame the millennium and a half theological dispute. However, he argued that the leaders who in the fifth century divided the church still deserved to be excommunicated because, "Whoever leaves the unity of the Church, in whatever degree he is deceived, he is subject to severe penance and to anathematization."[17] In other words, failure to maintain the unity of the Church is grounds enough for the rejection of the wider church. The Church must consciously strive toward the maintenance of this unity. Arrogance, stubbornness, and *idiorhythmacy* (self-rule) lead to division and schism, which are worthy of punishment. Thus one of the foundational attrib-

---

[16]"The Metropolitan of Preveza Meletios Responds," *The Local Voice*, no. 26820 (November 10, 1982).

[17]Metropolitan Meletios, *ΑΠΑΝΤΗΣΗ ΣΕ ΑΠΟΡΙΕΣ Γύρω ἀπὸ τὸ θέμα τῆς ἑνώσεως τῶν Ἀντιχαλκηδονίων* (Ἀθήνα, 1992). Translated by author. Hereafter cited as "*ΑΠΑΝΤΗΣΗ ΣΕ ΑΠΟΡΙΕΣ.*"

utes of the communion we share with other Orthodox Christians must be the pursuit of unity in humility and love.

PRINCIPLE 4: THE CHURCH MUST CULTIVATE THE EXTERNAL ELEMENTS OF FAITH IN PARALLEL TO THE INTERNAL ELEMENTS.

When someone gains a reputation for being "spiritual," it is often assumed that his or her focus is exclusively in the spiritual world. The "things of this world" are said not to influence the spiritual person. He or she is assumed to be "above" the material world. While Bishop Meletios stresses the ultimate importance of the internal world—the spiritual world—he does not disregard the role of external elements. Rather, he recognizes that they have their place within the development of the spiritual life of those within the Church and thus should not be trivialized. In the imagery of his spiritual father, Father Joel Yiannakopoulos, the spiritual life is like an egg, which is composed of the yolk inside and the hard shell outside. The shell is necessary to keep the yolk intact and must be preserved, but what is ultimately important lies inside.

As a result, Bishop Meletios seems to spend an inordinate amount of time on externals. He insists that his clerics have a disciplined exterior appearance, especially in public; he rebuilt churches in Byzantine style, replaced Venetian painting with Byzantine icons, and improved the chanting by establishing a school for Byzantine music; he stresses the importance of external preparation to receive Christ, especially during Great Lent, by fasting, simplicity of dress, and manually helping the poor. In all these things, Bishop Meletios never stresses the importance of external elements in and of themselves; to isolate and highlight them apart from his instruction for the internal development of the spiritual life presents a warped image. However, the stress he places on external elements of the faith is noteworthy and when recognized in parallel to the internal stress reveals interesting insights into theology and psychology.

Bishop Meletios recognizes that in this fallen world, there is a symbiotic relationship between external discipline and internal development. In the heavenly world, any external appearance will reflect only the inner beauty; but, in this fallen world, the internal life and the external life are intrinsically linked. He notes that this connection is inherent in humans. When asked about the extensive program for Great Lent in the Metropolis, he responded:

> Great Lent is the greatest preparation for the feast of the Resurrection and together with it [this preparation], the primacy of the Resurrection and of eternal life. The practices of the people are internal and external preparation for the great events of life; humanity demands it so. In other words, the correct conception for the spiritual nature of man—this is the best condition to make one understand easily the utility of Great Lent.[18]

Preparation for any state, especially a spiritual state, requires both external and internal development. Our psychology demands it. And they must be cultivated in parallel; it is a consequence of our living in a fallen world:

> Bishop Meletios says (though he is just taking it from the Bible) that first you clean the inside and then it does not say *then* you clean the outside but the outside will be cleaned. If the inner life is clean, pure, and tidy then the external life will be so. But until we reach that stage, we need to put some effort into it, especially for the clergy who live outside in the world but also for the monks.[19]

The deified person exudes the imperishable light of Christ in his or her every action and even in appearance. However, before that time, we cannot wait for deification to reflect Christ in every part of our lives. Bishop Meletios argues that people must put effort into the externals with the hope that the light of Christ within will one day outshine any human effort offered.

Bishop Meletios then maintains that the condition of the external state serves as an indication of the inner spiritual state. There can be no division between the external and the internal in the presence

---

[18]Interview, SLM.
[19]Nun E.

of God. If one has an authentic relationship with Christ, it *will* influence the external elements of his or her life. As we saw above (but deserves repeating here), Bishop Meletios makes this point when commenting upon the relationship of the older generation to the younger generation in the Church. He says:

> [The older generation] warped it because they introduced an opposition between internal conviction and external action. The older generations, although they lost the correct conviction, they maintained a compulsory surface of decency, but one which could not be imposed upon the youth. Because the youth want authenticity! And when looking at the inauthenticity of their elders, they rebel. Truly, they rebel! Truly![20]

Authenticity requires that inner conviction has external ramifications. Faith without action is dead. Thus while humans should never place their hope in appearances or behaviors, these externals must reflect their internal faith, if that faith is authentic. Any discrepancy between the two becomes a sign of spiritual sickness; a sign that others, particularly the young, are quick to recognize.

When the alignment of external and internal is achieved, they serve as a means of communication and witness. After the arrival of Bishop Meletios in Preveza, the "smartening up" of the clergy externally became a sign of the seriousness by which they were taking the spiritual life. Their external appearance and behavior sent a message to the people of Preveza of their renewed dedication to the Church. As one hieromonk recalled:

> He told us to be careful with our cassocks; we must teach with our external elements. When you see a priest with a cassock and *kalimavhi*: his appearance must be a *kerygma*. Because respect cannot be enforced, but rather radiates from the priest. You cannot force respect. The dictators force respect, not the priest. Respect must emanate.[21]

---

[20] *Orthodox Globe.*
[21] Monk C.

External discipline alone would have had no effect on the spiritual reputation of the clergy. However, when combined with the development of their inner spiritual life, the external appearance and behavior of the clergy became a *kerygma*. The "shell" came to reflect the glories within. However, this does not mean that the external appearance and behavior should become a marketable good. Bishop Meletios responded to this misguided interpretation in response to a question regarding how visible the bishop should be. He said:

> The Lord taught us that everything must be done in "secret" and not to be "on display" (Matthew 6.4, 6). Consequently, the bishop, as the one sitting on the high throne of the apostles, is visible; and indeed very visible. However, if he wants to be faithful to the word of Christ, being visible must show the joy, the truth, the mercy of Christ. Not his own work nor his own virtues. And if he is holy, to try to continue to be, without ever transforming his own obedience to the will of God into a worldly marketable good. This is valid for all the world and all the more for the kingdom of Christ.[22]

The clergy and especially the bishop must walk a fine line. His external appearance and behavior must speak to Christ but they must not be the final word. If his external life—even his asceticism or love— become ends in themselves rather than indicators of Christ's work through him, then they have become idols. In this case, the glory of the bishop individually has come to supersede the glory of Christ, and the Church has been led astray.

Of course, Bishop Meletios is quick to point out that the value of human beings lies in the inner man and not the outer. However, he also recognizes that the external elements have a role in the spiritual life of the Church. This role is healthy and needful in this fallen world as long as they do not become ends in themselves. That is, the external must not be ignored altogether but rather kept in proper perspective. The work of the Church is ultimately spiritual work but all spiritual work in the world has a corporal dimension.

---

[22]Interview, SLM.

PRINCIPLE 5: THE CHURCH SHOULD INTEGRATE THE MONASTICS INTO THE COMMUNITY TO THE EXTENT THAT IT DOES NOT COMPROMISE THEIR HIGHER PURPOSE.

The primary orientation of society today is not toward God, and perhaps it never was. There is always a mix of influences, purposes, and trends that shape society. However, monasticism consciously strives to be permanently oriented toward the divine. The walls are there to allow them to focus on the spiritual rather than the material, the eternal rather than the temporal, and the unchanging rather than development. This orientation provides the monks with a unique witness: the monks can offer the Gospel to the world in clarity. When called upon, the monk must offer this witness, for the love of the world. If there are humans in authentic need, to reject their pleas in the name of acquiring virtue or conquering passions is a farce. Monks must not retreat to their four walls in the face of authentic needs, even out of fear of contamination from the world. They must use their vantage point to teach, exhort, and serve their fellow humans.

After all, the Church is one. Every monastery is a part of the universal Church; every monastery within a metropolis is part of the local Church, regardless of its articles of incorporation.[23] There cannot be two parallel Christianities in one place. The monks do not operate in a separate, higher realm but are subject to the same Gospel injunctions as all others. Thus if monks choose to deny this necessary role to reach out to people, then they are denying the unity of the Church. However, this unity also means that the local bishop is responsible for the spiritual good of all Christians in his metropolis, including the monks. Out of love for them, he must respect their goals. He must not compromise out of selfish desires for *his* vision for the Church the legitimate roles that the monks play.

The *raison d'etre* of a monastery is primarily the spiritual perfection of its monks. The monastery is a spiritual boot camp that devel-

---

[23]Some monasteries have been granted a special charter to be directly under the patriarch, usually because they have had tensions in the past with local bishops. This practice does not lead to long-term healthy spiritual environments.

ops souls; it is a place where the cares of this world—money, gender relations, politics—are all deliberately set aside to focus on the spiritual; it is a spiritual laboratory wherein every method has been tested over hundreds of generations to lead those called to this height. As such, the bishop should keep in mind that the monastery, at least in Orthodox Christianity, does not exist in order to "do" anything but rather to create individuals who "are" something. This realization does not mean the monks should not have a role in society. It means that the primary role for monks in a local community is to be a light to others; that is, by their complete dedication to Christ and by their holiness, they will inspire others and allow them to see God more clearly. But as with any light, it needs certain conditions to burn: a single candle can illumine an entire room when protected but blows out instantly if brought into the wind and rain. Similarly, in order to remain a light, the monk's life must be protected. His protection is his fellow monks, the rhythm of the monastic life, confession to an elder, extended prayer and services, and so forth. To force the light out of these conditions will ultimately make it burn out, even if it seems to be brighter for a period of time. The bishop who takes the monk out of his monastery too much is dousing one of his potentially brightest beacons for his community.[24]

The bishop and the monks in the region must balance the need to serve others in need with the requirement that the conditions for spiritual growth are maintained. Ultimately, the health of the relationship between the bishop, monastery, and surrounding community is closely tied to the health of its constituent parts. A corrupt or unmotivated bishop will rarely harness the presence of a monastery for the spiritual good of the people, or worse he will destroy the

---

[24]If service to others becomes burdensome to the extent that it threatens to compromise *permanently* the integrity of the monastic purpose, the monks must help find other means to meet the needs. Invariably, service to the world disturbs the rhythm and hesychia of the monastic life. However, only in the rarest circumstances is a monastery such a sensitive spiritual ecosystem that it cannot reach out to those in genuine need until permanent resources are found. Discernment and periodic reflection are required to know when the desire to bring aid and comfort is in danger of permanently damaging the community.

monastery by creating conditions by which it cannot function. Likewise, an internally divided, bitter brotherhood (or worse, an arrogant one) rarely will embrace the local community or the bishop in Christian love. Finally, a community must be open to accepting the presence of monks; a cynical or spiteful local Christian community will not respond to the overtures of even the most saintly of monasteries or bishops. Each constituent element must be spiritually healthy in its own right before a successful environment can ensue. The bishop, as the shepherd of all in the area, must set this tone, as Meletios has done.

†

The particular context of Preveza is in many ways unique. Bishop Meletios is the shepherd of a comparatively small, homogenous community. The largest city in his metropolis has only 15,000 inhabitants and the Metropolis serves a total population of around 80,000, nearly all of whom can be reached within an hour's drive. For all practical purposes, the bishop is the sole source of spiritual authority in the region. There are no yoga centers, no theosophical societies, no tele-evangelizers, no Buddhist temples—in short, very few organized groups exist that are actively seeking to draw people away from the Church. While there had been no active monasticism in Preveza for a generation, the Greek people have a long-standing relationship with monasteries so the presence of monks is neither totally novel nor totally innovative. Furthermore, Bishop Meletios was the spiritual founder of the monastery of the region, thus there is no competing spiritual figure for the monks.

By contrast, the context of a bishop in a non-Orthodox country is likely to be very different. He might serve a region that has tens of millions of people, very few of which are Orthodox, who are continually being offered alternative spiritual opportunities. He not only does not represent all spiritual authority in the region but also does not represent all Christians or even all Orthodox Christians, since there are competing jurisdictions. There is no monastic history to speak of outside Orthodox countries, so most of their people would never encounter a monk in their lives. The few monasteries that do exist have more often than not been in tension with the local bishop and have often positioned themselves in opposition to the "worldly" church. As a result, the value of any program, especially one that involves the monastics, would seem limited. However, the task of the Church is always the application of the timeless to the specific. The principles outlined above are intended to help navigate this process.

When Bishop Meletios was enthroned as the Apostolic Metropolitan of Preveza and Nikopolis on that March morning in 1980, the enthronement service reconstituted the local manifestation of the universal Church; by nature, the service is always a harbinger of something new, since each new shepherd shapes his Metropolis. At the same time, however, it is something ancient, for it has been repeated countless times for nearly 2000 years. The stories that played out that day under the surface were inherently interesting ones: the sex and blackmailing scandal that had caused the moment; the diverted path of the charismatic spiritual elder from Athens and his educated and zealous spiritual children; the political undercurrents that were shifting the relationship between the Church and the state. These stories were all new, but the process of applying the Gospel's message to the world is perennial. Bishop Meletios' gift is for a contemporary generation to observe and learn from this process.

CHAPTER SEVEN

Monks and Modern Society

When I was nineteen, as I spent my first day in Athens walking through the parks, I encountered a group of men engaged in an argument that I thought was going to lead to physical blows. Unaccustomed to vocal public arguments, I grew nervous until the two protagonists yelling at each other nose-to-nose ended up in an awkward but hearty embrace. I learned that day that Greeks love to argue with gusto, yet it is rarely as serious as the apparent tension suggests. More familiar with Greek norms, when I encountered a similar argument on a cool spring evening more than a dozen years later at a local tavern in Preveza, I knew it was typical. Voices were raised, ouzo was flowing, and the night was rapidly turning into early morning. The subject, however, was not typical. The patrons were debating which of the monks of the Monastery of Prophet Elias was "the best." An older man missing part of his index finger pointed up as he emphatically exclaimed that his candidate chanted the best. A younger man just back from his army duty argued that the waistline was all telling and "his" monk was clearly the most ascetic. His younger sister merely mentioned the name of another monk—one particularly tall and handsome—and fluttered her eyes. An older woman said that she knew well only one monk, the one who comes to the village to hear confession, but he was "divine." I, the only foreigner, was asked to arbitrate. I wisely stayed silent. As with most taverna debates, no consensus was ever reached and the only winner was the one pouring the drinks.

As I told this story the next day at the monastery, I noticed that one of the "candidates" had a sling immobilizing his arm. Being familiar with his driving and fearing an accident, I inquired as to its

cause. "Throwing snowballs," he replied. It seems the youth catechism class that he oversaw ventured to the mountains the previous
days and a snowball fight ensued. The monk lost, despite a valiant
effort that led to his shoulder being dislocated. These were not typical monks or typical townspeople.

The monks of Prophet Elias have woven themselves into the very
fabric of Christian society in Preveza. In doing so, they have balanced
their fervent desire to preserve their monastic vocation and their
equally fervent desire to reflect God's love to those placed in their
care. In a sense, this balancing act was caused by their unique calling
to be linked to a spiritual father who became bishop of an area of great
spiritual need. However, it is also an ancient tension within monasticism and indeed Christianity itself. How does one separate oneself
from the world yet love those within it at the same time? How does
one preserve the unique spiritual conditions of the monastery that are
so conducive to growth without growing insular and detached from
the real needs of all the children of God? How does one be a monk
in society?

MONASTICISM AND SOCIETY

Monasticism is a mystery of the Church traditionally defined by two
sets of relationships: the complete dedication of the individual to God
and a conscious rejection of the world as it stands. Long-standing
reflection on the former relationship has produced the fruits of the
monastic tradition: the prayer patterns, spiritual literature, and traditions of monastic life. In a way, this relationship of total dedication to
God is timeless, since neither God nor humans fundamentally
change; the details of this relationship need only to be adjusted based
on the characteristics and peculiarities of the monks.

The relationship to the world and to the church is more complex
and is currently in the midst of tremendous change. The great monastic centers of Orthodoxy, such as Mt Athos, St Katherine's on Mt
Sinai, and Valaam in Northern Russia, have traditionally been difficult for most people to visit and this isolation has led to development

largely outside the hierarchy of the Church. In fact, the great monastic centers rarely developed near to the people, and perhaps as importantly, near to the close scrutiny of bishops. This traditional isolation brought with it certain advantages. Being removed from the world, these monastic brotherhoods could control their interactions with non-monastic influences. Sometimes there were natural protections, such as the physical hardships it takes to visit remote areas such as Mt Sinai, but other times these interactions are artificially controlled as well, such as Mt Athos' *dimaterion* system. This system limits the number of pilgrims to four non-Orthodox and a hundred Orthodox pilgrims per day, effectively enhancing the natural protections against outside influence. As a result of this enforced isolation, the monks did not need to concern themselves with other Christians because there were really no Christians who were not monastics; there were no new social trends that swept through the monastic countryside; there were no pressing evangelical causes. The monks were alone with God. In these conditions, the monasteries created self-contained laboratories of the spiritual life, without the worry of outside infections.

Throughout Orthodox history, the monastic centers close to population centers rarely obtained long-standing preeminence due to conflicts with the local Church hierarchy that dissipated their strength and vitality. This misalignment with the bishop often led to the monastery closing itself off from the local community or to the opposite extreme: the bishop through force of will draws the monks into servicing the bureaucracy of the church, usually leading to the eventual dissolution of the monastery, as was the case with the Monastery of Velanidia in Bishop Meletios' story. Alignment between the bishop and the monastery such as currently exists in Preveza is rare. As a result, one can arrange monasticism historically in the table on the following page.

Today the barriers that once protected these great monastic centers are lessoning with the rise of technology and globalization. They are no longer isolated. Previously too difficult to visit on a regular basis, Mt Athos can now be a relatively easy visit; the British Prince Charles himself flies helicopters to the Holy Mountain for quick visits on a regular basis. Despite their best efforts to regulate visitors, hundreds

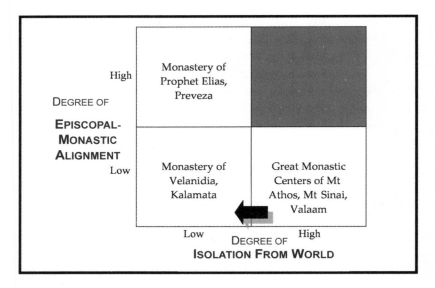

of pilgrims visit Mt Athos each summer day. Only a few generations ago, that number might have been in single digits. St Katherine's of Mt Sinai has nearly a hundred tourist buses a day visit when once they may not have had a hundred people in a month. Valaam has daily ferry service and even tour boats visiting. As a result, locals who once went to their parish priest for advice now have increasingly sought out spiritual fathers in once-remote monasteries. And even if one is on the other side of the globe, as was the case with an Australian friend, their Athonite spiritual father is just a phone call away. Some monasteries and *sketes* are even dispensing advice via the internet. And this increased contact with the world has led to conflicts with the Church hierarchy, especially when monastic spiritual fathers offer spiritual direction contrary to the clergy "in the world."[1] In short, the distance and separation that once protected the great monastic communities such as Mt Athos are vanishing, and this new reality is leading to new problems. There are no isolated monasteries anymore, and so the pri-

---

[1] For example, in response to complaints by bishops, the abbot of Vadopedie on Mt Athos has recently told his spiritual fathers that their spiritual children must also have spiritual fathers in the world. When conflicting advice arises, the Athonite spiritual fathers should defer to the spiritual fathers in the world.

mary vector of alignment is the degree to which the monastery and the bishop are in alignment with each other. Faced with these new circumstances, the Athonite communities can learn from the monks of the Monastery of Prophet Elias in Preveza, who have reflected upon these relationships for nearly three decades.

Not surprisingly, Bishop Meletios never sought to create an updated monastic program for the contemporary world. Quite the contrary: they sought to follow the Byzantine monastic tradition as closely as they could, given their unique circumstances, personal weaknesses, and the age in which they operated. They sought to preserve the ancient monastic way, not invent a new one. While the monks themselves dedicated little time to abstract discussion on the state of modern monasticism, certain guiding principles can be identified that shaped their decision-making process. These principles have never been expressly articulated by the bishop, the abbot, or any of the monks, all of whom see their primary task as living and sharing the Gospel rather than developing social and theological formulations. Nevertheless, they witness to the recurrent process of monasticism searching to discover its relationship to those around it.

Principle 1: Be prepared to change in order to remain unchanging to God.

If one asks the monk whence the monastic life began, he will undoubtedly say with the apostles and Christ himself. While perhaps historically anachronistic, this response is in a deeper sense accurate. The monk is merely trying to live the commandments of the Gospel in their most complete sense, refusing to compromise to the fashions of the world. In this sense, the goal of monasticism was and is to remain monolithically unchanging in the face of an ever-changing world. While the morals and social values of a society will alter over time, the world of the monk changes very little; he is transfixed by the unchanging call of Christ.

This goal does not mean that monasticism is destined to be forever unchanging, bound to be forever fundamentalistic. On the contrary, in order to preserve its unchanging character, the monastery must continually change vis-à-vis the world; that is, to preserve their life of total dedication they sometimes must change the character of their relations to the world. They must adapt to the world in order to stay the same. For example, monasteries have typically offered hospitality to any pilgrim who can come any day of the week at any time. If, however, the ease of transportation means an inordinate number of visitors come to the monastery and the hesychia within is threatened, a monastery may have to reconsider its hospitality pledge in order to preserve the important hesychia, as the monks of Prophet Elias have done. It may have to change to remain the same. Furthermore, monastic fasting rules historically allow for the consumption of shellfish on fasting days for it was considered unseemly food in ancient times. However, modern civilizations, particularly in some parts of the world, see shellfish as one of the finest delicacies. If a monastery is feasting on crab and lobster on its fasting days, perhaps they need to strengthen their local fasting rules in order to keep to the spiritual intent of the monastic tradition. The monks of Prophet Elias recently banned soy products that make their meals seem like meat, even while keeping the letter of law concerning the fasting requirements. In this case, they altered the fasting requirements in order to remain the same.

Reactionary fundamentalism is a danger to which monasteries easily fall prey in the modern world. In their noble thirst to remain unchanging, they reject the new even when it contributes to their final purpose. Instead of preserving the monastic tradition at all costs, the goal should be continual reflection upon the monastic life vis-à-vis the unchanging commandments of Christ and the particular circumstances in which monks find themselves. Healthy monasticism strives for such reflexivity.

PRINCIPLE 2: AIM FOR "HOLY OBSCURITY" WITH WARMTH, TOLERANCE, AND LOVE.

Having visited literally hundreds of monasteries in my research, I have collected a great number of mementos bearing the insignias of particular monasteries. I have calendars with pictures of abbots with various famous people; I have glossy books filled with pictures of religious treasures and the monastic way of life; and I have CDs of their choirs chanting. I can show friends publicity newsletters and web sites of monasteries I have visited. Many contemporary monasteries seem to excel at self-promotion.

The monastery in Preveza is very different. It has no newsletter, no colorful calendars, no picture books, and no web site. It does not sell a single item in its store bearing its name. It barely has a sign indicating its presence in Flamboura. This anonymity is not due to a lack of organization but rather to a conscious emphasis by Bishop Meletios that one of the primary virtues of the monk should be *afania* (anonymity). As one monk told me:

> He doesn't want to make publicity because he says it is a great shame for a pastor to say that I helped the poor or I built this thing or I went and preached in the churches—this is my job; it is not something to be proud of. It is the least I can do. So, you don't write in the paper that I celebrated the liturgy in this or that region. It is much more serious than that and you have to do much more.[2]

The history and context of Preveza is conducive to avoiding the publicity seeking that poisons some monasteries. They do not live in a historic building, and they have no renowned relics or icons; they are far from any major population area, and they have no history of great spiritual confessors. However, there is also a conscious recognition that part of the holiness they seek as monks means actively maintaining the obscurity that is nothing more than corporate humility.

This desire for anonymity is grounded also in a historical lesson: the great monastic centers did not begin by seeking out worldly glory

---

[2]Monk A.

or recognition; they did not want to become great. Rather, they sought out authentic holiness. Their rejection of the world was not done out of misanthropy but rather out of their sole desire to seek out holiness here on earth. And it was this holiness that brought them fame, not vice versa. Many modern monasteries seem to reverse this relationship.

The value placed on anonymity and seclusion from the world could lead to an anti-cosmic attitude which would condemn the world and those in it. Visitors could have easily come to be seen as a "threat" to the serenity and seclusion the monastery cultivates. Precisely the opposite is, in fact, the case with the Monastery of Prophet Elias. The brotherhood embraces every visitor brought to its door, which in an average year is more than 12,000. As one monk said, "You can say that we have open arms for the community."[3] The warmth of its hospitality and care with which they attend to guests are well known. As one resident noted, "It has a friendly atmosphere and is not judgmental, not strict like many monasteries."[4] The monastery has developed a reputation for tolerance and understanding. Unlike so many monasteries in Greece, no one is turned away because of what they are wearing or their personal faith. Each person is welcomed with joy no matter who they are, without qualification. As one monk noted:

> We have to be tolerant. If a woman comes to the monastery wearing pants or a man comes in sport pants and the monks scold them, what will be their impression of the Church? We have to be tolerant in order to bring them into the Church, and then we tell them about this and that. The monastery in Preveza is very open and tolerant. They welcome the people without judging them in order to bring them to God.[5]

Underlying this relationship to guests is a belief that God brings each person to the monastery for a reason, which may be beyond human

---

[3]Monk A.
[4]Lay Person, NK.
[5]Monk C.

capability to know. The visitor is Christ in their midst, an opportunity to serve rather than condemn.[6] They are to be embraced in fraternal love, not sent out in the cold. A monastery without love has no hope for the cultivation of holiness in any form.

When warmth and tolerance attract many people, as it has in Preveza, the pressures on the virtue of obscurity are that much greater. Word tends to spread about monasteries that are truly seeking authentic holiness. As one local resident noted about the monastery in Preveza: "Really, this [monastery] has become a spiritual magnetic pole. The word has spread very quickly that there you have good spiritual fathers and they are doing a great job without talking about it."[7] Ultimately, genuine holiness attracts people more than clever publicity. Balancing the command to show warmth, tolerance, and love to each person with the virtue of holy obscurity is the struggle of monasticism everywhere and always. However, in a contemporary world where advertisement and publicity is nearly ubiquitous and the pressures on isolation are immense, cultivating a healthy sense of holy obscurity with brotherly love is particularly challenging. The great monasteries of the next generation will balance the desire for holy obscurity with the command to love one's neighbor.

---

[6]Bishop Meletios reflects this posture required during confession by saying, "Every community, small and great, of villages in the countryside and of the great cities, has many weak people in faith. And has many who despise the faith and the life in Christ by their own choice. Every preacher of the Gospel and most of all the bishop must create opportunities for the 'door' to be opened; in other words, so that his message will be heard with eagerness. He must avoid the air of the public prosecutor. And when such an air is necessary, he has to use it for those within. Only for those who accept his message, 'For what have I to do with judging those outside? Is it not those who are inside that you are to judge? God will judge those who are outside' (1 Corinthians 5.12). The shepherd reproaches only those 'within,' the faithful; to the alienated, he must direct his message of conciliation and counsel." Interview, SLM.

[7]Lay Person, NK.

Principle 3: A monastery must always maintain its unique roles in the local and universal Church.

One of the perennial conundrums of monasticism from its beginning in the fourth century is that rejection of the "world" has come to mean rejection of a society that claims to be Christian and is guided by the Church. In other words, in taking a stand against the worldliness of society, how does it avoid condemning the Church that leads it? The traditional response is that the Church traditions support two modes of life—marriage and monasticism—which are in need of each other and whose worlds often coincide. They share common Scripture, a common goal, and a common Lord, but they are not the same. The community models that have evolved for these modes of life—the parish and the monastery—have been tailored to address their unique challenges so as to offer environments that foster spiritual growth. These are the communities where lasting, authentic fellowship is best found. For this reason, canonically speaking, one cannot be baptized, married, or buried in a monastery because these are seen as community events.[8] Nevertheless, they are equal parts of the Church that both need to be present for the Church to be complete.

Too often the search to isolate itself from worldly pressures has led a monastery to build a metaphoric and sometimes literal wall between itself and local Christians. These monasteries have created an unhealthy hierarchy that divides Christianity and often implicitly or explicitly judges other forms. They ignore the needs of the people around the monastery on the pretense that they are not inside the monastery. They presume that care for those in need is the duty of the clergy, not the monks. However, those in a monastery must always keep in mind that they are first Christians and then part of a monastic family. The demands of the Gospel extend beyond the four walls of the monastery. To deny those in need in the name of preserving

---

[8]Just as a monk will not find the conditions for spiritual growth in the world, the layperson who abandons his or her parish misses out on the conditions that will foster a long-standing healthy spirituality in the world. Periodic visits to a monastery will be spiritually refreshing, but if the monastery replaces the parish, it is only escapism.

traditional conditions conducive to holiness is the sin of the Pharisees in the Bible. It is the denial of Christ in the false pursuance of him.

Highlighting the need to serve one's fellow human does not mean that monks do not have a unique purpose. For Orthodoxy, the *primary* goal of the monks is not service to others. As Abbot Ephraim of Prophet Elias notes, "The apparent influence of the monks in the area in which they find themselves is the result and not the goal."[9] God may use the monks for good in the community, but that is not the intent of their vows; it is, rather, the byproduct of their spiritual struggle. In fact, seeking out service would be seen as immaturity from the perspective of the monk. Abbot Ephraim explains:

> The service to the spiritual work of the parishes is something which is practiced by the hieromonks who are considered worthy by the bishop for this work and are asked by him. If the future ecclesial authority of the monastery does not desire the service of the hieromonks in the parish work, they should stay in their monastery and not consider this a loss in regard to their goal. Something as such would prove that the parish activity had harmful effects on those hieromonks since it caused them to forget the goal for which they became monks.[10]

The monks' primary goal is not the service of those around them; they are, as a famous saying from Mt Athos states, like good dogs: they come when you say come and go when you say go. If there is a genuine need, they will come, but it is not their purpose. Bishop Meletios recognizes that we all "must live in the measure which God demands. He will find the ways to save his world; 'because he cares for us' (1 Peter 5.7)."[11] In other words, if the service of others is unduly comprising the purpose of the monastic life, the monk should first and foremost be a monk seeking spiritual development. God will see that the work will get done.

The danger of service to the world is not only missed opportunity for individual spiritual development. The graver danger is that the

---

[9] Abbot Ephraim.
[10] Abbot Ephraim.
[11] Interview, SLM.

monks may bring the world back into the monastery; that is, the world will inevitably creep into the mindset of the monks. The fear is that it will lead to, in the words of Bishop Meletios, a "gradual secularization." This "incursion" or "invasion" of society into the monastery should be the greatest fear of monks.[12] The monastery must first be a monastery—a place separated and consecrated for God.

The result is a careful balance, or what one monk calls a chosen "middle path."[13] This middle path requires the monastery to be not so secluded or detached as to be "outside" the local Church but not so integrated as to compromise the integrity of its monastic purpose. It preserves the unity of the Church and furthers Christ's evangelical mission on earth, but it also maintains respect for the variation of paths in which God calls individuals to live. Maintaining this "middle path" should be a goal of a healthy monastery.

For a healthy relationship to develop, the value of this "middle path" must be recognized by the local Church representatives, especially the bishop, as noted in the previous chapter. Some bishops view the monastery as a local resource which they can harness to its fullest extent for the good of the local community. When this occurs—when the bishop does not recognize the value of monasticism and does not desire with equal fervor to preserve its sanctity—conflict arises. Thus the bishop can also be a source of the inability to keep this middle path, as Bishop Meletios states bluntly:

> The tensions [between bishops and monks] derive always from sin, egoism. . . . One thing is to blame: the lack of humility and willingness to yield. The pursuit of responsibility for each person, each individual, is a spiritual quest and is found only if there exists a pure confession of thoughts with self-blame. Monasticism is not to blame. The hierarchy is not to blame. Whatever reference to whatever argument is nothing but a pretense for sin.[14]

Developing a successful relationship between a monastery and the local Church representatives requires humility, mutual respect, and

---

[12]Interview, SLM.

[13]Monk C.

[14]Interview, SLM.

shared recognition of the common goals. Unfortunately, these attributes have not always been common in the dynamics that govern the relationship between monasteries and their local Church.

The brotherhood of Prophet Elias exemplifies the middle path. The degree of involvement by the monks has always been driven by the natural response to the needs around them. However, they have been conscious not to seek out such service but rather respond out of love to those in need. As the Abbot states, "The love for all the world is the duty of every Christian, but especially for the monks." As Christians, they reach out in love to all those in need, but only to the extent that they can help without compromising their monastic purpose. Yet as one monk noted:

> We are not activists. It would be good if more of the roles of the monks in the community could be fulfilled by the married clergy rather than the monks. The most important thing for the monks is prayer. But, by the nature of things, we have to get involved. . . . [Our involvement in the community] is driven by need. It is not a particular vision for monasticism, but it is a response to a need. The best vision for monasticism is to dig within. Then, the monk can help better the community . . . we try to fulfill the needs of those around us. We must keep a balance so that there is not too much involvement but there are needs.[15]

While recognizing that monasticism at its heart is centered on prayer and the internal struggle, the monks like the one above have an innate awareness of the needs of those around them. Reflecting the love of Christ, they have a desire to assist in those needs but their success lies in their ability to balance serving others and preservation of the unique culture of monasticism. The monks have a different purpose in the Church that must be preserved.

Clear recognition of these different but related registers for Christian life is important in other areas as well. For example, the trend in Orthodoxy is that householders often have spiritual fathers in monasteries. However, less-mature monks have often modeled this

---

[15]Monk B.

relationship on their own relationship to the abbot, controlling nearly
every aspect of their spiritual childrens' lives. The monastic spiritual
fathers in these monasteries ask their children in the world to seek a
blessing for nearly every aspect of life just as a monk would. Furthermore, they promise great blessings for monastic-like obedience. The
monks at the Monastery of Prophet Elias reject this "guru" model,
recognizing important differences in the two relationships.[16] Bishop
Meletios states:

> The relationship between the monk and his *geronda* is a commit-
> ment that has been established before God. The monk has an obli-
> gation to keep absolute obedience to the demands of his *geronda*
> unto death. He vows this before God. And he undertakes this obe-
> dience for the Kingdom of God. And he accepts it, although he is
> weak, by the "hope of the power of God." And the commitment of
> the monk to his *geronda* is extended to the most insignificant and
> minimal: how many drops of water he drinks in his cell. . . . The rela-
> tionship of the married person with his spiritual father cannot exist
> in the framework that is in effect with the *geronda*-monk. The mar-
> ried person maintains his freedom to act on his own in regards to
> everything he wants. He limits his freedom only as far as he wants.[17]

Humans are by nature free to choose how they act at any given
moment. A monk chooses to limit that freedom in the hope of greater
rewards. To make this "choice to limit choice" possible, he confines
his environment to the four walls of the monastery. The person outside the monastery must act in a very different environment, with different pressures and different temptations. The spiritual fathers of

---

[16]"The role is to be a father and a guide and nothing more. There is a danger
that he becomes like a guru and does not cultivate maturity and responsibility in his
spiritual children so that he takes responsibility for everything." Monk B.

[17]Interview, SLM. Abbot Ephraim echoed a similar sentiment when he said,
"The monk according to the monastic tonsure gives some additional promises, which
do not burden other Christians. One of these is obedience to the elder and indeed
even 'unto death.' From this promise, a special promise follows of obedience by the
monk to his *geronda*, which the simple Christian does not have toward his spiritual
father. Because he never gave this promise and because it is nowhere evident that he
or she must give any such promise." Abbot Ephraim.

Prophet Elias recognize these different forms of Christian life and keep them separate.

The healthy monastery thus will always find a balance between its universal command to serve those in need with its unique monastic methods and goals. This is particularly challenging in the modern world because the spiritual needs of the people are great and the corresponding opportunities to serve are magnified at precisely the time when the pressures on the traditional monastic life in the form of encroaching worldliness are particularly intense. A healthy monastery serves without losing its unique identity.

PRINCIPLE 4: HEALTHY MONASTERIES MUST BE PREPARED TO WITNESS TO ITS LIFE.

The monk stands as a living testament to an ancient ideal, for when compromise is inevitable in the world, the monk represents someone who has left the world in order to consciously not compromise. He is not a saint but one struggling earnestly to become one. His devoted effort more often than his virtue inspires the layperson to greater spiritual depths. Thus even the neglectful monk can be a light unto others. Bishop Meletios remarks:

> For the lay people, the monks are light: even in the person of the neglectful monk, they see that which they themselves find difficult to accept; the monk lives in poverty. He prays a lot. He has a very well-disciplined life. He knows to be yielding. He lives noiselessly. For the layperson, all this is a dynamic example. And for them, who in all they do act in accordance with their internal impulse, the monk (and even the neglectful monk—the one who is unstable) is a teacher of the Gospel.[18]

This light becomes brighter as the monk conquers his passions and cultivates virtue. When a monk obtains such passionlessness and comes to embody the love of Christ—rare in monasticism but cer-

---

[18]Interview, SLM.

tainly not impossible—the impact on the world cannot be measured. Even if monasticism produces only one such beacon every generation, the "institution of monasticism" has value because the impact of that beacon is so great. Yet strictly speaking, such a beacon "does" nothing. He does not change the world by his actions but by his presence, his inaction, his stillness. As Bishop Meletios noted, "The role of the monks is elucidated clearly by the fathers: it is to radiate light. Not to act."[19] Within the monastic tradition, this embodiment of the light that inspires others has been presented as the traditional role of monasticism in the world.

It is one of the ironies of the modern world that while communication is easier than ever, the monastic example is increasingly becoming less prominent. This dearth of influence is not because there are not holy monks worthy of emulation, as some people argue; rather, the monastic light is more often than not drowned out by the massive amount of competing messages people receive. The simple monastic example is lost amidst the noise of modernity. In the words of Bishop Meletios, the people have become "intoxicated" by all the competing messages.[20] People can no longer find themselves or know their place in the world. This leads to an unsettled feeling. Abbot Ephraim observes:

> The chief characteristic of our era and even more in the era to come, appears to be fluidity in not only social, political, and cultural things but also religious, perhaps even in Church affairs. The static, stationary, secure have been replaced by new, continually unsettled elements. This involves a continual change to the form of difficulties that the Christian will encounter in the modern world, but also the monk.[21]

The authentic monk represents something grounded in the midst of this constant flux and message overdose. His unchanging commitment to the Gospel provides him the perspective that is required to

---

[19]Interview, SLM.
[20]ΟΡΘΟΔΟΞΙΑ.
[21]Abbot Ephraim.

see clearly in the world, even, or perhaps especially, now. Thus, according to Bishop Meletios, the "modern" monk must be prepared to educate and shed light upon the world. The bishop stated:

> Today it is necessary, as never before, for the monks to intercede with their word. Because today the people no longer understand every-thing according to the Christian way. So, it is desirable for the monks to know and to be able to explain, to elucidate, to clear up questions. The occupation of the monk in preaching and in confes-sion fulfills this role. As regards to the fundamental attitude or spirit, monasticism must never change. Simply, the same spirit is being experienced slightly differently within a somewhat different world.[22]

The result is that the monks should be prepared to discuss the Chris-tian life in the changing world. They are in a unique position to do so because one of the fruits of undistracted dedication to God is the abil-ity to rise above the clatter of competing worldly messages to discover something deep, stable, and true for all generations. This role has always been part of the monastic vocation, but it is acutely needed in the modern world.

The spiritual danger accompanying this role is that it can often turn into crass publicity that stands in direct contrast to the impor-tance of holy anonymity. However, the monks of Prophet Elias pro-vide a model. They are often teaching: the youth catechism classes, Monday or Wednesday lectures at the spiritual centers, Sunday litur-gical homilies, and frequent lectures in Athens and throughout Europe. During these talks, the stress is never on themselves but on the life in Christ according to the Gospels. When a question is asked regarding them personally, they deflect it with self-deprecating humor. For example, I once asked a respected father of the monastery about the tradition of the prayer of the heart. He responded by telling me what others had told him personally and a few insights from what he had read. He came across as a fellow seeker. Afterwards, a fellow monk who had overheard a portion of our conversation asked me to

---

[22]Interview, SLM.

repeat it for him because, as it turned out, this monk was one of the foremost thinkers on the prayer of the heart in Greece, having published numerous articles about it. None of this preeminence had come out during our conversation. He had mastered the art of witnessing with humility.

A healthy monastery will be able to identify the monks who have the maturity and discernment to speak to the world without seeking worldly glory. In the din that comprises the muddled messages of modernity, the voice of the monk relaying the ancient message of monasticism is critically needed. Ultimately, both the message and the light of the messenger will transform the world.

†

The Athonite "renaissance" of the 1970s and 1980s was truly a rediscovery of Byzantine monasticism. The charismatic leaders of the monasteries sought not to reconsider monasticism but rather to be as faithful as possible to what had come before. By doing so on the protective peninsula of the Holy Mountain, they avoided the three relationships that historically have created tribulations for monasticism: the relationship with the local bishop, the relationship with the local Christian community, and the relationship with the world. The isolation that made that possible is now vanishing, and monasticism is forced to reconsider its place in relationship to these three arenas of society.

The healthy monastery will balance with maturity and discernment the various goods that are available to it: the desire to remain anonymous yet also embrace all who come with warmth and tolerance; the desire to serve their fellow Christian in need, without compromising the monastic life; the need to educate and speak out, without losing sight of the understanding and compassion that comes from authentic love of Christ. The sign of failure is usually fundamentalism or activism; success means finding some middle path, as the brotherhood of Prophet Elias has.

The Monastery of Prophet Elias is a modern community continually seeking to forge itself upon an ancient model. When I first arrived, the monastery did not seem like a "real" monastery to me: it was not ancient, the beds were too comfortable, the icons were too new, and the monks were too jovial. I had confused antiquity and seriousness for sanctity. Holiness is not found in stones or grimaces, famous relics or deep prostrations. Holiness is found in faces struggling to emulate Christ, serve him, and transform the world in the process. The monks of Prophet Elias commit to this struggle with wit and wisdom. Though their purpose is of utmost seriousness, they rarely seem overly serious. They rely neither on pretense nor on worldly glory to demonstrate their holiness, but they have a refreshing spirit, shared with Bishop Meletios, that is unmistakably divine in origin. They have an ancient faith that is in so many ways perfected for the modern world.

CONCLUSION

Preveza Today

"Seek first the kingdom of God and his righteousness; and all these things shall be added unto you." Matthew 6.33

Every Sunday for more than a decade, Bishop Meletios of Nikopolis and Preveza is driven through his metropolis to a small village which has become its center. Amidst the fields filled with flowers and sheep, he arrives at a gleaming-white edifice, the Monastery of Prophet Elias. A quarter-century prior, many of the monks within used to come to his small apartment in the middle of Athens to chat about spiritual things. Now, he comes to them. He is not alone. The dining hall is nearly full of people from near and far, young and old, Greek and foreigner, rich and poor. There are doctors, students, laborers, teachers, businessmen, and government officials. They, too, have come to talk with the monks about spiritual matters. Laughter erupts from one part of the room, as one of the monks finishes passing along a joke; in another part, a monk and two young men look at the text of the *troparion* for the feast of the day, pondering its meaning. The bishop enters quietly, hardly looking up. Everyone naturally quiets and looks to him. The scene is the fruit of a quarter-century of spiritual dedication and a microcosm of the Metropolis as a whole. He rings the bell and the prayer begins, "Let the heavens rejoice; let earthly things be glad . . ."

On one level, the spiritual struggle of the Church is everywhere and always the same. There are no new struggles; whenever critical observers highlight some new social trend that will supposedly spell disaster for the Church, Bishop Meletios reminds his people that all such trends are nothing but "gnats on the horns of a bull. They are powerless."[1] The Church has faced these challenges time and time again. In this sense, then, the work of Bishop Meletios and the monks would be the same in tenth-century Constantinople or contemporary Los Angeles or modern-day Preveza. Details will differ, but most of these concern only externalities. The life of the Christian and even more the call of the Christian leader does not change based on place or time.

On another level, every Christian story is different. In March of 1980, the people of Preveza were suffering under years of spiritual neglect, caught between national political currents, and above all scandalized by the behavior of their Church leaders. However, as Bishop Meletios reminds us all, God had plans that no human could conceive. No one knew or could have predicted what followed: a place, a people, would be transformed. This transfiguration occurred through hard work, sacrifice for others, and fervent prayer. There were no miracles. Or perhaps there were. Hundreds of smaller, daily ones. The "holiness" of Preveza is the accumulation of these moments. It is a unique tale that I have been privileged to tell.

I began researching this story because my sense was that there were many other places in the modern Christian world that were like Preveza. The specifics are always different and usually less dramatic, but there are countless Christian communities around the globe that have suffered from spiritual neglect, have uninspired leaders, and seem to be wandering in the spiritual wilderness without a map. In researching this story, I hoped that I could provide this map by extracting a spiritual program out of this story that could be replicated elsewhere. I discovered no such program, and as with so many other people, Bishop Meletios has made me reconsider my starting points. Instead, I discovered the simplicity of the Christian message in the world: it is nothing more than to allow God to work. This is the ancient faith.

In a mechanized and multifaceted modern world, this seemingly simple task has become all the more difficult. We have become a soci-

---

[1] *ΟΡΘΟΔΟΞΙΑ*.

ety guided by plans, programs, and proposals. We want change quantified and measured. And we want it right away. My sense after being with Bishop Meletios is that our ancient faith does not work that way. Christianity—at least any form consistent with the ancient beginnings—is then oddly out of place with the modern world. God's timeline does not have our dates or deadlines on it but eternity balanced on a cross. It does not rely on propaganda or publicity but on emptied wills and quiet hearts. It does not try to build up what is seen, but what is unseen. This is the contemporary story of Preveza: an ancient faith in a modern world.

Homily Offered by Bishop Meletios at His Ordination as Bishop of Nikopolis and Preveza

Your Beatitude,
Most Reverend Hierarchs,
My Holy Priests and Deacons,
Blessed People of the Lord,

Our Lord and Savior Jesus Christ, when he was going to the Cross for us, responded to the pleas of those who had loved him earthily by saying: "This cup, which the Father gave to me, should I not drink of it?"

And this cup was very bitter. So bitter. So that, in thought alone, He, who was all-God and all-powerful, knelt down, wept, imploring with beseechful prayers, with cries, and mighty tears, perspired drops of blood from the agony, and was in need of his angels to come to strengthen him. Never has a man on earth experienced such pain or felt such contrition as our Lord in the garden of Gethsemane; but he did not retreat. Because the salvation of the world does not happen by proclamation but only with suffering and sacrifice. For this reason, Christ not only did not avoid the Cross but also he made it his desire, his aim, his glory. And so the Cross became the great glory of the super-glorified Lord of Glory, Jesus Christ, who is the great glory of the Holy Trinity.

O, Cross of Christ, all-holy, thrice-blessed, and life-giving, instrument of the mystical rites of Zion, the holy Altar for the service of our Great Archpriest, the blessing—the weapon—the strength of priests, our pride, our consolation, the light in our heart, our mind, and our steps; Our Lord and Savior nailed to you revealed and instigated his priesthood for us. For this also, the priesthood saves and glorifies only as a Cross; only the one who bears it radiates virtue, which the Cross symbolizes and inspires, illumines and sanctifies; only when it has something from God and the inexpressible beauty of the virtues of our first and great priest, Christ.

For this I implore you, immaculate Theotokos, the bold vestment for the naked, the boastful veneration of priests, entreat your Son, who considered me faithful and placed me into His service, to vouchsafe His grace and give strength to my feeble hands and to my paralytical spiritual knees.

Holy and glorified martyr St Eleftherios, who blessed me to offer liturgy and confession for twelve years in your church, entreat our common Lord and Master to give also to my service as a bishop a mere drop from the grace and the spiritual fruitfulness which was given to you, unto salvation of the pious people of the apostolic Church of Nikopolis, to which I have been appointed preacher of the Cross and His Resurrection.

Holy and glorified hierarchs of Christ, Donatos and Attikos, pillars and champions of Orthodoxy, intercede for me who in a few minutes will be your successor, to become and participate in your way, for the good of the people of God.

Your Beatitude,

To you, who are at the pinnacle of worldly hierarchy, first in honor, first in responsibility, first and chief cause of goodness but also first in accountability. And for this more lofty to the Cross, in the Greater Cross, accept my humble assurance that I will subject myself to every sacrifice in order that you will have a good apology at the fearful judgment seat of Christ and I will be united with you by the bond of peace, love, deserved respect, and prayer.

I call upon the blessings and prayers of those present here, the reverend hierarchs and likewise of the eminent Metropolitans Jacob of Mitilini, Barnabas of Kitrous, and Chrisostomos of Messinia, under whom I worked and came to know their virtues and benefited from their experiences.

I call upon the blessings and prayers of my co-workers and my beloved in the Holy Synod, distinguished ministers of the Almighty, co-priests in my parish church, with whom I feel that I am one in body and one in spirit. In particular, I call upon the prayers of the good angel of my over twenty-five years of priesthood, for whom I have deep-seated respect, Father Agathangelos.

Finally, I call upon the prayers of my venerable mother, of my spiritual children in Christ, and of all pious Christians, of parishioners of this holy Church, who in judging my work until now in the Church, who by the goodness of their hearts assess it greater than its actual worth, come to pray for me and my service from now on. I pray the Lord rewards all their love bountifully.

Lord Jesus Christ, the source of our salvation and priesthood, I am not worthy for You to come under the roof of my soul because its all desert and ready to collapse. But as you deigned to enter into the house of Simon the Leper, come also to me and may your light illumine me, in my soul, in my mind, in my heart. And make your light always pour forth from my heart, my words, my hands. So when men see it they will glorify our Father who is in the Heavens. Amen.

Homily Offered by Bishop Meletios at His Enthronement in Preveza

Friday
March 28, 1980

The Cathedral Church of St Haralambos
Preveza, Greece

Most Reverend Hierarchs,
Reverend priests and deacons of the Church,
Worthy and respected leaders; Mr. Prefect, Leader of the armed
forces, and Mayor of Preveza,
Worthy representatives of the political and judicial authorities,
Blessed people of the Lord,

I feel very small in front of the greatness and the gravity of the responsibilities which the laying on of hands and the election by the Hier-
archies has placed upon my feeble shoulders, in front of our great
Archpriest Jesus Christ, who is "over all, the eternally blessed God.
Amen."

"As the Father has sent me, so I send you."

The mission of Christ was to save the world. Not to judge it. To
save it. The mission of the apostle of Christ, the bishop, is the same
mission of Christ.

"As My Father has sent me, so I send you."

But how great a difference! The height of the mission is hard to
contemplate even more for the angels! And what an abyss of
wretchedness are we! I am very much aware of my smallness, bearing
to my mind the problems with which our Church is confronted in its

entirety and especially the local Church that I am called to shepherd. How? In the name of Christ. With Christ as the model. Imitating Christ.

The Lord said: "Take my yoke upon you, and learn from me; for I am gentle and humble in heart, and you will find rest for your souls." And the Archpriest is the messenger of God. The proclaimer of peace. And whoever hears his words and imitates his good works, finds rest.

Once, when our Lord was sleeping in the boat, the holy apostles, frightened from the fierce storm which had arisen, awoke him with the words, "Master save us, we are perishing!" And then the Lord got up and "rebuked the wind and the sea." And tranquility was restored. Also, the bishop, and each cleric, must be a messenger of peace, a fount of tranquility for the souls who suffer from whatever causes anxiety.

And in order to be as such, he need not seek out honors but imitate Christ, who "when he was reviled, he did not revile in return."

And to be always willing to say from the depths of his heart: "to those who hate us and have wronged us, forgive them, Lord; and give to them your rich mercy and Your Kingdom."

But for the mission of the clerics, this is little.

The chief mission of our Lord Jesus Christ, was to offer his soul, his entire self, as ransom on behalf of the world. And in this way of "mystagogy," the Lord taught his disciples saying, "Pay attention dear friends. Nothing separates you from me. For if I suffer, it is for the sake of the world. Therefore, if you are friends of mine, imitate me."

Christ, in order to save us, ascended the Cross and descended into Hades; from the hands of those, he benefited and blessed.

Why?

In order to save them from the tyranny of the devil and the founding of their life upon deceit and delusion, in order to make them realistic and to bring them down to earth.

And true imitation of Christ, even if stoned and crucified, is to preach always the truth; because only the truth makes one free. "You will know the truth and the TRUTH shall make you free."

The bishop sits in the place of Christ. His throne and glory is the Cross. His joy and jubilation are persecution and reproach from the men of this world, who live far from God. . . . His comfort, his power, and his consolation are the love and devotion of the faithful.

Holy land and land of the saints, who shined in the spiritual firmament of the Church—this is the Metropolis of Preveza. It was and it is, but it must remain so, by thriving in holiness and bearing fruit—if possible—multiplying it a hundredfold.

This must be my aim. Because Christ seeks this. "In doing this," says the Gospel, "my Father is glorified, just as you go and bring much fruit and your fruit will remain."

Did you hear what he said? He wants much fruit. The more, the better.

Let us prepare ourselves. Work is necessary. Struggle. Battles. War. Tough war, merciless. Merciless for our own selves. Not for others.

I, like a responsible father and your director, call upon you to stage an uprising. A glorious uprising. An uprising of Christ. For the good of all. For the bad of none.

"Let us stand with awe. Let us stand with fear of God," calling out as the Archangel Michael did once to the unsettled angels. And the holy Angels were gathered around him and defeated the power of darkness, for the good of all.

And we, the lovers of Christ and Christified, who rally together and are united in one heart, one soul, one mind, one intellect, one will, one action, let us struggle for the glory of God and the salvation of his people.

This is my work! This and nothing else.

Because I am a servant of Christ and nothing else!

I am a priest, and nothing else. Nothing less; nothing more. Nothing higher; nothing lower. Nothing more to the right; nothing more to the left. Nothing more to the front; nothing more to the back.

I am a priest and nothing else!

I am a worker of the Kingdom of God.

And as a priest, a servant of Christ, I greet you all with the greeting of Christ, the greatest of all blessings:

Peace unto you, peace unto all. And I pray, this is my greeting and my blessing, to find you all sons of peace and to rest one for all in all, and in all of your loved ones, throughout your houses; and to lead you all to your loved ones, in all your houses; and to lead you all to full knowledge of the glory and of the Kingdom of God, of the Father, and the Son, and the Holy Spirit. Amen.

Peace to you. Peace to all.

"Come, O Christ"
by Metropolitan Meletios

You can live without a father, you can live without a mother, but you cannot live without God. Russian proverb

PREFACE

A contemporary young man tells us:

- how he found Christ.
- how from a lifeless, purely sentimental faith he was guided to true knowledge.
- how he fought against sin; that is, against himself, how true happiness and peace came into his heart, how he became a friend of Christ.

He describes the struggle that occurred inside his heart: between Christ and those things that, until then, had been a source of his happiness, comfort, and enjoyment. Let us follow his struggle. It has something to teach us because the problems of others are not that different from our own.

COME CLOSE TO ME ...

The first years of my youth were not lived in a Christian way. I was young, and I wanted to enjoy the "good things" in life. I wanted to celebrate my youth, and I did many foolish things.

Up to that time, I had heard plenty about Christ and about the Christian way of life, both at home and at school. However, I used to put it aside and consciously closed the door of my heart to Christ.

They say that longing for happiness is blind and that it blinds you. I used to live it up. I had decided to keep my life free from any moral principles. I didn't want morals! I wanted happiness! I wanted "enjoyment!"

I wanted so much to be able to erase a few things from my heart and from my memory with the sponge of forgetfulness, but that did not happen. No matter how much I tried to do this, avoiding systematically everything that was related to religion, the image of Christ never erased itself completely from inside me. Occasionally I would still catch myself calling Him; sometimes at the most unlikely moments. I used to plead with Him not to allow my soul to perish!

Why?

Because, although I enjoyed that lifestyle, deep inside me I felt really terrible. I felt a strange inner turmoil. I had a feeling as if I were sinking in quicksand.

One night my thoughts came back to Christ more intensely. And as I was lying down comfortably, those simple thoughts became a prayer! I said to Him: "My Christ, do not let me sink in this quicksand!"

I said it and tears filled my eyes.

"Come close to me, Lord! . . ."

Christ heard me and came instantly. I felt His presence near me, beside me, a living reality! From then on my life changed. It became enlightened. The darkness of my soul dissolved.

Up until that time, I had felt bitterness, a lamentation inside me that I tried to cover up with wild, crazy rock music; by living it up, with wild antics, dancing, sex, and with any sensual pleasure I could find.

All this was extinguished at once within me and a sound of sweet music now took its place. I was full of calm, peace, and happiness.

I was not the only one who had this strange experience. Somebody else had a similar but somehow more intense one than mine.

He also had not followed the correct road. He had not lived close to God. He had made plans to "enjoy" his life and had indeed enjoyed all the sensual pleasures. He was proud of that. He used to rub his hands with satisfaction and used to see himself as being clever and alert. He would do any "job" without hesitation or moral scruple whenever he found (or thought he found) the chance. But one day they caught him, and he ended up in jail for years.

One day a priest visited him there and with God's help began a conversation with him.

"How is it going in here?" the priest asked him.

"Better than outside, Father!" he answered.

The priest was amazed.

"Surely you must have confronted many difficulties and felt deprived in the outside world," said the priest with sympathy.

"Difficulties?" replied the prisoner, "what are you saying Father? None at all. I had everything I wanted! I had it easy. I had good buddies; friends I could trust."

The priest was amazed! He didn't know what to say. He asked again:

"How can you be happier here 'inside,' without your freedom, than you ever were on the outside?" He answered calmly:

"You know Father, I have time to think in here, and I have done a lot of thinking about my situation, about myself. Most of all, about God! Do you know what God is, Father?"

What could the priest say?

The prisoner continued, "Father, God is peace. If someone stays far away from God, he does not have peace, the inner peace of the soul. Father, how can someone have true joy and happiness without inner peace?"

"Then my dear young man," said the priest, "have you found peace in here?"

"Yes, Father," he replied, "I have. You know about this stuff. In the tranquility of this place, day and night, I began a conversation with myself; about the things I had done and the course my life had taken. And I decided to correct myself. Then a strange thing happened, Father! As soon as I had those thoughts, I felt that I was reconciled with God right there and then. I felt Him inside me. From then on, my life overflowed with peace and joy."

†

What a pity not to have these kinds of experiences in time! What a pity to hear about them and not to pay any attention! What a pity to ignore them!

The famous philosopher Blaise Pascal says: "True happiness is not found outside or even inside of us. It is found only in God. When we find God, happiness is everywhere."

†

And so, the door of my heart had opened. I didn't regret this. Not at all. (With every day that passes I feel better.) I felt really content. One day I prayed with all my heart: "O Christ! . . ." And before I knew it, before I had even finished calling to Him, I felt Him next to me, saying: "Here I am, beside you."

"O Christ," I responded, "I want to belong to You. Stay with me! I cannot live without You!"

"If you want Me to come close to you," Jesus said to me, "and to stay with you always, it is entirely up to you! Make the necessary changes in your outer behavior and within yourself, and I will stay close to you always."

"I love you! . . ." I said.

"Thank you," He said to me, "however, it is not enough. Prove it to Me by your actions."

I nearly choked! I was lost for words!

He said to me: "That's how it is. Whatever someone has within comes out in how they act. It becomes his way of life. Show Me, therefore, what you have 'without you': in your home and surroundings, so that I can understand what you have 'within you.' And if it's possible, and if it's beneficial, I will come."

How could I refuse? I got up, "With pleasure," I said to Him warmly, and so we began.

†

There isn't one life here and another life elsewhere! Life is one, only one. And that is life close to God. It starts here and continues there, unto the ages of ages. Far away from God there is only eternal death.

†

In my library

The first room that we visited was my library. It was a room full of wisdom and spirit. I had collected all the books that I liked and that fascinated me. However, the books that fascinate us usually shape us and express who we are!

I entered the room with pride; I was expecting admiration and praise. As we entered, I began to feel dreadful, seeing our Savior looking carefully at each one of my books. He stopped to look at some of them, particularly those which I did not want Him to have seen at all. I felt very bad. Up until that time I had not realized how unsuitable some of my books were! Now that He was looking at them, I understood and became ashamed as never before.

Christ was shaking His head with sorrow and bitterness at my sad state. I remembered the saying: "A man is what he eats." And I froze. "Oh my God," I said to myself, "if my heart has become what I gave it to eat!" Surely something was not going right with me. And I whispered:

"O Christ, I give you my promise. They will go. Both from my library and from my life."

He smiled, like He wanted to say to me: "Good! Well done!"

Suddenly I saw Him begin to frown again. I searched to find the cause, and I saw Him looking at some pictures with which I had decorated the room! They were disgraceful. He asked me:

"What feelings are stirred inside you, each time you stare at them?"

I lowered my eyes and said to Him: "I know Lord, that this room needs a radical change. It will happen. I beg you, help me. Help me to correct all this."

He responded: "I will help you, but you need to lend a hand also. First, throw away from here whatever is impure and unclean. How will your heart be cleansed if you feed it with such filthy images and thoughts? Fill your library with religious books that speak about Me.

Study them if you want things to go well with you. Study them regularly. It is food for the soul. Take care of the food for your soul in at least the same way as you take care of the food for your body."

From then on I started to study the Holy Bible. By studying it, I realized that it is the best book in the world. Another young man with slightly different experiences to mine writes:

The Holy Bible:
  • I read it for the first time to show obedience to my mother,
  • for the second time I studied it, concerned about my soul,
  • now I study the Holy Bible mostly out of love for our Savior.

†

I asked the Lord faint heartedly: "So, what about the pictures?"

"Surely," the Lord replied, "those images must have been deeply imprinted in your heart, which is not good! However, have courage! There is a cure."

He gave me a large Icon of Himself with fine features, and said to me: "Here! Hang it there, opposite your study desk. Look at it when you study."

I did that, and as time passed, I found that His divine image was attracting my attention. When I looked at it, His purity and His strength would drive away each bad thought from my mind. His Sacred Icon taught me "To bring every thought into captivity to the obedience of Christ" (2 Corinthians 10.5).

†

Our joy, our peace, our comfort, the end of our every bitterness is only God. Fortunate are those who turn their heart towards Him! Saint Augustine on Psalm 84.10

†

IN THE KITCHEN

The kitchen is a place for appetites. It is a symbol of appetites and desires. Many, when they are at home, are always in and out of the kitchen munching and nibbling at something. I used to do the same.

"My kitchen and fridge are always full! Do You mind," I asked the Lord, "if we have something to eat?"

He agreed, and we sat down.

"What is on your menu today?" He asked.

"Well, what isn't on it!" I said bragging, and I started to bring out the dishes and place them on the table. Many different dishes, all very tasty. I was ready to sit down to enjoy them again.

However, Christ was standing without interest, indifferent and unmoved!

I said to Him: "Aren't You going to have something Lord?"

He answered me: "I want a different kind of food, which you who are carnal do not understand! It is much better than all this, more satisfying. Whoever eats from this food is never hungry or thirsty again. If you want to taste it, start searching to find ways to do the will of My Father in Heaven. Search with a little more appetite than what you have for these futile things that can never make a man happy. I imagine you agree with Me!"

How strangely Christ acts sometimes! There, at the table, the table of wastefulness and gluttony, He taught me to appreciate simplicity and tasting and to understand that a different sort of food exists: doing the will of God.

I followed His advice, and it didn't take long for me to understand that this is the tastiest food in the world. Was it possible for Christ to make a mistake? Does Christ ever make mistakes? This food causes a man to be filled once and for all.

†

The Lord said: "Blessed are those who hunger and thirst for righteousness" (that is, those who make it their main concern to obey the will and commandments of God) "for they shall be filled." Matthew 5.6.

†

In my living room

We went into the living room. This room was very quiet and comfortable. You could stay there for hours. Christ said to me: "It is very charming. It is set up in such a way as to create the suitable atmosphere for close company! Let's come here often."

His words inspired me. Since I was young, I enjoyed having pleasant and intimate company, Christ's company was the best, the sweetest, and the most intimate! We sat and talked for a long time about many things.

The Lord said to me: "Every morning, nice and early, I will be waiting for you in here. We will be starting the day together."

From then on, every day at seven in the morning, I had a meeting with Christ. I used to take a spiritual book and sit comfortably, and I would study it. The Lord sat beside me, guiding me so that my heart would fill with His Sight, the light that is hidden in His words. Afterward I would talk to Him about my weaknesses, my passions, and my mistakes, and He would talk to me about His love and His charity. How good were those moments! How much I used to long for them! How much I used to seek them! What could be more natural? This room was so linked with its new use that I had forgotten it was called a living room. I had named it a place for meditation.

However, this did not last very long. My zeal started to evaporate. The time put aside for communication with Christ started to become shorter and shorter. This was because: Sometimes, I was late getting up! Sometimes, I had something important to do! Sometimes, an urgent distraction would come up! Sometimes, this! Sometimes, that! . . .

As time went on, I began to realize that I did not have time; I did not have the extra time to occupy myself with Christ. I did not do this on purpose. Things developed like this of their own accord, without my realization. Sometimes days would pass without me visiting the place of meditation at all. I had nearly forgotten what the words study and prayer meant.

One morning I was late getting up, and I was rushing, eager to be on my way. Passing by the living room, I saw the door ajar. As I quickly glanced in, I saw Christ there, waiting for me. He was thoughtful and a little grieved. This stirred me, and I said to myself: "Christ is waiting for you, and you are running?"

I humbly went close to Him. I fell to my knees and worshipped Him. With my eyes lowered, I said to Him: "Forgive me Lord. All those mornings that I have not come in here, have You been waiting for me?"

"Yes," He replied, "I have been waiting for you every morning because I love you. Do not forget that I shed My blood for you. Furthermore, I made a promise to you. I keep My word and I am faithful to My promises. I think that even if you don't realize this, even if you don't want to do something for your soul, you should at least do something for My sake!"

†

Do not forget your obligation to Christ. Do not forget your relationship with Christ. Do not leave Him waiting out in the cold. It is not in your interest. Do everything possible to find enough time for study and prayer. Spiritual life and spiritual progress just can't happen without study and prayer.

†

An evening out

One evening I was ready to go out. Within me, I was used to mixing and matching the most inconsistent things. I loved Christ. However, I did not want under any circumstance to let go any of my old habits. I used to find them very enjoyable, even enthralling. And I couldn't understand what problem Christ could have with these things. As often happens, the things I liked I found absolutely rational and correct! That was as far as my understanding went then.

However, as I stepped outside and was ready to close the door behind me, I suddenly heard (to my surprise) within me, the voice of Christ: "Hey, where are you going?"

"I have an engagement to attend to very soon!" I answered.

The Lord responded: "Great. I'm coming with you."

I was stunned. I didn't know what to say. Was I going to go out on the town with Christ? "Eh . . . No Lord," I said, "I don't think that You can come with me today. Can You leave it for tomorrow? In my program tomorrow, I have something that will please You. I will attend a good lecture. Today is something else."

Christ responded to me: "Let Me tell you My friend. Were you not the one who called Me sometime ago to come close to you, to continually be close to you? Here I am. Now I realize that you don't want Me any more! Or rather, you want Me to be brought down to your level, to ring the bell when you want Me to come, and to make a sign when you want Me to go. Like the masters used to do with their servants in the 'good' old days, and what some employers do to their staff today. However, can you imagine that? Can something like this happen, and continue to happen?"

His words were irrefutable. However, I didn't want to back down by any means and so I cut Him off: "Come with me today? No way!" I turned my back on Him and left.

Yes, I left. I wanted to distance myself from Him and to escape His glance. But who can hide from Him what is deep inside his heart? I felt His glance following me everywhere, and that made me feel really bad. I felt upset all night. I did not enjoy myself at all. No matter how much I tried to entertain myself. On the inside, I felt as if I were at a funeral.

When I returned home late that night, I had a conscious understanding that: It was very dangerous to allow your soul to get used to inconsistency, between what you say and what you do, even for small things. I stood in front of the Icon of Christ and said to Him: "I have learned my lesson. I understand now. Without You, far away from You, life becomes a tragedy. From now on, O Christ, I won't make the mistake of giving preference to the things that give pleasure to the flesh, and delight to the senses. I will be very conscious of the harm they do to my soul and to my spiritual relationship with You."

There is no worse mistake for a human being than trying to find a joy and happiness here on earth that is greater and better than the joy that comes from having the grace of God!

†

The quest for joy and happiness is not a delusion. Our Creator God has put it inside us. However, if you do not take care to follow the road that leads to joy, true joy, then your pursuit will certainly lead you along the wrong roads, and you will end up in a blind alley. Saint Augustine (*De libero arbitrio* II, 9.26)

†

I ALWAYS HAD IT LOCKED . . .

A long time had passed since then. Somebody would have thought that everything was going fine during all this time. I was feeling quite good, and I was trying to be consistent with all that we had said. I very much liked discussing some matters with Christ. Just as much, I liked discussing with others about Christ! I used to feel Him very close to me. My soul was filled with the grace and the calm that was spread by His presence.

But it seems that things were not going as well as they appeared on the outside. Something was hidden inside me, in the house of my soul. There was one small, tiny, and secret cabinet hidden away in an unknown "room" of my soul. I always had it locked. Double locked. In it, I used to keep different objects (books, cassettes and other little personal things) that I did not want anyone entering my house by chance to notice. In other words, inside this little cabinet I used to lock away my other self, the one I was not showing. I used to lock up my deepest yearnings, my secret desires, the ones that fascinated me but I never had the courage to talk about with others, or with anybody!

But now the time came for it to be opened. And it was opened!

One time, as I was entering the house of my soul, I saw Christ beside me, holding His nose, and simultaneously pointing with His finger at that little cabinet that held my secret desires and acts. His expression was clearly saying to me: "Something smells inside here! Something is not right in here!"

I pretended that I did not understand where! Very soon however, I realized that I couldn't hide any longer!

†

"Playing." The more you try to hide one sin with another, the more you will be ridiculed. A sin is not hidden by another sin, it is hidden only through repentance and confession. When we want to hide a sin with another, we are like little children playing "hide and seek." Saint John Chrysostom (on Matthew, Homily 48.5).

†

I knew well that from some little place in my heart offensive odors were being emitted, odors of death! I used to smell them. I used to "listen" to them continuously. I knew both from where and from what they were coming! However, I did not want to be deprived of them! I liked them! I considered them precious for my life. I knew they smelt bad. This is why I never wanted to mention them anywhere and to anybody! I completely kept them secret! In addition, I used to be very careful not to allow anything to be smelt, not the slightest odor.

For this purpose, I was using every kind of deodorant: weak, strong, medium, depending on the bad smell I wanted to hide and from whom! Each morning before going out, I would spray the apartment of my soul with "discretion." I was arming myself with every kind of pretence and hypocrisy. Those wonderful deodorants not only neutralized every bad impression coming out of my soul and my acts but also gave my general behavior a charming fragrance! The comments kept circulating:

"A wonderful young man! . . ."

"Excellent character! . . ."

"Splendid manners! . . ."

People see only the outside. Whatever you show them. The mask is effective and I was doing well with other people. However, with Christ, the masks and the deodorants are not effective at all. How I unlocked myself! For Christ nothing is hidden. He can see everywhere. His eyes can see in the dark, and inside deep into our heart. Even if we double lock them! "What is going on in there?" asked Jesus.

I am trying to pretend to be the innocent child. I ask: "Where, Lord?"

"There, inside there!" He replied.

"Well! . . . It's nothing! . . . " I responded.

Jesus then said: "Open up, let Me see. Some carcass has to be in there, in a state of decomposition. Can't you see how it stinks?"

I tried to hide with the usual method. I mobilized all my hypocritical humor and skill, summoning all my deodorants: A smile, apparent surprise, jokes. But they did not work on Christ!

"Open, I tell you!" said Christ commandingly, "Something smells bad in here!"

He gave a stern look! I had no intention to lower my glance. I was being stubborn. I was like a wild beast; I got angry with Christ! Yes, with Christ. My thoughts inside me in an uproar:

I thought I could live a little with Christ too. That I also could give Him something. But not so that I'd be left with nothing of my own! What? Am I supposed to give up what I am? Am I supposed to become a slave? A servant of Christ? These concepts are old-fashioned!

And I burst out with anger: "Oh! You are unbearable! However, it is not Your fault, I am at fault. I was the one who wanted to be close to You for a while. I was the one who imagined that I had something to gain by being close to You."

He told me straight: "Very well, I am leaving. Follow your way. I don't want to force you to be close to Me. What can I do with you now? What can I do with you, if you are only close to Me physically, and your heart is elsewhere?" and He turned to leave.

†

"What do you want?" When you want to remember your sins, God wants to forget them. When you want to forget your sins, then God wants to remember them. Which of the two do you want? Saint John Chrysostom

†

The words of Holy Thursday's hymn sounded deafeningly in the ears of my soul: "Two evil deeds were committed by My people Israel: He forsook Me, the source of the Living water, and hewed out for himself a broken well. . . ." I remembered that Christ is Life. Then I realized that whoever distances himself from Life dies. The further away from Life we are the closer we are to death.

Humbled, I bowed and said: "O Christ, do not leave me. Do not go away! Do not let me die! You can see that I do not have the strength to deny my passions. I am tied to them. I like them. I like them so much that when someone is threatening to deprive me of them, I do not feel him as a liberator but as an executioner. Yes, executioner, torturer! As if he is skinning me alive!"

Warm tears poured out from my eyes and became streams on my cheeks.

Humbly, I whispered: "Have pity on me Lord! Cleanse me. Correct me!"

I felt ashamed of myself. A young man like me, with arms of steel, crying!

Then I saw Christ smiling at me; as if He wanted to say: "Well done, My son. Now you are starting to have hope, hope of salvation. And you will achieve it, if you unlock your soul for Me. Do it, and then you will see that you won't be skinned alive! Then, you will understand a man's deliverance from his passions is not like being skinned alive but like being set free."

WAS THERE A MORE LOGICAL SOLUTION?

I remembered our ancestor Adam. Christ had demanded from him that he must also unlock his soul to Him! "Adam where are you? Adam, what is your inner state? What are you hiding within you? Are you alive? Have you died? Adam, where are you? Where are you hiding? Leave these foolish games. Come close to Me!"

But Adam preferred to hide! And when he saw that he could not hide, he became spiteful! He acted on the defensive and put on a mask. He double locked his soul and played the innocent child! He tried to clear himself, and he thought he had achieved it. . . . With the mask. . . . And the deodorants. . . . Oh the poor wretch! . . .

But why condemn our ancestor? Are we not the same? Are we not locking away deep inside our heart some details of our life? Yes, we are. With locks, and safety keys! And we never allow anyone even to attempt to unlock them!

How carefully we avoid allowing a word to be said about the details that captivate us! And above all when we have with us respectable people we use all the hypocrisy at our disposal. All our diplomatic abilities are brought into play, so that we can keep these hidden details unknown, inaccessible, secret, and undisturbed! We manage to keep them secret from people with little expertise. But from Christ?!

Christ searches deep in our heart. Is there anything hidden from Christ? Is there any greater torment than for someone to try to hide something from Christ?

With this thought. I felt wretched! Like Adam and like Eve. For then, shortly after they committed sin, they heard the sound made by the steps of the Lord of Glory walking inside Paradise (Genesis 3.8), and they ran to hide!

I also wanted, if I could, to run and hide. Somewhere where Christ would not find me. But where? I remembered the words: "Who can hide from You Lord, what he has deep in his heart?"

Christ's gaze falls everywhere. He sees everything. With His glance and with His appearance He gave me to understand that a day will come, when all that is hidden in the dark, that is, all those things that we keep and do in secret and in the dark, will be revealed! And I wish that they would simply be revealed, because there is a possibility of their even being held up to ridicule in the presence of angels and people.

A person is saved from this ridicule only if they ridicule their indecent acts. That is, if they criticize them in the presence of the

Lord as acts which are not permitted. This only happens in Holy Confession. And how could it be otherwise?

So I made my confession.

With a trembling hand I gave Him the key to my heart. Then my tongue was loosened, my hesitations cast aside, and I made my confession.

Was there any other rational solution?

Then for the first time in my life I understood and accepted that I would be saved only with the Lord's mercy. I made up my mind to live, as far as possible, according to the will of Christ and to become worthy of His mercy and compassion.

Christ asked me: "Do you want Me to cleanse you from the infectious passions that you have created in your heart, that restrain you in every good thought and decision?"

"Yes Lord," I replied, "I want You to."

"Be careful," said the Lord, "guard your heart. As time passes, do not allow yourself to start forgetting the words that you say now. Stay firm, steadfast, and immovable. Do not yearn for the old. Do not turn back like Lot's wife (Genesis 19.26). And I will be with you always."

†

As long as the passions exist and prevail you will never be able to achieve inner peace. Saint Augustine (*City of God* 19.27)

†

Join Christ?

Something from the service of Holy Baptism came to my mind. I remembered that for someone to become a Christian, they first have to separate themselves from all their indecent and sinful works: "Do you renounce Satan and all his works? And all his worship? And all his pomp[1]?"

---

[1]Vain display.

All of us, except for some who worship Satan, have a bad idea about the devil. And we answer very willingly: "I do renounce him."

But, having renounced three times the devil and all his works, we also have to declare that we join with Christ.

"Do you join Christ?"

Here is where things get tricky: God wants something from us. But we want and like something else! Before us, there are two different wills. Which one of the two shall we follow? To follow the will of God we must first correct our own will! That is, correct it in line with the will of God! Is it permitted to have even a single thought that the will of God should be corrected (i.e., bent!) to fall in line with our will? Our will is crooked; the will of God is the proper measure and a model. With God, frivolous words are not permitted.

"Do you join with Christ?" Answer! Directly and with consistency: "I do join Him."

It seems that all this is not enough! It's as if there is a fear that we will go back on this affirmation! That is why the priest asks again: "Have you joined Christ?" Definitely? Forever? Is your decision binding, definite, and irrevocable? Or are you having second thoughts? What do you have to say? Have you joined Christ? Have you joined Christ once and for all?

"Yes, I have joined Him once and for all."

Then show it with the customary actions that indicate your devotion, your complete and total dedication. These confessions are so serious that each one is repeated three times.

"Worship Him."

"I worship Him as our King and God."

Then, for the first time in my life I truly understood the meaning of the questions and answers exchanged between the priest and the person to be baptized (or the godparent, when the person is an infant) during the service of baptism. Up until that time whenever I heard them I used to laugh. I found the word "join" especially funny. And I laughed with all my heart. But now, when I think about it, I can hardly hold back the tears.

Of course, we never keep these confessions with as much consistency as we should. But as Saint Gregory the Great says: "The most precious thing which we can offer to God, is our good disposition, our eagerness to keep His will" (Homily A, 5.3).

And I said to the Lord: "Yes, my God, Jesus Christ. You are my Lord, I am Your servant. And I always want to be Your servant. I leave everything in Your hands. Everything. I put my entire self in Your hands, to do with as You wish."

He replied to me: "Yes. That's how it is. He Who created you, without asking you whether you wanted to come into His life (how could He have asked you, since you did not exist?), cannot save you unless He first asks you whether you want to be saved."

I remembered then the words of Saint Augustine: *Qui fecit te sine te, non potest salvum facere te sine te* (He Who made you without you, without you cannot save you) and I understood that the first precondition for salvation is our good disposition. That is, our willingness to sacrifice all those things that prevent us from coming close to Christ.

My workshop

Naturally, after all these things I was looking quite shame-faced. Wishing then, it seemed to me, to give me a little courage, Christ asked me: "Tell Me, do you do anything in your spare time?"

"I try Lord!" I replied.

"Let us go and see," the Lord said.

We went down to the basement together. There, in a corner, I had a workbench that was rather poorly equipped. Every now and then (once in a blue moon), I used to go down there and tried to do something. As soon as Christ saw the workbench, He told me:

"Nice workbench! Nicely polished! But what do you do here? What are you producing with your life for the Kingdom of God?"

I showed Him something from my "works." The best I had up to that time.

He looked at me sadly and told me: "These little toys are the only things that you have made for the Kingdom of God?"

I was ashamed. I felt really bad. For myself, I kept the best of everything in my house. And yet the only things I was making for the

Kingdom of God were these worthless and miserable toys! . . . I lowered my head and said: "I know Lord. There aren't very many, and they're of no value. I have done poorly in respect of doing good works. But I would like to do something. Help me. Guide me."

"Do you want to succeed?" He asked.

"I want to! But how?" I asked.

"I will help you," He replied. "I know that you are weak, and without Me you can do nothing. Put it deep inside you that you are My disciple, and try to follow My suggestions. Start working with eagerness and consistency, and one day you will succeed."

"Where should I start from, Lord?" I asked.

The Lord replied, "By studying the Gospels, and continuing steadfastly with prayer, fasting, and self-restraint. Little by little you will find it all, and you will be filled with the gifts of the Holy Spirit."

"Which are they, Lord?" I asked.

He answered: "Love, joy, peace, longsuffering, kindness, goodness, faithfulness, gentleness, self-restraint" (Galatians 5.22, 23). "What more can a person desire? And you must know that the more you struggle, the more I will give you. Those who labored hard reached great heights. Therefore, do not be afraid, I will be with you always, I will support you and give you strength, joy, and peace."

†

"Christ is everything to us!" Are you in pain? Looking for a cure? He's the Physician. Thirsty? Do you want a drink? He is the Well. Need help? He is Strength, Are you afraid of death? He is Life. Do you long for Heaven? He is the way. Are you afraid of the dark? He is the light. Are you hungry for truth? Taste and see that the Lord is good.

†

How small I am!

Was anything more needed for me to understand how small I was and how great is our Savior Jesus Christ? I had invited Him to come inside me, into my heart. And He found Himself in the stables of Augeas.[2] . . .

I knelt and said to Him: "Now I understand, Lord. I am not worthy for You to come inside me. You will not find a place worthy to rest Your head. Cleanse me Lord. Cleanse the filth of my soul."

He replied to me: "That's the way! Now you are on the right track. And you should know that the more humble the thoughts you have about yourself, the more I will love you and the more effective I will be in helping you. And I tell you again, now you have entered the right track. The first step is humility."

†

Brothers, if you want to be saved, first find a good and experienced spiritual father, who you can confess to, so that you can be cleansed of the filth of your sins. Saint Kosmas the Aitolian

†

He looked at me seriously and asked: "Do you want never to stray from His road?" "Yes, Lord," I replied, "I want to, with all the strength of my soul. And for this I am willing to sacrifice everything."

He replied to me: "You do not have to sacrifice anything. On the other hand, you will gain many gifts and everlasting imperishable heavenly riches. You need only do one thing: make every effort to realize that you must not trust your thoughts, because they do not guide you correctly. Your thoughts are very easily misled by the passions and by the devil. They lead into things and actions that are not permitted, and do harm. Therefore, if you want to follow Me, take care to entrust the guidance of your spiritual life to an experienced and honest representative of Mine, a spiritual father from the priesthood. Close to him you will find what My disciples found close to Me: guidance, protection, cleansing, remission, grace."

---

[2]Augeas is a mythological figure who had very large and dirty stables.

Four … Hairs!

Saint Kosmas the Aitolian used to say:

Brothers, If you want to cure your souls, you need four things! Shall we make an agreement? From the time you were born until now, whatever sins you committed, I will take on my back, if you're willing to lift only four strands of hair in exchange! Is that too heavy or hard for you?

And what will I do with your sins?

I have a bottomless pit and I will throw them in!

What is this bottomless pit?

It is the compassion of Christ.

The first hair is: When you want to confess your sins, the first foundation is to forgive your enemies. Do you do this? If you do, you have lifted the first strand of hair! …

The second hair is: Find a good, educated, and virtuous spiritual father to whom you can confess your sins. The time to be ashamed is when you commit sin. When making your confession you should not be ashamed. When confessing, tell all your sins clearly. First, say to your spiritual father: "Father, I will go to Hell because I don't love God and my brothers with all my heart, as I love myself." Have you done this? Then you have also lifted the second hair.

The third hair is: When you have confessed your sins, the spiritual father will ask you: "Why, my child, did you commit all those sins?" Be careful not to accuse others! Accuse only yourself and say: "I have done them through my own wicked will; I am to blame." Is it too much for you to accuse yourself? It isn't? Then you have lifted the third hair also.

Now we come to the fourth hair. When you finish confessing your sins, and your spiritual father gives you his blessing and you leave, decide with a firm resolve and decision that it is better to die, better to shed your blood in martyrdom, than to fall again into sin. Do you do this also? If yes, you have lifted the fourth hair as well.

These are your remedies, brother. As light as lifting four strands of hair![3]

---

[3]From the *Fourth Teaching of St Kosmas*.

CLOSE TO CHRIST!

So now I am close to Christ!

Perhaps somebody will wish to ask me: "Well, so what? What was the big achievement?"

I reply: My heart and my life are filled with the gifts of the Holy Spirit. My life is filled with love, joy, and peace! My life is filled with states of mind and feelings that previously I used to seek for in vain, by going to parties, through entertainments, and through sex. Back then, the more experience I had of that lifestyle, the emptier I felt! I could feel that something was missing, and I was searching to find it where it did not exist. Now nothing is missing. I am full of peace, joy, and love. And above all with hope! With hope of life, true life. With hope of everlasting life.

Do you too want to obtain this? Follow me. Imitate me. Taste and see that the Lord is Good.

†

Isn't it a miserable thing not to tolerate even the smallest speck in your eye? But in your soul, for it not to bother you to see a whole mountain of wicked deeds and passions? Saint John Chrysostom (PG 57:456)

Bibliography

Formal Interviews Conducted

Abbot Ephraim, unpublished written responses, Monastery of Prophet Elias, Flamboura, Greece, Spring 2003.

Lay Person, ΣΤ, digital recording, Preveza, Greece, 18 May 2003.

Lay Person, IT, unpublished written responses, Preveza, Greece, Spring 2003.

Lay Person, LS, digital recording, Preveza, Greece, 15 May 2003.

Lay Person, NK, digital recording, Preveza, Greece, 29 April 2003 and 1 May 2003.

Metropolitan Meletios, unpublished written responses, Spring 2003, Preveza, Greece.

Monk A, digital recording, Monastery of Prophet Elias, Flamboura, Greece, 3 December 2002 and 16 December 2002.

Monk B, digital recording, Monastery of Prophet Elias, Flamboura, Greece, 11 February 2003.

Monk C, digital recording, Patras, Greece, 2 March 2003.

Monk D, digital recording, Preveza, Greece, 19 March 2003.

Nun E, digital recording, Monastery of St Dimitrios, Zalongo, Greece, 18 April 2003.

Priest A, digital recording, Preveza, Greece, 15 May 2003.

Published Greek Interviews with Metropolitan Meletios of Nikopolis and Preveza

Κείσογλου, Γιάννη. "Ένας Σύγχρονος Άγιος: Ο δεσπότης που προηγείται της εποχής του και απολαμβάνει της καθολικής αποδοχής λαού και εκκλησίας." *ΕΠΙΛΟΓΟΣ*. 5 January 1996.

"Ο ΜΗΤΡΟΠΟΛΙΤΗΣ ΝΙΚΟΠΟΛΕΩΣ ΚΑΙ ΠΡΕΒΕΖΗΣ ΜΕΛΕΤΙΟΣ Μιλάει για τη ζωή του χριστιανού και το έργο της Εκκλησίας στον σημερινό κόσμο." *Orthodox Globe*. May 1996.

Φερούση, Δημήτρη. "Απειλή για την Εκκλησία η αθλιότητα των εκπροσώπων της." *Ορθοδοξία*. April 1998.

Μακρή, Διονύση. "Κλήρος καριέρας με ενδοκόσμια φρονήματα." *ΣΤΥΛΟΣ ΟΡΘΟΔΟΞΙΑΣ*. January 2001.

General Bibliography

Βαγγέλης, Γ. *Πρέβεζα: 1945–1990*. Πρέβεζα: Δήμος Πρέβεζας, 1991.

Bowden, W. *Epirus Vetus: The Archaeology of a Late Antique Province*. London: Duckworth, 2003.

Chrysostomou, P., and F. Kefallonitou. *Nikopolis*. Athens: Ministry of Culture, Archaeological Receipts Fund, 2001.

Κόλλια, Ιερέα Ιωάννη Αλ. "ΕΝΟΡΙΕΣ ΖΩΣΕΣ ΚΑΙ ΑΓΩΝΕΣ ΚΛΗΡΟΥ ΤΗΣ ΠΟΛΗΣ ΠΡΕΒΕΖΑΣ ΕΠΙ ΤΟΥΡΚΟΚΡΑ-ΤΙΑΣ." *ΠΡΕΒΕΖΑΝΙΚΑ ΧΡΟΝΙΚΑ* 27–28 (1993): 79–96.

Κούρτη, Γεώργιος. *Η ΙΕΡΑ ΜΗΤΡΟΠΟΛΗ ΝΙΚΟΠΟΛΕΩΣ ΚΑΙ ΠΡΕΒΕΖΗΣ ΚΑΙ ΟΙ ΑΡΧΙΕΡΕΙΣ ΤΗΣ (1881–2000 μ.Χ)*. Πρέβεζα: ΙΕΡΑΣ ΜΗΤΡΟΠΟΛΕΩΣ ΝΙΚΟΠΟΛΕΩΣ, 2000.

Κραψίτη, Βασίλη. "Οι επισκοπικοί θρόνοι Ευροίας, Φωτικής και Βουθροτού." In *Θεσπρωτικά. Δεύτερη έκδοση*. Αθήνα, 1973.

Melek, Delilbasi. "The History of Preveza in the XVIth Century according to the Ottoman Taxation Registers." *Η Ιστορία της Πρέβεζας*. Πρέβεζα: Δήμος Πρέβεζας, 1993: 57–65.

Μελέτιος, Μητροπολίτης Νικοπόλεως, "Ο Νικοπόλεως Ευγένιος και η σύνοδος της Χαλκηδόνος." *Αναφορά Σάρδεων Μαξίμου*. Γενεύη III (1973): 367–376, 468–469.

Μελέτιος, Μητροπολίτης Νικοπόλεως. "Ο Νικοπόλεως Ευγένιος και η Σύνοδος της Χαλκηδόνος." In *Πρακτικά του πρώτου Διεθνούς Συμποσίου για τη Νικόπολη (23–29 Σεπτεμβρίου 1984)*. Πρέβεζα, 1987: 269–277.

Μουστάκης, Γιώργος. *Τα Πρεβεζάνικα*. Πρέβεζα: Δήμου Πρέβεζας, 2002.

Μπιτζιλέκη, Ε. *Νικόπολις: Ιστορία – Μνημεία*. Πρέβεζα, 1966.

Οικόνομου, Φώτιος Γ. *Η ΕΝ ΝΙΚΟΠΟΛΕΙ ΚΑΙ ΠΡΕΒΕΣΗ ΕΚΚΛΗ-ΣΙΑ ΑΠΟ ΤΗΣ ΠΡΩΤΗΣ ΔΙΑΔΟΣΕΩΣ ΤΟΥ ΧΡΙΣΤΙΑΝΙΣΜΟΥ ΜΕΧΡΙ ΤΩΝ ΚΑΘ' ΗΜΑΣ ΧΡΟΝΩΝ*. Αθήνα, 1973.

————. *Η ΕΚΚΛΗΣΙΑ ΤΗΣ ΗΠΕΙΡΟΥ*. Αθήναι, 1982.

Ortayli, Ilber. "Preveza during the Tanzimat Era (1864–1895)." In *Η Ιστορία της Πρέβεζας, Πρακτικά Α´ Διεθνούς Επιστημονικού Συνεδρίου (Πρέβεζα 22–24 Σεπτεμβρίου 1989)*. Πρέβεζα: Δήμος Πρέβεζας, 1993: 241–248.

Πάλλας, Δ. "Οι Χαρακτήρες και η ακτινοβολία της εκκλησιαστικής αρχιτεκτονικής της Νικόπολης." *Πρακτικά τού πρώτου Διεθνούς Συμποσίου για τη Νικόπολη (23–29 Σεπτεμβρίου 1984)*. Πρέβεζα, 1988: 226–229.

————. "L'edifice cultuel chretien et la liturgie dans l'Illyricum orientale." *Πρακτικά του 10ου Διεθνούς Συνεδρίου Χριστιανικής Αρχαιολογίας, Θεσσαλονίκη 28 Σεπτ.–4 Οκτ 1980*. Θεσσαλονίκη–Citta' del Vaticano, 1984: 85–158.

————. "L'Illrycum Oriental. Apercu historique." *Θεολογία* 51 (1980): 53–73.

————. "Monuments et textes. Remarques sur la liturgie dans quelques basiliques paleochretiennes de l'Illyricum oriental." *Επετηρίς Εταιρείας Βυζαντινών Σπουδών* 44 (1979–1980): 37–116.

Παπαγεωργίου, Γιώργος. "Οικονομικές και Κοινωνικές όψεις του καζά της Πρέβεζας κατά το β μισό του 19ου αιώνα." *Η Ιστορία της Πρέβεζας*. Πρέβεζα: Δήμος Πρέβεζας, 1993.

Pietri, C. "La Geographie de l'Illyricum Ecclesiastique et Ses Relations avec l'Eglise de Rome." In *Villes et Peuplement dans l'Illyricum Protobyzantine, Actes du colloque organise par l'Ecole francaise de Rome (12–14 May 1982)*. Rome: Ecole Francoise de Rome, 1984: 21–62.

Σακκελλαρίου, Μ.Β., ed. *Ήπειρος 4000 Χρόνια Ελληνικής Ιστορίας και Πολιτισμού*. Αθήνα, 1997.

Θεοχαρίδου, Γ. *Ιστορία της Μακεδονίας*. Θεσσαλονίκη, 1980.

Τσαγκαρόπουλος, Σπίρος. "Ο ΑΠΟΣΤΟΛΟΣ ΠΑΥΛΟΣ ΚΑΙ Η ΕΚΚΛΗΣΙΑ ΤΗΣ ΝΙΚΟΠΟΛΕΩΣ." *ΠΡΕΒΕΖΑΝΙΚΑ ΧΡΟΝΙΚΑ* 27–28 (1993): 49–62.

Φιλάρετου, Βιτάλης. *Ή ιερά μονή Ζαλόγγου*. Αθήνα, 1959.

————. *Το παρά αρχείον της ιεράς μητροπόλεως Νικοπόλεως Ηπείρου εκκλησιαστικών μουσείων*. Πρέβεζα, 1972.